1

JUST CALL ME SIR PERCY

The Ventures of a Boy Done Good
1920 - 1993

An illustrated biographical novel
by
Jane Sherwood

ISBN-13:9798613021918

Dedicated to Percy's grandson, Sam.

Percy (Chic) Sherwood left school at 14 with no prospects, to work as a delivery boy for a green grocer. After seizing the opportunity to train as an apprentice car mechanic at a local garage, he enlisted as a sapper with the Royal Engineers in 1941. He saw action from D-Day through France, Belgium, Holland and Germany during 1944 and 1945 and was demobbed in 1946. The army changed his life. This is his story. A sensitive and creative man who never talked about the war, he refused to claim his medals, but left a diary that was not discovered until after he died. Read how the war and military service influenced his journey through life, the people he met, the places he saw, and the enterprises he embarked upon as a skilled mechanic, chauffeur, husband and homemaker in his pursuit of health wealth and happiness.

Contents

Contents

Sapper Edward (Stead) Stevens & Sapper Percy (Chic) Sherwood.
Sapper Melinen Melling, Sapper Joe Cunnew & Sapper Verner (Jenni) Jensen.

Photograph notes.

1. THE DIARY.

Sapper Percy Ronald Sherwood celebrated Christmas early in 1943. He was with the Royal Engineers under the command of Major General Percy Hobart, Eleventh Armoured Division, in Yorkshire. He had been engaged to Joyce Cheshire, a country lass from Cambridgeshire for six months. They met at Foxton Village Hall back in the winter of 1942, when he was stationed with the 12ᵗʰ Field Squadron *(later to become the 612 Field Squadron)* in the neighbouring village of Harston. Joyce and her friends organised dances and shows, to raise money for the war effort. The Foxton hops were very popular with all the military personnel stationed in the area, not least Percy, known as Chic by his army mates. He like many others enjoyed a bit of female company, along with some light entertainment. Chic and Joyce got on famously, she was not only a great dancer, but beautiful and clever with it. However, their new romance was soon to be thwarted, by the spring the squadron was back in Yorkshire. The sapper was given ten days leave in May 1943 to visit his girlfriend, he took the opportunity to propose. Joyce accepted and her parents approved of their engagement. A small gathering was held on Tuesday 25ᵗʰ May in The Black Boy on Foxton High Street, with friends and family.

Chic's Christmas leave was brought forward to November, his third trip down to Foxton that year to visit his darling. They went dancing in Cambridge and to the flics, before having a slap-up meal at home with her parents. They also exchanged early Christmas gifts. Joyce gave him a blue leather pocket diary, with a sepia portrait photograph of herself tucked inside. She made him promise to write in it every day. Christmas passed by with Chic in Yorkshire, and Joyce in Cambridgeshire. On Christmas morning he took out his 1944 diary and completed the address page: Joyce first, then Aunt Martha, his school friend Alf *(another sapper)*, cousins Des and Molly, and lastly his home address, 32 Lenelby Road, Tolworth, Surrey.

On New Year's Day he was upset with Joyce and wrote a letter that he thought may start a row with his fiancée. There was no work on and he was brooding, so he went to the pictures. The following day was Sunday, still no work, so he went to the pictures again. In the evening he was bored, so he completed the personal notes page in his diary:

"Telephone number; BLA
Ration Book No; 000
P.O. Savings Book No; 999
Cycle Makers No; 1
Life Policy; Why.
Premiums Due; Sat afternoon.
Height; 6ft 2in. Eyes of Blue.
Weight; Not Enough.
Wireless Licence Due; Yesterday."

He expected a letter on Monday and went to the garrison post office, but nothing. He was down in the dumps and wrote another letter to Joyce.

On Tuesday: Chic, Johnno *(Sapper John Rooke),* Jenni *(Sapper Verner Jensen),* and Mel *(Sapper Melinen Melling),* were told to report to the gas chamber wearing their gas masks. The quarter-master sergeant had set light to a small tin in the middle of the floor, it was smoking profusely. The men were ordered to remove their masks on entry, only to be choked by the putrid sulphurous fumes, making their eyes smart. They were then marched around the room twice, with their eyes streaming before being released into the fresh air. Chic's chest was on fire with fluid pouring from every orifice, coughing, retching, tears streaming down his face and strings of snot dripping from his nose. Johnno and Mel were lying on the grass clutching their chests. Chic remained standing, hunched over trying to clear the debris from his tubes. It took him a good fifteen minutes to recover, his eyes stung for days afterwards and his chest rattled. He wrote to his good friend Alf in 1ˢ Field Squadron, who had already experienced the pleasure of the gas shed. Alf had told him what to expect, with he now realised, quite a few omissions.

The sapper wrote to his boss Mr Fox, one of the owners of Fox and Nicholl, a garage in Tolworth. He was due to take his trade tests in a couple of weeks and was enjoying the work. He added that he was not much keen on army life and looking forward to coming back to civvy street.

He had left Tolworth Boys School at fourteen, and went to work as an errand boy for the local greengrocer in Red Lion Road. He was a likeable lad and given a good reference from the headmaster, Mr Stokoe;

"A steady and persevering boy, always trustworthy."

He was given menial tasks, unloading, sweeping and making a few local deliveries on the cumbersome grocer's bicycle, that sported a huge basket in front of the handle bars. In 1935 the grocer bought a motorised delivery van, Percy scrounged a ride at every opportunity and was eager to get to grips with the van's mechanics. He was delighted when given the responsibility not only to keep it clean, but also to check the dip stick and put distilled water in the radiator. The vehicle was serviced regularly at Fox and Nicholl, only a short cycle ride away on the Portsmouth Road. Sometimes Percy was sent down on the shop bike to collect parts; spark plugs, cables, and the like. He loved going in the workshop to see what the mechanics were doing.

Mr Fox and Mr Nicholl built racing cars and sometimes a Bentley or Lagonda was being worked on, he was fascinated. The mechanics were always willing to chat. Mr Fox could see this young lad was keen. Would he like to earn some pocket money by sweeping up at the end of the day, after he had finished at the greengrocer? Well, ask a silly question! By Percy's sixteenth birthday, he had saved up enough money to buy an old motorbike from one of the boys. Mr Fox called him into the office to congratulate him and then asked if he would like to work at the garage as an apprentice mechanic. It was poorly paid, but he would learn a trade. Percy could not believe his ears, he did not have to think about it, and could not wait to get home to tell his parents.

Wednesday 5ᵗʰ January 1944 was quiet with nothing to do, but Chic received two letters from Joyce, he was happy again and immediately wrote back to her. Saturday the 20ᵗʰ May was underlined in his diary;

"To be married I HOPE."

13

Their engagement was back on. He also sent his mother a letter with some money for her forthcoming birthday. He didn't mention the gas chamber to either of them, they would only have worried. On Thursday Chic and Johnno were woken at 0430 by their corporal. They were selected as the strongest swimmers, to go out with the Bridlington fisherman for a training exercise, to develop their sea legs. Chic was looking forward to something different, but he was disappointed. The fishing boats did not go out, the weather was too bad, they both had another half day off and were bored, again. The next day was an even earlier start at 0400, the fishermen cancelled again due to a 50mph gale force wind. It was irritating to be woken for no reason, but Chic had no experience on the waves, his insides had not recovered from the gassing three days earlier, it was probably for the best. They were both browned off despite having another half day to themselves. Boredom had set in, so they decided to go to the pictures again before returning to their billets.

Saturday the same tedium, same afternoon off, same picture house, same film. On Sunday Chic was feeling under the weather and went to bed in the afternoon. The remains of the tear gas was working its way up, he was coughing like a train. He thought about where he was this time two years ago, with his new girlfriend Joyce, dancing the night away in Foxton village hall. How he wished he could be back there now, he decided to write to Joyce there and then, and tell her how much he loved her. The following week at last he was given something to do. He was assigned to loading a munitions transport truck for an inspection, he passed with flying colours. The afternoon was spent at the flics again, a new film was showing things were looking up. He also started growing a moustache and was looking quite dapper along with his mate Johnno. The lads were running a book on whose tache grew the quickest. He received another letter from Joyce and replied the following day while it was snowing heavily, perfect letter writing weather. By the time he ventured outside, the snow had disappeared to slush and the air a little warmer. All the lads in Chic's unit were in jubilant mood, they had been given seven days leave in February. The news did not go down well with 3 Troop, who were told on the very same day that all their leave was cancelled. Chic and Jenni tried to make a joke of it, but none of them laughed. Chic thought it was very unfair, surely the whole squadron should go on leave? Especially now, when there was nothing to do in the camp! What none of them knew, was that Mr Churchill and his generals were hatching a grand plan.

On Thursday the whole unit was sent off to practise on a PIAT *(Projector Infantry Anti-Tank)* gun. It was a hefty beast and not everyone managed to master the technique. Chic was OK, but only just. After being told to put both feet on the butt, he turned the body of the gun at the same time as locking the firing pin into position. He then had to bend double to pull the gun body upwards and cock the mechanism. Now it was ready to fire. He released the spring, pushing the firing pin forwards, the bomb launched throwing him flat on his back. He managed the task adequately but he would never be a sharpshooter, it was not an experience he enjoyed. He was then ordered to re-cock the gun and do the whole process again, the pin got stuck, he was ordered to do it again and again. The end of practise did not come soon enough even though there was not much doing for the rest of the day. He sauntered off to the garrison post office to see if he had any letters, there were three, one each from Joyce, Mum and Alf.

The end of the week brought a medical inspection. The powers that be wanted to make sure every soldier was fit for purpose, despite poisoning them with tear gas, depriving them of sleep and trying to drown them in the North Sea. Chic passed the medical with a satisfactory report, although the medical officer questioned his rattling chest. Chic was not too bothered about it, he had stopped coughing and had received another lovely letter from Joyce, as well as a parcel from his mum. The afternoon was spent at a lecture on mines and planes. All the lads were in high spirits, they had a free week-end and planned to go to Bridlington. On Saturday a dozen or so headed off to town in an open backed army truck, with Stead *(Sapper Edward Stevens)* driving. Chic and Johnno went straight off to the shopping parade to get their photographs taken for the purposes of judging the *"tache"* competition. They caught the others up for a few beers, a trip to the flics and afterwards dancing at The Spa. Everyone had a great time and arrived back late. Sunday was quiet, Chic stayed in all day writing letters and preparing for his trade test on Monday.

The first test was theory and only lasted a couple of hours, he sailed through it. As soon as it was done, after a meal of hash and hotchpotch *(bully beef and potato stew)* served up by Sapper Walt Atkinson and Corporal Sam Whitaker, they were all sent up to the firing range at Boynton. Each man was told to fire two shots into the bank to warm up the gun barrels. Walt hit two bull's-eyes straight off, what a star. The rest of them hit a bit wide, but they all improved by the end of the afternoon apart from Walt. He never hit the target again, his beginner's luck had gone AWOL *(Absent Without Leave),* and by the time they arrived back at HQ he was renamed, "Walt *(two in the bank)* Atkinson." He took it in good part and gave them all something to laugh about for a few hours. The next few days passed without incident, there was a kit inspection and a very welcome trip to the showers. It was now only three weeks to Chic's leave, he could not wait. The practical trade tests were not due to start for another week, so he was assigned to packing up stores, a job that he didn't mind doing, even if it was a bit repetitive. On Saturday he went for a drink with Johnno, Mel and Stead and afterwards dancing at The Floral Pavilion. Sunday was yet another quiet day apart from going to the pictures to see the film he had missed the day before, and then he wrote several letters.

The trade tests were held at Divisional Headquarters and started with a vengeance on Monday 31ˢᵗ January 1944. Passing these examinations would upgrade him to a Group A, Grade 2 motor mechanic. When he enlisted into the army three years previously in February 1941 at the age of twenty, Sapper Sherwood was accepted as an engine and pump fitter. He had not completed his Group B trade tests at Fox and Nicholl, but despite that, he was listed as Trade Group B, Grade 3. The first thing the army did was push him through the outstanding tests to get him up to speed, they were desperate for mechanics. By the end of March, he had the paperwork to show his trade as a B3 motor mechanic. This was all carried out during the sixteen weeks of sapper recruit training at the Royal Engineers No:1 Training Battalion in Clitheroe, Yorkshire. The following year after taking more tests, he was upgraded to B2. Now these current trade tests would raise him to A2, with the promise of higher wages when he returned to civvy street as a married man with responsibilities. The tests were practical, Chic was an enthusiastic student and not fazed by the tasks, he knuckled down happily with the constant thought in his head of his forthcoming leave to Foxton.

16

On the fourth day of the tests he was told all leave was cancelled. That knocked him for six, he was angry and struggled to keep his mind on his work. There was not much doing after the test, he was sent to stores and issued with a ration of three oranges, he felt like throwing them at the sergeant. He wrote to Joyce straight away, she would be upset. The next day he went into Bridlington with Johnno to pick up their photographs. Chic won the sweepstake and collected his winnings of 8/6d. He decided to save it for when he went on leave, God knows when that would be! By Saturday he was tired, he'd had tests every day for two weeks, with another today. As soon as he finished he went back to the billet and promptly fell fast asleep on his bed, with the light on. He was woken by the unmistakeable voice of Sergeant Wickham;

"Stand to, now.
What are you thinking of Sherwood?
Don't you know there is a blackout?
Pull down those blinds.
You are on charge."

He was annoyed with himself, what an idiot! He went off to the flics to stop himself fretting, but he had seen the film before. He still hadn't finished his trade tests and should have been going on leave in three days. Now to make matters worse, he would probably be put in the slammer. He was unaware that all leave had been cancelled because General Montgomery was due to visit the division.

On Sunday he went along to a service at the YMCA *(Young Men's Christian Association)* with the promise afterwards of light refreshments and a brass band. He told his mates with a wry smile, that he needed to;
"Get God on his side."

The lady volunteers were a cheerful bunch. Chic always enjoyed a joke with the fairer sex, he liked a bit of brass, and the band were good too! The entertainment took his mind off things for a couple of hours. He had three more trade tests to go, but one was delayed because Monty had arrived in camp. All ranks were rallied for inspection including Major-General Pip Roberts, who had recently taken charge of the whole division. On Friday after his final trade test, Chic was re-mustered as an A2 motor mechanic. He was very pleased with his results but did not get a chance to celebrate with his pals, instead he was sent before the sergeant-major and given two days jankers. He was confined to

17

barracks. His mates all went to town while he was put into stores to help pack up for the scheme that was commencing on Sunday; codename Operation Eagle.

At first light on Sunday morning the whole squadron moved off to the moors. The weather was freezing cold with a bitter north wind, and there was mud everywhere. Chic's first task was out in the field, repairing a Dingo scout car. The centre belly plate had come adrift and the drivetrain that powered the wheels, needed adjusting. He managed to get it going after several hours of struggling on his back in cold, dank, mud, before driving carefully in reverse to complete the job at the temporary workshop, set up in an even muddier field. The Dingo had five gears and could go just as fast backwards as forwards. It was great fun to drive but you had to know what you were doing. He had learned to drive a Daimler Dingo, on the earlier Mark 1 model. He and his pal Jenni, would practise driving to The Blacksmiths Arms and back in reverse across the North Yorkshire Moors, when they were both in the 12ᵗ Field Squadron up at Keldy Castle. They had some great times together; lots of laughs, singsongs with Sapper Collins at the piano when every tune came out as *"We'll Meet Again",* and Sapper Joe Cunnew doing his best to upset the locals with his irreverent sense of humour;

"Missed the last ghost train, granddad?"

The next day Chic and Bill were issued with a motorcycle each, they were expected to go out on reconnaissance to reach and repair any stranded vehicles. It was like being an AA *(Automobile Association)* officer but without the salutes, that tickled Chic. He was chuffed to bits with his bike, but the second day brought muddier ground, he had to be very careful not to come a cropper. His experience of motorbike scrambling on the steep chalk slopes of Box Hill with his mates Dave and Alf, came in very useful, but these conditions in Yorkshire threw up different problems. Major General Roberts intended Operation Eagle to be a realistic practice manoeuvre for what was to meet his troops in Europe, but most of the lads were blissfully unaware of this. The armoured traffic quickly churned the sodden ground to a quagmire. Progress was slow, two trucks were stuck, abandoned, and in the way. Then it started raining, and how it rained. Surely the conditions could not get more difficult, but the rain continued they were all sinking in a sea of mud.

Chic changed a wheel on his bike, checked the dynamo on the Dingo and fiddled with the drivetrain, all in mud a foot deep. Lorries were blocking the road and now the bridge was broken with no way of getting through. He went out on the back of Bill's bike to help out, they nearly went over in all the mayhem. Now the Gin Palace had broken down; a solid bodied truck for housing the signallers and all their communication equipment. The pressure was on. On the seventh day of Operation Eagle, Bill and Chic were working flat out on repairs until 2100 hours. The following day was a bit easier, apart from having to rescue Sapper Wilson who smashed up his lorry. Chic was sent to Hull to collect a replacement centre plate for the Dingo. The journey made a welcome break and while he was there he picked up Bill's wedding permit. Bill was getting married on Saturday.

At last the scheme was over. The mood in the camp was a happy one, everyone was shaved, showered and squeaky clean. Bill went on leave to get married and everyone else had the day off. It was time again to go the flics and dancing at Bridlington Spa, the boys had a great night out. They woke to heavy snow the following morning. It was settling on top of frozen mud and there was a biting wind. Chic was working on trucks that had been in the sea, he felt like he was doing a useful job, despite the cold, and was revved up for this new project. The checking for water damage and planning appropriate waterproofing was a satisfying task that continued for several days. At last his unit was eligible for some leave, the lucky recipients were drawn out of a hat, and Chic got the 10ᵗʰ of March, only two weeks away. He wrote to Joyce to tell her the good news. The days that followed were busy and flew by. It was a Leap Year, the 29ᵗʰ of February brought slightly warmer weather allowing a temporary thaw despite the snow still falling. The whole division seemed to be waterproofing, but the sappers bore the brunt of it. Every single vehicle whether it be a tank, a gun carrier, truck, lorry, van, or scout car, had to be treated with a rubberised gluey substance that was painted or stuck to the undersides and lower bodies of all vehicles. They were then driven through deep water to check they did not get waterlogged. Some worked, some didn't, Chic took on the challenge of solving the problems with great enthusiasm.

He was enjoying his work and excited about his forthcoming leave. In the first week of March he wrote four letters to his darling Joyce, and received two back, one telling him that some close family friends from Cambridgeshire had been in a car accident, but escaped with minor injuries. He was concerned and could not wait to see Joyce to catch up properly with all the news. He went to the flicks two days running to see *"Coney Island"* with Betty Grable and Alexander's Ragtime Band. It was a brilliant film, a cheerful comedy romance with great music, exactly what he needed. He also pressed his suit and army greatcoat in readiness for the 10ᵗʰ March when he would see his darling. Friday could not arrive quick enough. At last it was the end of the week, he packed up some gear in his newly waterproofed kit bag, and Stead drove him to Bridlington Station to catch the train to London, via York. He arrived in Kings Cross at 10.45 pm and eventually got back home to Tolworth in the early hours. His mother had gone to bed, but Frank Sherwood was dosing in the chair, he was startled from a deep sleep when he heard his son walk in the back door.

Operation Eagle.

2. LEAVE.

On Saturday morning, Annie was so pleased to have her youngest back home, she could not stop smiling while she fried him an egg laid by one of their two hens, along with three sausages and fried bread. The bangers were compliments of her other son Charlie, who was now married and an expectant father. He was always up for a bit of wheeling and dealing, the bangers were given to him in lieu of a gambling debt taken on his milk round. He took bets on the horses from housewives and local tradesmen and was not averse to a bit of black-market trading. Charlie was seven years older than his brother, and managed to evade conscription due partly to his flat feet, but mainly to the gift of the gab. Charlie was a harmless rogue, he hedged his bets by keeping a couple of local policemen and a town councillor on his books!

Straight after breakfast, Chic walked to Surbiton Station and travelled up to Kings Cross on yesterday's ticket, he could also do a bit of ducking and diving when necessary. It was easy to dodge the ticket inspectors; the trains were heaving with troops and he was good at keeping his head down. He met Joyce off the Cambridge train and they went straight to the pictures in Kingston, to see *"Coney Island"*, Chic knew she would love it. They caught the trolleybus back to Tolworth and stayed at Lenelby Road, for a few days. They also visited Charlie and his wife Phyllis, who was six months pregnant, and excited at the prospect of motherhood. They were living in a modern terraced house just a mile down the road, on The Sunray Estate. Charlie had recently bought this pretty little house with saved money from his illicit betting business. Joyce and Chic *(AKA Perce to Charlie)* were pleased for them, it was also something for them to aspire to. The four of them played gin rummy and had a good laugh. Charlie was a terrible cheat but it was all light hearted, they gambled with a pot of pennies that were returned to the jar at the end of the session.

On Monday, the couple went to The Kingston Empire to see *"Sid Seymour and his Mad Hatters,"* but they weren't very good. The rest of the week they visited friends, played cards and went to the flics. They enjoyed each other's company and had a lovely time. On Saturday it was time to go back up to London to catch the Cambridge train and stay with Joyce's parents. Chic gave his mother a big hug and shook his father's hand, he didn't know when he could visit again. It was only a couple of hours to Cambridgeshire and Joyce's house was an easy walk from Foxton station. They arrived in good time for afternoon tea with semolina tarts, Mrs C was a fantastic pastry cook. There was a dance in the village hall that evening, Joyce and Chic danced the light fantastic to; *"The Gordon Revellers,"* a band that made regular visits to the village. It was great to be back in familiar surroundings where they had met, and fallen in love less than two years ago, it seemed like a lifetime.

Sunday was a quiet day. Edie went to church, while her husband worked on his vegetable patch in the front garden. March was a busy time of year for vegetables, manuring and double digging being an essential part of a healthy allotment. Joyce's father took digging for victory very seriously. Chic helped Joyce peel some turnips and potatoes to go with the rabbit pie that her mother had prepared earlier. After a delicious Sunday dinner, the couple played dominoes in the front parlour while Joyce's parents amused themselves in the back parlour, they only used the front room on high days and holidays.

Joyce had to go back to work on the Monday so Chic went for a long walk along the lanes that he had got to know so well last year, when his squadron was stationed in Harston. When Joyce finished work at 6 pm, they hopped on a bus and went to the flics in Cambridge, it was their last date before Chic returned to Bridlington. His leave ended on Wednesday, he was required to be back before evening curfew, unless he wanted more jankers. His final day in the village was spent sorting out and writing letters and then a quiet evening with Joyce. They went to bed early and the following morning, not long after Joyce had gone to work, he made his way ..... alone ..... to Foxton Station. It was a testing journey back to Yorkshire with several changes, many delays and a few dodgy incidents. The military police could be rather heavy handed with anyone in uniform who didn't have an official pass and a ticket. Chic was safe, he had both, but he was miserable.

3. HAMPSHIRE.

On returning to the billet, he discovered that everyone in the unit had all
been inoculated and now it was his turn. The whole camp was
employed in the packing up of stores and Chic was ordered to square up
his kit, they would soon be on the move. The only break in the routine
over the next five days was an ENSA *(Entertainments Nation Service
Association)* show at Bridlington Spa. It made a change but it was far
from entertaining, the hecklers got more laughs than the acts. On the 28
March the whole division was on the road. Chic rode his motorcycle
one hundred and forty miles southward with troops and vehicles nose to
tail, it seemed like the whole country was on a military exercise. His
unit stayed overnight at Lutterworth, before moving on the next day
down the Great North Road past Cambridge and Foxton. If only he
could have contacted Joyce to tell her, she could have waved to him on
his way through, maybe even stop for a few moments to give her a last
kiss and cuddle. The convoy continued through the bombed ruins of
London's East End and along the Portsmouth Road, past Fox and
Nicholl at Tolworth and eventually after two long days, Aldershot. The
town was a seething mass of troops and military equipment, with a
heavy Canadian presence. Chic's unit was billeted in Nissen huts
(buildings with rounded corrugated steel roofs), it was noisy but
adequate. They were on the verge of something, but none of them knew
exactly what. Chic wasn't far from home, he wrote to Joyce to tell her,
so near and yet so far.

The whole squadron was given the week-end off; some caught the train
to London, others painted Aldershot red, but Chic borrowed Bill's
motorcycle and played April fool on his Mum. She thought it was
Charlie coming through the back door, and could not believe her eyes
when she saw her other son standing there. On returning to the barracks
Chic wangled a day pass to visit Joyce the next day. It was three hours
to Foxton, he set out at first light and met army convoy after convoy,
mostly travelling in the opposite direction. He arrived before Joyce and
her mother left for church. Joyce was so delighted to see him that she
missed church and they went for a walk up to the clunch *(chalk quarry)*
pits. Chic had just been paid, he gave her some cash and all his coupons
to buy their wedding rings, they would have to be utility there was no
choice. He left Foxton at 6 pm to get back to camp before curfew. Joyce
promised she would travel down to Tolworth next time he had leave
and they parted company reluctantly. It took longer to return back to

23

Aldershot, he was now riding among the endless chain of convoys travelling southwards, but arrived back at camp in the nick of time.

Monday morning brought hard graft, he was assigned to de-coking the engine on a transporter truck and it took several hours. As soon as he was done, he was sent out on the heath with the rest of the squadron for military exercises. Then at 2130, he was told to go and collect a motorcycle that was designated to him personally, his new acquisition pleased him immensely, but he soon came back down to earth. Hard graft continued all week, with training on top of long working days. The worst part was the route march at running pace across the heath before breakfast, four miles was a bloody long way, when you had to follow it with eight hours of hard graft in the repair shop, with only a couple of short breaks. The work was piling up, they were overloaded, then suddenly out of the blue all leave was cancelled until further notice. It was Easter, but Good Friday and Easter Sunday passed by without mention, apart from hot cross buns in the NAAFI, *(the Navy, Army and Air Force Institute, provided catering and other facilities to ranks other than officers.)* To make matters worse, it had started raining and the lads were waterproofing trucks, outside, with no cover. They were all soaked to the skin and had not been for a night out for over a week, they were all thoroughly browned off. The damp pervaded every nook and cranny of their hut, the noise of the rain on the metal roof was deafening, and the heavy condensation added to their misery.

Chic's parents Frank and Annie Sherwood arranged to visit Annie's brother Sid Plant on Easter Monday. She wrote to her son hoping that he would be able to come to, Frensham was only a few miles down the road from Aldershot. Sapper Sherwood invented an essential errand related to his forthcoming wedding, his block sergeant allowed him to take a couple of hours off in the afternoon to join his family for tea. Uncle Sid and Auntie Millie were not attending Chic's wedding in a couple of weeks. If the truth be known they couldn't afford the train fare, but they wanted to give him and Joyce a small gift and wish them both all the very best. It was an enjoyable afternoon, Uncle Sid was always good fun and Auntie Milly had made a Simnel cake with dried fruit, semolina and almond essence. They reminisced about the good times at Lenelby Road when they were all living in the two up two down, Percy with his brother Charlie and their parents sharing one bedroom, Sid, Millie and their son Desmond in the other. Not forgetting Grandpa Charlie sleeping downstairs in the front room where he made his baskets, and of course Pants the dog.

Private Desmond Plant was in an anti-tank platoon with the 2/4ᵃ Battalion of the Hampshire Regiment, he had seen active service throughout the war, including evacuation at Dunkirk. Now he was out in Italy up against Mussolini as well as Hitler, his parents had not heard from him for several weeks. The two cousins always got on well as children, Chic hoped Des would be OK. It was great to see Uncle Sid and catch up with all the family news, despite them all being worried about Desmond. He counted his blessings.

The division had now done as much waterproofing as possible. It could only be carried out on vehicles that were being transported, the rest had to wait until they arrived at the docks, wherever that might be, it was a waiting game. Boredom had set in again, Chic, Johnno, Stan *(Sapper Stanley Groom)* and Stead, all walked up to Aldershot Hippodrome on the Wednesday evening to watch a variety show. There certainly was a lot of variety, some good mostly dreadful, but Chic talked the usherette into getting them all some chips and they had a jolly good laugh. There were hundreds of soldiers in the audience, many three sheets to the wind, the heckling was hilarious. There was also a fight, the military police were called in but it was far enough away not to bother the lads.

The following week-end, Joyce travelled down to Tolworth and Chic managed to grab a pass for a couple of hours on the Sunday. He also sneaked off on Saturday, but made sure he was under the radar. Joyce had brought her wedding ring and she wanted to give it to her fiancée for safe keeping. The wedding was just over a month away, she nagged him to go and see the camp verger to get their Banns read. She was making her own dress from figured white satin, purchased with clothing coupons scrounged from relatives. She also made the chief bridesmaid's dress from a length of pale pink crepe that her mother had purchased before the war. There were two matrons of honour, Joyce's best friend Joyce who had just married Creighton Romine, a GI from Texas, and Audrey her newly married school friend. Joyce made their powder blue dresses from a bedspread she found in The Foxton Yokels dressing up box. Her little cousin Pearl was going to wear a blue figured silk dress with matching bonnet made by her mother, Joyce's Aunty Rose.

The whole family had been saving coupons for months to get enough rations for the wedding cake. Edie was eager to put on a good spread and called in the help of the Women's Institute who were delighted to assist. It seemed to Chic, like the whole village was invited to the wedding, there were fifty guests expected, only six of which were on his side. His mother bought herself a yard of silk petersham *(corded tape)* ribbon and silk flowers for her hat. Frank borrowed a suit from his son Charlie who had already told his brother he could not see him get hitched because of his wife's confinement.

Chic's great pal Jenni was now transferred permanently to the 13ᵗʰ Field Squadron, they no longer worked or went on manoeuvres together but they still managed to meet up socially in Aldershot. They both preferred dancing to standing around drinking and were in demand with the ATS *(Auxiliary Territorial Army)* girls, who were keen to partner them not just for the dancing, they were good fun. Jenni was three years younger than Chic, but they hit it off as soon as they met as rookie sappers together, back in 1941. They were always playing harmless pranks on the other lads and each other, when they were stationed down in Cambridgeshire. Chic asked Jenni to be his best man, who was thrilled by the compliment. He knew Joyce from the Foxton dances and thought they made a delightful couple, he would be honoured to support his friend and see them get hitched.

The following week-end Chic put in for a pass and got it, he was very happy indeed, but he did not arrive in Foxton until 10.30 pm on Saturday night. The trains were packed to bursting with delays due to bomb damage on the lines, just north of Kings Cross. His train was supposed to stop at Foxton, but it went straight through to Cambridge to make up time. He then had to wait ages for a bus back to Foxton, by the time he arrived at the village hall the dance was nearly finished. He and Joyce managed to fit in three dances together before the band packed up, and Chic supped a very welcome bottle of brown ale. They walked up to the clunch pits again on Sunday morning, it was a beautiful day and they had a lovely time together, but it was all too brief he had to be back in camp that night. Joyce's head was full of wedding arrangements they were both excited. Over the following week he wrote to his darling no less than six times, covering all her questions and assuring her everything was in hand. There was still nothing much doing in the camp apart from the endless errands Joyce had given him, but he did go and see *"Maurice Winnick and his Band"* at the Garrison Theatre with Jenni. It gave them the opportunity to compare speeches.

On 29ᵗʰ April Chic rode his motorbike back to Tolworth from Aldershot to go out with his brother Charlie and a few mates. Most of Chic's friends were away serving in the forces, but Charlie was determined to give his brother a good stag night. They were up half the night, but Chic did not really enjoy it, or at least what he could remember of it! He arrived back at Aldershot on Sunday evening with a monstrous hangover. To add to his malaise, Jenni had left a message to say his leave was cancelled, he could not attend the wedding. Chic was going to have to find another best man. Maybe Johnno would do it? The following Friday Chic managed to wangle some extra petrol from stores and rode up to Foxton on his motorbike. He did not want to rely on the trains again, he had too much to do. Joyce wanted to take him shopping in Cambridge on Saturday morning and then he was riding down to meet a couple of school chums for a final drink in the evening at The Red Lion, in Tolworth.

He was due back in Aldershot before 1000 hours on Sunday morning. A new operation was starting in two days, it looked like the big push might be on the horizon. On Monday all the lads were given new sets of felt signs *(bull and stripes)* to sew onto their uniforms, after removing all the old insignia. Chic also went to see the verger at the Royal Garrison Church to collect the Banns, but he wasn't there. He saw the chaplain instead, a personable chap who cared for the welfare of his congregation, despite the fact that he had little time to get to know any of them before they moved on. He checked the name Percy Ronald Sherwood, gave him the Banns and talked to him about the sanctity of marriage. He hoped that Sapper Sherwood would have a long and happy relationship with love, affection and trust. He also spoke about carnal matters and asked the prospective groom if there was anything he was worried about. Chic was a little apprehensive, but he didn't say so. The chaplain gave him a small booklet called;

"How to Treat a Young Wife. A guide to sex adjustment in marriage."

It was a glorious afternoon, so Chic went to listen to a military band in the park and started reading his book. The first paragraph began;

"One of the writers responsible for this booklet recently received a letter from a Naval Chaplain saying that men frequently consult him about their wives. These men complain that their wives are cold towards them, are continually irritated, or have even left them and won't live with them ….. When questioned closely they all confess, to have been, to a greater or lesser degree, inartistic, blundering, impetuous, forcing, etc., in their early attempts at sexual intercourse. They state that trouble began there."

He lost concentration when he reached page 10. The writer told him he must try to be as attractive as possible in a bodily way, well-shaved, clean teeth, bathe regularly and not stink of beer or tobacco. Well of course he knew that, he was not an imbecile. He walked back to the Nissen hut and showed Johnno the book, they had a good laugh over some of the practical suggestions. Johnno was older than Chic and a married man, he offered a few tips of his own. Chic kept the booklet anyway for future reference and asked Johnno if he would be his best man. Johnno agreed as long as he could use Jenni's speech.

The new scheme began on Wednesday the 10ᵗʰ of May 1944. After having nothing to do for weeks, suddenly there was so much work it appeared to the men that the powers that be were demanding an impossible task. In addition to an influx of mechanical repairs and servicing, there was waterproofing to be done on a major scale. Everyone was working flat out, starting early and finishing late, battling to get everything ship shape. On Friday Chic didn't finish until 2245 and was up again at 0400 on Saturday morning, preparing the armoured vehicles that were being transported. They were required to be fully waterproofed and ready for inspection by 1300 hours. He was given the afternoon off and rode to Tolworth for a couple of hours. On Sunday he did another twelve hour shift. When he got back to the hut there was a nasty letter from Joyce accusing him of not getting on with the wedding arrangements. She suggested he was too busy enjoying himself, Chic was mad with her and wrote back immediately to put her straight. He was exhausted.

Chic was extremely relieved when Johnno finally got his week-end pass along with Stead and Stan, for the wedding next week. The following two days were also long and hard, but at the end of it, another letter arrived from Joyce, she was most apologetic, he was happy again and in a few days time they would be married. Harry, a draughtsman by trade and a talented artist was not one for going out with the boys, he preferred to sketch or read poetry whilst smoking his pipe. He liked Chic and the feeling was mutual. He always carried a leather-bound copy of;

"Lord Tennyson's Poetical Works,"

given to him by his mother. He knew much of the poetry by heart. Sometimes when the lads organised a talent night he would give a short recital, Chic loved listening to him speak. He asked Harry to draw a portrait of Joyce from a photograph she had given him. Harry was more than pleased to do so and presented him with a good likeness of his darling, drawn in pencil on the back of a cereal packet with a cardboard hinge. Chic was delighted, he gave him a tin of tobacco. Harry then produced a sheet of typed paper, a poem dedicated to the happy couple, called *"Spring Wedding."* His gift to them, it was delightful.

As Chic was packing up his kit, for ten days compassionate leave due to start at 1700 hours on the 19th May 1944, Johnno dragged him down to the NAAFI where some of the boys were having a brew. Jenni had organised a collection and given it to Johnno. The boys all gathered around and Johnno presented his friend with a money bag containing 41 half-crowns, a total of £5 2s 6d. Chic was overwhelmed and dead chuffed, he valued their comradeship. They all wished him the very best. Johnno arranged to meet Chic with Stan and Stead at Kings Cross first thing on Saturday morning. At precisely 1700 hours Stead drove him to Aldershot Station to catch the train to Surbiton. He arrived at Lenelby Road at 7 pm where his mum was bubbling with excitement. The next morning, they were all travelling up by train to Cambridgeshire together. Frank had already fired up the copper, both he and Annie bathed before their son arrived home. He was able to enjoy a long hot bath, went to bed early and slept well. He woke at the crack of dawn with butterflies in his stomach.

Annie, Frank, Joyce, Pearl, Johnno, Chic, Joyce, Harry, Gwen, Audrey, Edie.

SPRING WEDDING.

Church, old and grey, where Spring's fragrant blossoms
hang in a cascade upon the bough, where the lich-gate,
rustic and ancient, stands open as if to welcome you now.

Windows of stained-glass through which sunlight filters,
weaving gold patterns o'er hassock and pew. Alter and
organ, choir-boys singing hymns which though old remain
ever new.

Here in this church, two hearts, in their seeking, find
the fulfilment and wonder of love. Blessed by the radiance
of God's gracious glory, strengthened with hope from His
heaven above.

4. THE WEDDING.

Frank, Annie and Chic were up with the lark on Saturday the 20ᵗʰ May 1944. After a light breakfast of scrambled egg with toast and dripping, they caught the trolley bus up to Surbiton Station. They were meeting the boys under the clock at Kings Cross Railway Station at 10 am sharp. They had to fight their way across London, the underground was congested with what seemed like thousands of military personnel. It was rather overwhelming for Frank and Annie, they had never travelled this far before and were not used to the crowds. They met up with the boys on time and caught the Cambridge train. It was standing room only, but Chic managed to find a bench seat for his parents, after chatting up a couple of squaddies and giving them some ciggies in return for their seats. Meanwhile the lads were winding Johnno up about his speech, he was not a natural speaker. Chic gave him Harry's poem and suggested he read it out after the telegrams. The groom had been writing his speech for weeks and knew it off by heart, but that didn't stop him being nervous, he couldn't believe this day was finally here.

They arrived at Foxton Station just after one-o-clock with over an hour to spare and walked up Station Road to Saint Lawrence Church, where Chic had attended occasionally to hear Joyce playing the organ at Sunday matins or evensong. Frank insisted that all the lads should go on ahead, he and Annie would follow at their own pace. Annie was nearly sixty and sprightly for her age, but Frank, four years younger, suffered with his chest and walked with a limp. He fought in The Great War as a private foot soldier with the East Surrey Regiment and was taken prisoner on the Western Front in 1916, after being shot in the leg. He served hard labour at Saint Quentin in France for three years, where he was forced to live in a hole in the ground, enduring severe weather conditions and a daily food ration of just one hard biscuit with a cup of hot water. He was a navvy by trade, better equipped than many to suffer the backbreaking toil that the Germans imposed on their POWs in the labour camps. Frank was a survivor, but the hardship had taken its toll on his body, he did not want Percy to suffer a similar fate or worse.

Frank and Annie stopped frequently on Station Road when an appropriate garden wall presented itself at just the right height to perch on. They had plenty of time and would easily make it before the bride's family appeared. The lads were the first to arrive at the church, the vicar welcomed them. Most of the congregation were walking to the wedding ceremony and the church was rapidly filling up. Joyce's parents lived just around the corner in one of The Press cottages, her relatives were all gathered in the house. Joyce's mother arrived first with her sister's family, including little Pearl along with the chief bridesmaid and the two matrons of honour. Joyce's mother looked very summery in her floral dress and straw hat, a great contrast to Frank and Annie in their dark suits. Chic introduced his parents to Mrs Cheshire, they had not met before and made polite conversation, they were all rather shy. The army lads knew the two Joyces and Gwen and Audrey from the Foxton hops, they were all getting on well. Now it was time to go inside the church, while the bridesmaids waited outside for Joyce and her father.

It was a very personal service, the Reverend Rowlands knew Joyce and her family well, they were all enthusiastic participants in village life which centred around church and chapel. There were two hymns; *"Praise my Soul"* and *"The Voice that Breathed O'er Eden."* Chic and his mates did not know the second hymn, but apart from that all went smoothly. Johnno did not lose the ring and neither the bride nor the groom fluffed their words, it was all perfect and Chic was;

"Over the moon."

He was a married man, his darling looked beautiful in her homemade satin wedding gown, an orange blossom headdress and a bouquet of yellow tulips, with lily of the valley. Her veil was made from a lace curtain. A local amateur photographer took a few snaps outside the church and then everyone followed the newlyweds on foot, around to the village hall next door.

Chic and his parents were amazed at the spread before their eyes, the WI had worked wonders. Joyce's mum was very proud of her cake hidden under a cardboard shell decorated with white silk flowers and silver foil leaves. The Black Boy provided a barrel of beer with sherry for the ladies and gooseberry wine for toasts. Now it was time for the speeches. The father of the bride was an extrovert chap with a jolly disposition; he told a few jokes, made some references to his daughter's shortcomings, and finally mentioned her brother who was stationed on a naval ship somewhere out in the exotics. He toasted to absent friends. Chic thought about Jenni.

Johnno talked in his strong Yorkshire accent of when he first met Chic.

"I am standing in today for our great friend Sapper Verner Jensen who has been moved to a different squadron and refused leave. We all met as new recruits in 1941, at the Royal Engineers Territorial Brigade in Clitheroe and have had some great times together. There is always the chance of a laugh when Jenni and Chic are around. Now you may be wondering how Percy became Chic? Well, we all have to take our turn on spud duty at the NAAFI, but when Chic is on duty the hens always got more scraps. He can often be found talking to the chickens and giving them a few treats, he says they remind him of home."

Johnno added a few anecdotes about their nights out in Scarborough and Bridlington and of course their time stationed in Harston, when they met the Foxton girls. He then read the telegrams including one from Joyce's brother Doug, saying;

"Don't be late, Love."

And another from Jenni;

"Congratulations, lasting happiness to you both."

Finally, Johnno read Harry's poem; *Spring Wedding.*

Now it was Chic's turn to stand up.

"I am the luckiest man alive to have such a beautiful and clever bride, Not only is she a great dancer, she can act, play the piano, is a fantastic needlewoman and a good organiser, her versatility is endless. I remember our first dance in this very hall in October 1942, when the

squadron had only just moved down to Harston after being told we were not being sent to the middle east. "The Stirlingaires" were playing; a great band from Marshalls Aircraft Fitters in Cambridge, who have a brilliant Glen Miller repertoire. The hall was packed out, Joyce and I jitterbugged to "In the Mood", and then we got talking. I suggested we teamed up to raise money for the Foxton War Effort, by putting on some more dances. The following January we organised a dance together and made a fantastic £6 profit in just one night.

I was devastated when our squadron was moved back to Yorkshire and missed Joyce desperately, but managed to get leave in May to ask for her hand in marriage and to my delight she accepted. I am grateful to Joyce's parents for welcoming me into their family and for this magnificent spread. The lovely bridesmaids have done us proud. Thanks to Johnno for stepping in at the last moment as my best man. I am a very lucky man and will do my utmost to make Joyce happy."

Harry Cheshire had brought his wireless down to the village hall, after the toasts the BBC world service entertained the wedding party with *"Forces Favourites"*. The youngsters danced to Glen Miller and then Joyce's father led a sing song with *"Boots"* when Peter Dawson came on the radio.

It was now time for the bride and groom to depart on their honeymoon. Joyce changed into a two-piece suit with matching hat and said her goodbyes to family and friends. The sun was still shining as they made their way on foot to Foxton railway station. Chic's parents and the boys followed at a discreet distance, they were all catching the same train back to Kings Cross. The newlyweds would be back in Foxton on Thursday, because Joyce was appearing with *"The Foxton Yokels"* in a play at the village hall in the evening. Their honeymoon was spent at home in Lenelby Road, Tolworth. They went to the flics on Sunday afternoon and again on Monday afternoon, after sleeping in until 10 am. They then went to see *"Adelis and Hall"* at the Kingston Empire in the evening, Chic was on top of the world. The following day they went to the pictures again, it was the only place where they had a bit of privacy, Joyce never felt totally at ease at her in-law's house, despite them making her very welcome. On Wednesday they went for tea at brother Charlie's house, their baby was expected in less than two weeks and his wife was more than ready. They played gin rummy before going to the Whitsun fair at Epsom Downs which made a nice change. They all had a super time on the dodgems and roundabouts, eating toffee apples. This was Joyce and Chic's last day in Tolworth.

On Thursday morning after another long lie in and a delicious sweet snack at Peggy Brown's, opposite Surbiton Station, they took the train back up to Waterloo and made their way across London to Kings Cross for the Foxton train. They arrived just in time for tea before Joyce and her father were due backstage at the village hall, Harry Cheshire had been fretting, his daughter always cut things fine. Joyce didn't want Chic to attend the show, she was not well rehearsed and wouldn't be very good. It was agreed he should go the following evening, when *"The Yokels"* were appearing in Melbourne. The evening on his own gave Chic time to reflect, he did not want to leave his wife and go back to Aldershot. It was raining when they woke on Friday morning, they decided to go to the flics in Cambridge. In the evening, Joyce's friend Jimmy gave Chic a lift to the show in his lorry, Joyce and Harry had gone on ahead. The play was rather boring but no matter, Chic only had eyes for Joyce, he was besotted by his darling's performance and loved her to bits. Saturday arrived, it was their last day together, the newlyweds stayed in bed until 11.30 am, while Edie and Harry were out doing their chores. Chic took all the empty bottles back to the village shop and collected a few pennies, while Joyce made a sweetbread casserole for dinner.

The rain had stopped enabling them to spend all afternoon in the park. Chic had to leave at 5.30 pm to catch his train back to Aldershot.

ALONE.

The honeymoon was over.

24 Wed. ~~~~
Had tea with C + P.
Played cards went to
their at Eloom.
Empire Day.

25 Thurs. ENGAGED 1 YEAR.
Got up about 11 AM.
went to Factory, layer
in play at Village Hall

26 Fri. Went to
Pictures went to Haw...
to see layer in Hall.
Queen Mary b. 1867.

27 Sat. Got up 11.30 AM
Took empty gattcoozok
lay in park in Afternoon
lay... teeth (how 2)

28 SUN. Have been busy
watering ... until 500 PM
wrote to my Darling
wife and baby
Whit Sunday ... all

29 Mon. checking over
truck's am feeling
browned off wrote
Whit Monday to my Darling wife

30 Tues. had I hrs off
to do shopping wrote
to all made out will
to my wife.

31 Wed. Wrote to my
Darling wife, set
Head lamps.
Union Day, South Africa (1918)

5. D - DAY.

On Sunday the 28ᵗʰ May he worked all day waterproofing and did not get a chance to write to his darling wife until after supper. It was the Whitsun bank holiday week-end but Chic's day, along with most of the troops, was spent waterproofing again. All the vehicles were being inspected by the commanding officers, and some came back. They were all browned off, particularly when they were then ordered to go out marching after yet another day of jolly hard graft. On Tuesday he was allowed two hours to go shopping and given a form by the quarter-master, to make out a new will to benefit his wife. This was a worrying development as it suggested that active service was imminent. Chic didn't give it a second thought, after all he had just got married.

Percy Ronald Sherwood was instructed to make his first will back in August 1942, when his commanding officer had just been told that all units should prepare to mobilize for going overseas. They were all sent to Thetford, Norfolk in readiness for travelling to North Africa, but after only a few men and their vehicles had departed the scheme was aborted, leaving most of the division back in England, with a new commanding officer; Major General Brocas Burrows. Chic had counted his blessings again, another reprieve from active service. His squadron was one of many being sent to Cambridgeshire, a very pleasant part of the country, little did he know what delights that would hold. Back then when he was only just twenty-two, he made his father executor and left all his worldly goods to his mother, Annie Sherwood, all he had was his motorbike. His father Frank would have struggled to be executor because he could only just read and write, but this young sapper did not consider that, he thought it was the right thing to do. Frank never went to school, he was taught to read by his future wife Annie Plant when he lodged with her family before The Great War. They married in 1913.

This time around, Percy Ronald Sherwood was a bit more canny. He wrote his rank and army number; Driver 2140769 RE and appointed his wife Joyce Sherwood of 3 Addison Cottages, Foxton, Near Royston, Herts. as both executor and beneficiary. He still didn't have much more than his motorbike, just a few pounds in the post office. He duly completed the small slip of paper and signed it on the back in the presence of Arthur, a clerk at the garrison and Bob Wolstenholme, a Lancashire lad with a flamboyant writing style who happened to be in the office at the same time, for exactly the same reason. While he was there Chic witnessed Bob's will for him and posted some letters to Joyce, Mum, cousin Molly and his friend Alf.

The last day of May was spent setting headlamps to work on the right, rather than the left. He wrote to Joyce again and was disappointed that he had not received any letters back, perhaps they were delayed. The beginning of June was a waiting game, he was bored. He sewed on his new bulls and flashes *(felt badges showing the squadron insignia),* but all he could think about was his darling wife and the holiday they had together less than two weeks ago. He wrote to Joyce again despite still not receiving any letters in return, he was upset. Tension was building in the barracks, with an air of expectancy. Chic was not sleeping well, he had one particularly restless night with bad dreams causing him to fall out of bed. That did not help his state of mind.

On Saturday there was no work but all leave was cancelled. Chic visited Jenni down at the 13ᵗʰ Field Squadron, they went into town for a beer and spent the whole afternoon reminiscing, from when they were in the 12ᵗʰ Field Squadron together. Jenni reminded Chic of the day the sergeant major was standing on the small bridge at Harston, when 1 2 & 3 Troop from HQ scared him half to death by charging down the road to breakfast. It was hilarious to see the expression on the sergeant major's face, he thought the Germans had arrived and he was a gonner. They could not stop laughing.

While he was in town Chic bought Joyce a birthday card, when he got back to the hut he had received two letters from her, he was happy again. Sunday was another boring day, he wrote to Joyce again and sent her card, he hoped it would arrive on the 12th of June, her twentieth birthday. That evening *"Harry Farmer and his Organ Ensemble"* were playing at The Garrison Theatre, Chic liked a bit of organ music and had a good night out with Johnno and Stead. They walked back to the hut laughing again about the sergeant major in Harston. Everything was now in place ready and waiting to move off, with just a few last-minute adjustments. Chic and Bill were ordered to fix up some tail lamps on a couple of Crusader tanks that were being used to shift the smaller equipment. Everyone knew something was imminent.

Mr Churchill's great plan for D-Day had begun, although it was not yet public knowledge. The operation was delayed by twenty-four hours due to bad weather much to the annoyance of the generals. Nothing much happened on Tuesday for 612 Field Squadron at Aldershot, they were having an easy time of it. While the lads were having their dinner in the canteen, the BBC Home Service was interrupted with a Special News Bulletin. Chic and his pals, listened in silence;

"D-Day has come."

"Early this morning, the Allies began the assault on the north-western face of Hitler's European Fortress. The first official news came just after half past nine when Supreme HQ of the Allied Expeditionary Force, (SHAEF), issued Communique N.1."

....

"Under the Command of General Eisenhower, Allied Naval Forces supported by strong Air Forces, began landing Allied Armies this morning on the Northern coast of France." ....
"General Montgomery is in Command of the Army Group carrying out the assault."

This was them, this was action stations. Chic barely heard the rest of the bulletin that talked of the well trained and battle-hardened enemy, how the free men of the world are marching together to victory. It went on for about five minutes, he hoped Joyce had not heard it, she would think he was in those first troops that had just landed in France. He went back to the workshop and carried on with packing up but his mind was elsewhere. During the evening hundreds of allied aircraft flew over Aldershot, they were bound for Europe. This was not that unusual, bombing raids on Germany were a regular occurrence, except this time there seemed to be very many more and they were making a lot of noise about it.

The following morning, they were packing up to move and after being told to rest in the afternoon, 612 Field Squadron set off in convoy after midnight, under cover of darkness. They went northwards from Aldershot, along the blacked-out roads, each vehicle following the discreet lights of the one in front. Their predecessors travelled on route in daylight and were cheered along by civilians who offered cups of tea and wished good luck, but now most people were tucked up in bed. The convoy followed the Portsmouth Road, through Tolworth, across London Bridge and into the city. It was slow going but finally they arrived at the West Ham speedway track in London's East End, in time for breakfast. Camp T *(Thames)* 4 was the 612 Field Squadron's designated D-Day marshalling area.

Despite travelling all night there was still more waterproofing to be done on their own vehicles, in readiness for the invasion. And then it was time to wait, three days with nothing to do. Chic wrote a few letters, went to the pictures and had a good Saturday night out in the East End pubs with his best man Johnno. The locals were eager to wish them well and buy them drinks, they refused more than they accepted. They spent the last of their English pennies and tried to get some sleep back at the camp. Chic did not enjoy having time on his hands, the anticipation of what was to come was playing on his mind. He now had French francs in his pocket it looked like Monopoly money. He was camping out under canvas in the back of a lorry on a race track in London's bombed out East End, waiting for something to happen and it was raining cats and dogs.

Sunday morning brought orders to move off. They arrived at The Royal Docks mid-morning, despite the appalling state of the surrounding buildings, the actual dock area was fully operational, but the stevedores *(dockers),* were not. They had been on strike and now they were working to rule, with absolutely no sense of urgency or patriotism. This did not go down well with any of the soldiers, least of all Chic who watched on helplessly while cranes dangled their equipment and supplies in mid-air, in torrential rain, while the dockers had a tea break. Major Bowen was overseeing the whole operation from LST 543; a huge American tank landing ship in the Victoria Dock. Chic's unit was designated a smaller ship LCT 522, moored next door in Albert Dock, their loading up went remarkably well all things considered.

Chic's boat set sail for Chatham at 1900 hours. In less than an hour both docks were empty and Major Bowen's ship was on its way to Southend, where it dropped anchor to wait for the tide. Chic's ship moored up further south near Chatham, in the Medway estuary soon after midnight. He snatched a couple of hours sleep in a hammock, that was a new experience! He was surprised at how comfortable it was and managed to sleep soundly, despite being fully clothed including his boots. Everyone woke early to glorious sunshine, but Chic was itchy, he discovered he was sleeping under a lousy blanket. He rolled out of the hammock and smartened himself up with a shave and a quick brush down and went for a walk along the shingle beach with the lads, before tucking into an excellent breakfast. He took a snap with Johnno's camera, Johnno, Bill and Harry with a beautiful old frigate, the training ship *"Arethusa"* moored in the background.

They sailed out of the Medway estuary at 0800 to join the main convoy of ships, tugs and assorted smaller boats that were now well underway, with more vessels joining them all the time. A lot of the lads were sea sick but Chic was fine, he liked the smell of diesel fumes. They travelled around the Kent coast to Newhaven, where Major Bowen's ship moored up again, this time to collect foot soldiers. Their ship sailed on to Portsmouth before regrouping and making its way with hundreds of others across the English Channel. They travelled all day and night on the 12ᵗʰ of June with more craft joining them throughout the crossing. It was Joyce's birthday, how Chic wished he could be with her instead of here. It was like Piccadilly Circus in the middle of the Channel, destroyers were weaving in and out, acting as traffic police, making announcements over loud hailers, amber and the occasional, red alert. The spectacle stretched as far as the eye could see, many boats had barrage balloons for protection against the Luftwaffe. The sea was calm and the sun shining, perfect cruising weather, but the ominous task ahead was never far from the men's thoughts. The crossing was a relatively peaceful one in this sector, two ships hit mines and one caught fire when it was bombed by mistake, but that was easy going compared to what the lads before them had come up against. Major Bowen anchored at Courseulles on Tuesday morning, but Chic's ship was several hours behind, they did not arrive until the early hours of Wednesday.

He was both relieved and anxious as he drove his lorry out of the bowels of the ship and down a ramp between two rows of white ribbons, onto a beach that was littered with the macabre flotsam and jetsam of corpses, burnt out vehicles, ship wrecks and crashed planes. The sea was black with craft jostling for space. It took over an hour to disembark, he quickly set to with his de-waterproofing. Then there was the loading up, this took another hour or so, making it late afternoon before they moved away from the beach. They were now frantically camouflaging the vehicles and digging themselves in under a beautiful red sunset. Chic did not get much rest, there was erratic bombing throughout the night, loud enough to stir him from fitful sleep, despite it being in the distance. The Luftwaffe were bombing the allied ships in hit and run raids and as the navy returned fire the sky lit up in a series of spectacular firework displays. These last few days would be ingrained on his memory forever. He was woken at first light on Thursday morning to disturbing news, Sergeant Ramsden was lost. He had gone out with his driver Sapper Lawrence, after dark to look for the marching party and inadvertently driven into enemy lines. Their jeep was destroyed and Ramsden was injured. Steve had to leave his sergeant behind but managed to make it back to camp just before dawn. Sergeant Ramsden was their first casualty.

6. FRANCE.

Orders at 0900 were to move forward and Chic wrote in his diary;

"We are advancing."

As far as Chic was concerned he was going into battle, he was tired, frightened and his stomach was churning. That afternoon a survival pack was given to each soldier in the unit, Sapper PR Sherwood received issue number 232; a black tin box, the size of a small attaché case, with a metal handle and the following words stamped on the top;

"OUTFIT, FIRST AID, GENERAL, LARGE."

It contained two emergency ration packs, medical supplies including morphine and a housewife sewing kit. They were all on compo rations. These were packed in large wooden boxes and designed to provide three meals for fourteen men: breakfast, tiffin *(lunch)*, and dinner. Tinned everything: Spam, sausages, beans, soup, mash, vegetables, powdered egg, cheese, steamed and rice puddings, plus hard biscuits, dried fruit, chocolate and boiled sweets. The tins were self-heating, they just needed a match to light the fuse but that didn't always go well, Chic ate most of his rations cold. However, he did enjoy frequent cups of instant tea that were already mixed with milk and sugar and his daily ration of seven cigarettes. The hot water was provided by Corporal Whitaker and his catering team, who made sure there were always several pots on the go, either in the purpose dug cooking trench or bubbling away on a smouldering tank.

The unit was ordered to move all vehicles away from the beach which was duly done under sniper fire, their first encounter with the enemy. It was a hair-raising experience, but Chic felt relatively safe in his truck, he was grateful not to be in infantry. The unit survived unscathed and harboured in an orchard just beyond the village. Each truck parked up in a circle facing outwards and then every soldier dug his own individual slit trench to settle down for the night. Chic still had his boots on, he didn't dare take them off, despite his feet throbbing like mad. As darkness fell the hedges lit up with glow worms, what accommodating little creatures, now he had the chance to write a letter to his darling, he needed to do something normal. He was able to tell her the crossing was calm with no sign of Jerry planes and the weather was gorgeous, so far so good. He did not mention the mined ships, or that one boat had caught fire when it was bombed by one of their own allied planes. Nor did he say that he had been shot at by snipers and there was a rumour that some French women were being hanged that day for sniping and colluding with the enemy. He did tell his wife how shocked he was that some local women were married to Germans. The letter was shorter than usual, Chic had a painful boil on his wrist that sent stabbing pains up his arm every time he moved his right hand. He blamed that bloody lousy blanket on the boat. He should have got the infection checked out, but it wasn't worth going to see the medics, they were too busy with more serious stuff.

The next few days were quiet during the daylight hours, with sporadic air raids at night, but nothing too close. There was a bit of general maintenance required, the vehicles were sorted out and moved about to ensure everything was correctly placed in readiness for moving off at a moment's notice. No one had received any letters or parcels since leaving Aldershot. All post to all ranks had been embargoed before D-Day, but today the postman had arrived and the whole camp was engrossed in opening their letters and parcels. Chic received three letters and his marriage certificate, he would send that straight back to Joyce for safe keeping. There were two letters from Joyce, one telling him she thought she was pregnant. He wrote in his diary that he was going to be; *"a Daddy,"* he was thrilled and ready for anything. But his elation only lasted twenty four hours. A third letter arrived, Joyce was ill, she had lost the baby. In a flash Chic's mood dropped to zero, he was worried about his wife and full of doom and gloom.

All the lads were killing time, they just wanted to get on with the job in hand. Each individual dealt with boredom in different ways, Johnno played cards, Harry read his poetry and Bill did a bit of whittling. Chic enjoyed banter with the best of them, but he was in sombre mood and could not settle to anything. They were all sent to a lecture in the afternoon, the Frenchman spoke perfect English about *"The German Occupation of France."* There were more shocking revelations that just added to Chic's anxiety, he was distracted and wished he could be with his darling. News had also filtered through that there were plans to shoot a German prisoner the next day at the POW camp, just a mile or so down the road, Chic was not sure how he felt about that.

They were all playing a waiting game at the 612 FS HQ, there was no sense of urgency. Chic went out on his motorcycle to do a recce, his sergeant saw no reason to keep him in camp when there was nothing to do. He had a good run despite the roads being bad and it stopped him thinking. The following day he rode up to visit 2 Troop. The road deteriorated from bad to worse, it was badly cratered from incendiary bombs and littered with burnt out vehicles, but worst of all, there were dead cows everywhere. A permanent sweet sickly smell hung in the air wherever he went, it filtered through the dusty breeze and the hotter the weather, the worse it got. Some carcasses had been piled up and set alight with petrol, but most were just bulldozed to the side of the road. The cows that had been dead for several days were swelling up with their feet in the air. Every now and then, one would burst and send the disgusting stench of putrid guts and blood into the prevailing wind, it was the aroma of death! Chic felt bilious. At that moment, he was not thinking about the carnage, or the risk he was taking riding out on his motorcycle, his head and his stomach were in turmoil. He was oblivious to the dangers, but no harm came to him he was lucky.

On 26* June the lower ranks were informed that the big push past Caen was going ahead. This operation involved thousands of men in the 21* Army Group, Canadian and British, with Chic's division, the Eleventh Armoured bringing up the flank. The whole exercise commenced in the pouring rain. It was quiet for Chic back at HQ, there was not much to do and too much time to think. One good thing about the torrential rain, was that it diluted *"the stench of death."* He managed to eat some warm tinned sausages with mash, without gagging and enjoyed a rice pudding. However, the rain was not popular with the powers that be, it was hampering all operations and making progress for the advance parties very slow. Despite the weather, the following afternoon 612 FS moved up in column with the other support troops to Le Mesnil Patry. They immediately met evidence of hard-fought battles, the lads were returning with horrific tales of death and destruction. Men from both sides lay dead and injured among the mine fields. The noxious smell was now accompanied by the blood curdling screams of soldiers and the distant shouts of stretcher bearers, amongst constant gun fire and enemy shelling, searing them all.

The fields had to be cleared of mines, it was several hours, before they could bury the British and the German dead. 1 Troop, were tasked with sweeping a clear path for the bulldozer and came across a *"Bouncing Betty."* A booby-trapped anti-personnel landmine with a pull igniter that was designed to throw ball bearings in all directions, a very nasty device intended to kill and maim. It was defused without incident to the

45

great relief of the lads, who had already lost five men in the fighting, there were hundreds more from other units, all dead. Chic discovered that Sergeant Parker and Crowley from 2 FF Yeo (the 2ⁿ Fife and Forfar Yeomanry) were killed in their half-track at Le Haut-du-Bosq the day before, seventeen of their men were killed that day. They were all up against the highly trained combat engineer battalion of the 12 SS Panzer Division and the fighting was stiff. Morale was boosted a little when news filtered through that hundreds of German prisoners from the 12 SS Panzers were being brought in. Some progress was being made, but at what cost? Chic was cut up about Parker and Crowley, he had worked closely with these boys.

The shelling intensified, even the harbour at HQ was under attack. The Nazis had a new device called a Nebelwerfer; a rocket projector with six barrels that fired flaming, onion shaped mortar bombs into the air and took out everything in their path. They boys called them *"Moaning Minnies,"* they were designed to put the fear of God into those who could see and hear them coming. These short rocket fireballs, moaned and screamed all the way to their target as the recipients watched helplessly, knowing they had little chance of escape unless the gunners could shoot them down first. They exploded on impact, with repeated deafening bangs, spreading fragments of red-hot steel over a wide area. The whole landscape was now a wasteland with burning buildings and wrecked vehicles. The Germans were destroying everything that crossed their path as they retreated and leaving their dead, unburied.

On Wednesday 28ᵗʰ June, there was more stiff fighting, this time at Cheux. Sergeant Budd was one of many killed that day, Chic knew most of the lads who were killed and injured. Reality had set in, they were all in hell on earth. The whole division was now under fire, the shelling relentless and the gunfire continuous, with the deathly smell of high explosive all about them. 1 Troop returned having failed again in their task to make good the road ahead and 2 Troop had lost one of their half-tracks, Major Bowen's squadron was at stalemate. The fighting was too stiff and the going impossible for the armoured troops, in the drenching rain. The major called a *"stand to,"* and they all retreated back to where they had been a few days earlier, at Le Mesnil-Patry.

Chic's unit got off quite lightly with only a few minor injuries, including a lance-sergeant who was run over by his own driver and evacuated to a forward dressing station with a leg injury. The men were exhausted and stupid mistakes were being made. By Saturday the whole armoured division had been pulled back for a rest. Chic was thankful that he was not in infantry, they were only given twenty-four hours before being sent back in again. On 2ⁿᵈ July the weather had improved but now they were up against a battalion of the 1ˢᵗ SS Panzer Grenadier Regiment from the Adolph Hitler Division, a serious bunch of black shirts. The camp was told they were advancing, but no progress was made, they were pulled back again. The squadron was literally in the thick of it, with over a thousand big guns blasting out from first light, all through the day and long into the night. It was too noisy to sleep and Chic was scared out of his wits.

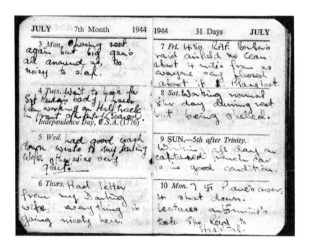

By Tuesday 4ᵗʰ July the fighting had eased a little, it was warm and the sun was shining through a haze of a fine ash that settled on and in everything. The landscape was now a ghoulish grey with splashes of red and the sulphurous smell of hell accompanying an eerie silence. Chic went out on his motorcycle to look for Sergeant Parker's body. Major Bowen thought it too dangerous for motorbikes to go out on the lethal roads, but that message did not get through to Chic. Five men were missing, there was no sign of any of them but Chic did find the sergeant's half-track, it was in one piece, but bullets had punctured the radiator. He was in front of infantry, terrified, and in a cold sweat, but a job needed doing. He gave himself a good talking to and managed to fix the radiator with the help of some water proofing putty and a few bandages. He stacked his bike up on the rack and limped back to HQ in the half-track. The ghostly apparition caused great hilarity in the camp until he told his mates there was no sign of Sergeant Parker. Chic felt lucky to be alive and desperately needed a drink, he was spitting dust. A nice cup of char, courtesy of boiling water from a billy can perched on a burned out but still smouldering German tank, did the trick.

The next day was pretty quiet, the camp was now at full complement and HQ had been informed that a medical officer was arriving to carry out an FFI *(free from infection)* inspection. The latrines were filled in and relocated and hot showers were laid on for all ranks, by the mobile laundry and bath unit. Chic was one of the first to get a good wash down, he was in heaven. He did a spot of sunbathing while his dirty uniform was swapped for a clean one, along with a pair of clean underpants and a shirt. The pants were too big, but they and he were clean! Then it was time to get in the queue for the doctor, every man had his private parts checked for the clap *(venereal disease),* most had a clean bill of health including Chic. Major Bowen was more than pleased, although to be fair, the men had not had much opportunity to misbehave despite there being an ever present contingent of prostitutes that could be found by the most earnest soldiers, but Chic kept well clear of all that. He mentioned the boil on his wrist to the doctor, it was healing nicely and nothing to worry about. He settled down to write to his darling wife.

612 Field Squadron were now resting and the following day Chic received a letter from Joyce, he was feeling very positive, and wrote in his diary;

"Everything going very nicely here."

The next couple of weeks were busy for the mechanics, while the boys were having a bit of R & R *(rest and recuperation),* the mood in camp was optimistic. Caen was bombed yet again by the allies, they watched the sky as hundreds of RAF *(Royal Air Force)* bombers targeted the Caen airfield, less than four miles away. Chic was working eight hour days in the makeshift garage, throughout this rest period. Busted vehicles were pouring in, many with major faults. It was pressured with uncomfortable working conditions, but then news arrived that only one allied aircraft had been lost in the Caen raid and the Germans were in retreat. The propaganda was working, and morale was high, despite those *"Moaning Minnies,"* or as some referred to them; *"the mother-in-law",* that were still spreading their evil work. A couple of the lads returned from a recce with a French car that had been in German hands and Chic was assigned to check it over. It was in very good condition and he enjoyed working on it. The following evening, seven Nazi planes flew overhead, four were shot down but one caught Sapper Reid in the strafing. In the morning Chic took him to the dressing station, he wasn't seriously injured and was back on duty in no time, but it was a wake-up call for Chic, it could just as easily have been him.

On his return from the field hospital, Chic was ordered to attend a lecture about Nazi mines and instructed to go on mine detection practice the following afternoon. He was given the morning off and decided to ride his motorcycle to Bayeux. The town was about ten miles south, the roads in that direction had improved slightly, they were drying out in the glorious sunshine but the dust got into everything. Chic bought a round of camembert cheese with his Monopoly money. He had never tasted French cheese before, what a rich and delicious treat. He was now hardened to the sickly odour that consumed the whole countryside, although the cheese did its best to out-do that particular perfume. He also tasted French cider for the first time, it was extremely strong. It probably wasn't a good idea to go mine detecting with a couple of pints inside you, but Chic did. He thought it was all pretty straightforward, the standard drill was to thread a piece of rope through the ring and then move back twenty yards, crouch down and pull the rope. It was easy when you knew you were not going to get blown up. He kept his head down and survived another day, this time with a hangover.

On Wednesday orders came in to move back to Saint Aubin where the squadron was required to build a rest camp. This was good and bad news, it was great to have a rest but they were going backwards. Chic had just received two letters, one from his wife and the other from his mother. He immediately wrote back to Joyce and talked of the fine weather, his trip to Bayeux and the delicious French cheese, he was missing her more than he could say. He also caught up with his diary, he had not written in it since the bombing of Caen. The next day Chic, Johnno and Bill walked out in Saint Aubin the sun was scorching hot as they strolled along the sea front still littered with the spoils of war. The town was in ruins, most of the buildings were bombed out, many razed to the ground. There were only a few residents left, food was in very short supply. The beach was covered in debris as far as the eye could see, created by a military machine that had rapidly moved on. They did not really notice any of it, they were all hardening to the reality of war and keen to enjoy the sunshine while they could.

Sunday was a busy one for Chic, he was working all day and thoroughly browned off, more from exhaustion than anything else. He badly needed a rest, but it didn't look like he was going to get one. Major General Pip Roberts had just been given the news that his own Eleventh Armoured Division was being moved up to the Caen area once again, to lead the next offensive, Chic didn't know that yet, which was probably for the best. He gritted his teeth and got on with his work, unaware that on Monday, the 29ᵗʰ Armoured Brigade with 612 FS tagging along, would be back within shouting distance from where they had been just last week, in readiness to advance behind artillery again. At first light on Monday morning, Stead and Corporal Whitaker led the convoy in their Bedford MWD ration truck, along the route, codenamed; *"Holly,"* to the designated field at Lasson where unit 41 was to be harboured. They carried a large wooden sign painted in yellow and blue with the sign of the bull, the number 41 and an arrow pointing left. After they parked up, Stead in his shirt sleeves and Sam wearing a jumper knitted by his mother, stood casually holding the sign directing the rest of the convoy. They were smoking cigarettes and looked like they were on a jolly camping trip. Johnno took a photograph of them.

On the 18ᵗʰ July the offensive began at 0530 hours with allied air bombardment. Artillery went in two hours later and 2 N Yeo *(2ⁿᵈ Northamptonshire Yeomanry)* advanced up to Cuverville. The weather was good but the fighting stiff. Sergeant King and eight sappers from 3 Troop were wounded, Corporal Gilbey and Sapper Williams died, Kingy was not expected to live. They were attached to the 8ᵗʰ Rifle Brigade just north of Grentheville, after fighting all day they were then confronted with six German tiger tanks in the dark, they suffered dreadfully. There was congestion on the bridgehead and progress across the river was slow, reinforcements were unable to get through. The 29ᵗʰ Armoured Brigade were stuck and exposed, the enemy was standing fast and shelling relentlessly, the noise was ear splitting. Close to midnight they began dropping flares which illuminated the whole of the camp at HQ. Bombing quickly followed creating mayhem, it was terrifying for them all but infantry got the worst of it, they had been fighting all day and now they were being attacked again as they tried to sleep. Chic did not sleep, it was hot and dusty with that putrid smell that never went away and then there were the insects, the flies and mosquitos were driving him mad. The groaning of men in pain, the unworldly screams of those caught in the shelling combined with the unrelenting noise of gun fire brought nightmares that turned out to be reality, he was frightened to close his eyes.

On Thursday he was sent on foot to pick up an abandoned half-track, *(jeep type vehicle with two wheels and tracking),* whilst being strafed by Nazi planes, this was becoming normality. A torrential rainstorm had come through in the afternoon soaking everything in its path, it continued to rain for two days making the going tougher as each hour passed and hampering the progress of reinforcements. They were all still stuck with no sign of relief. Chic's memories of Operation Eagle hung heavy, as he was lost in his thoughts an Ack Ack *(anti-aircraft)* gun, shot the tail off a Nazi plane just a few yards from where he was working. Then an RASC *(Royal Army Service Corps)* driver stepped on a mine in the next field, his screams echoed around the camp for what seemed like hours, he had lost both his legs. They were all in hell and Chic had an horrendous headache that he could not shake off. On 22ⁿᵈ July the whole section was ordered back across the river, where they were told to wait for the reinforcements that were so long arriving. On the same day Chic and Bill had to stay put, they were given five trucks to get functioning again. There was one consolation, the heavy work load took Chic's mind off the horrors of the last few days. The boys had been bombed and five of them were now hospitalised back in Blighty.

It was a rush to get the trucks ready while the rest of the unit was on the move. It took five days, a truck a day, and they were both dog tired by the time they finished. On Friday the 28ᵗʰ July it was time to move on, Chic went to the flics at HQ and watched Errol Flynn in *"Gentleman Jim,"* but he couldn't say what he thought of it, he fell asleep. The squadron was now moving over to help the Americans, they travelled in convoy by night and were all exhausted, there was no chance to sleep. On 30ᵗʰ July the attacks began and the 29ᵗʰ Armoured Brigade were doing well alongside the Yanks, but bombs blasted 3 troop, eight men were hurt and Harris stood on a mine. Despite all that morale was high. The allies were smashing through the German armour at Coutances and prisoners were rolling in from all directions.

At nightfall on the 1ˢᵗ August, Chic's unit were held up in the woods five-hundred yards south of the town with among others, the 13ᵗʰ Field Squadron. Everything was quiet. This gave Chic a chance to meet up with his friend Jenni *(Sapper Verner Jensen)* the next day. He gave him a wedding photograph and told him he was greatly missed at the celebration. Jenni was disappointed not to have been there, particularly as he was kicking his heels back in camp with all his squadron leave cancelled for no apparent reason. It was all rather frustrating, but a lot of water had passed under the bridge since then and they had another good laugh about some of their past antics, not least when they drove across the Yorkshire Moors backwards in the Mark 1 scout car, after several pints at The Blacksmiths Arms. They parted with strong handshakes and a hug, little did they know that would be the last time they would get the chance to speak to each other.

The allied troops up ahead were now advancing like hares, with little opposition. The beautiful Normandy countryside was a patchwork of fields, thick woodland, narrow lanes, high hedges and deep ditches, not an easy landscape for armoured tank warfare. They were harboured in the woods and almost continually under gun fire, along with those dreaded *"Moaning Minnies"* that were doubly dangerous here. They exploded into thousands of pieces as they bounced off the trees. Despite all that, the chaps in charge knew the enemy was flagging. On Friday Chic was sent down to 1 Troop, they had a BARV *(Beach Armoured Recovery Vehicle)* diesel tank, that had been abandoned at the front line. It was used originally as a recovery vehicle on the beach landings because it had a high hull. Most tanks had petrol engines, but this one was designed specifically to be exposed to sea water where diesel was the favoured fuel. Now the engine was playing up and it was in the way. If Chic could get it going, the tracked tank would be very useful for shifting the many obstacles left by the retreating Germans.

He walked through the woods and kept his head down, he was fastidious in every footstep, terrified he too might tread on a mine or meet a sniper. He had never worked on a tank engine before and in a weird way was looking forward to the challenge. The engine was quite different to what he was used to, but he knew about diesels and got his head around the mechanics. Eventually, after two days the mighty beast was up and running, Chic was very pleased with himself. Then he heard that 2 Troop had been bombed by friendly fire, this made him extremely angry. It was bad enough that they were all in this terrible situation without having to watch their backs from both directions. He never did like the gung-ho approach of the Yanks. The next day the Americans apologised but that paid short shrift with Chic.

What did cheer him up was the arrival of two parcels, one from Mum and the other from his maiden Aunt Martha, it was his birthday on the 8th of August. The parcels contained cards, writing paper, a pen and more underpants from Mum, with ciggies from Dad. His aunt had knitted some very colourful socks. Martha always favoured her almost youngest nephew, she was a little odd, but Chic liked her. She was the kindest and most thoughtful of his aunts and uncles, of which he had many. The Sherwoods were a bit of a rum lot. His father Frank was the second youngest of ten children, he suffered a dreadfully deprived childhood. His father was a brawling drunkard who beat his wife and assaulted his children on a daily basis. Frank's mother used to hide him and his baby brother in the loft over the cow byre, to save them from the drunken blows of their father, who died when Frank was sixteen years old. Neither Frank or his little brother were sent to school, they were both illiterate. Annie taught Frank to read, when he lodged with the Plant family before The Great War, they subsequently got married. Chic's father was a kind and cheerful soul and a good provider who made sure his family never suffered the hardships that he had done.

Chic celebrated his twenty-fourth birthday with a bath and swapped his filthy uniform, underwear and overalls for fresh clean clothes, all supplied by the unit's very own laundry facility that operated under the auspices of HQ. The shirt didn't fit, but no matter, he felt as fresh as a daisy. When he returned from the wash house there was news that the 147 Field Park Company's cook had been taken alive. That was a double blow, cooks were in short supply!

> *"With a bit of luck, the enemy might put him to work,*
> *and he could poison his captors."*

They were all supposed to be getting a bit of quality rest but no one could relax, who would be kidnapped next? Chic was pleased to be busy. He was now working on a captured T45 Citroen truck that had been abandoned by the Germans just beyond the camp perimeter. The Nazis took over the Citroen factory in Paris when they invaded, back in 1940 and subjected the French civilians into forced labour, to produce hundreds of vehicles for use by the German military. It looked like the engine had seized, a was a major job and towed back to the workshop. He and Bill worked on the truck all day, from dawn until dusk with shells falling less than 200 yards away. Luckily neither of them suffered any injuries but it was difficult to keep their minds on the job. After two days of hard graft; draining the oil, stripping the engine and replacing the bearings, they put the engine back together and Chic poured in the clean oil. The strange thing was the dip stick was showing full, when he had only put in half the amount of oil usually needed. He wondered if he had the wrong oil gauge but there was no time to investigate, the vehicle was working that was all that mattered. What he didn't know was that the French POWs attempted to sabotage production by adding false readings to the oil gauges, rendering the vehicles unreliable.

He settled down to writing his thank-you letters. Everyone had been told to be ready to move at a moment's notice, the unit had been packing up for a couple of days. That night he slept deeply, even the shelling did not stir him. When he woke in the morning, the Citroen truck had gone, in its place stood a cardboard sign with the word; *"DANKE" (thanks)* painted on it, the Germans had stolen their truck back, Chic and Bill had repaired it for Jerry *(the enemy)*. If he hadn't been so gutted he would have laughed out loud, they had found a German with a sense of humour! Chic consoled himself by writing to Joyce and sending her a gift, a small copper wishing well with a tiny brass bucket that wound up and down, something he had been making in idle moments from scrap metal in the workshop. Then bad news came in about Chic Williams, one of the sappers from their squadron injured at Cuverville, he had died from his wounds. The roll of honour was getting longer by the day, Chic took stock and counted his blessings once again.

The BBC world service reported on the 11[e] August that rabies was back in England after more than twenty years. This bothered Chic, rabies was highly feared in Britain. When he was little, Grandpa Charlie told him stories of mad dogs roaming the streets and attacking people, causing them to go mad. Rabies was still rife in Europe but nobody seemed worried about it in France, the civilians had worse things to fret about. Chic's anxiety was at high pitch, he was worrying about everything. To top it all he discovered that his best friend Jenni's squadron, 13 FS was being sent in alongside infantry because the British sector was so short of men. He thought it was only a matter of time before the 612 FS trod the same path. Allied bombers were coming in to hit twenty Nazi Divisions and the Eleventh Armoured Division was being moved up to lead an attack through the Falaise pocket. Chic wrote five letters, he thought they may be his last.

Two days later the squadron moved off and Chic wrote;

"Going storm."

There was news in camp that Jenni had suffered a shrapnel injury whilst working out ahead with infantry, it was only his hand otherwise he was fine. There were stories spreading that the Jerries in retreat, were setting mines, blowing bridges and felling trees to slow down their pursuers. Chic's unit was a few hundred yards back down the column, they progressed slowly but surely along the narrow lanes in a vast traffic jam. The lads up ahead were dealing with blocked roads, snipers, booby-trapped vehicles and horrific spectacles of suppurating bodies, both man and beast. Many of the dead men and animals had been driven over, causing the flesh to burst open and providing a haven for maggots and flies. As they proceeded, the debris was bulldozed out of the way, burned and the vehicles drenched in disinfectant or petrol. But this was not always possible, the stench was unimaginable. Every now and then the convoy came to a complete halt, while a few Germans were taken prisoner or a suspicious vehicle was investigated. At one point a Red Cross ambulance was being used as a hide out by snipers, nothing could be taken for granted. Despite all this the allies were covering twenty miles a day with little opposition.

AUGUST	8th Month	1944	1944	31 Days	AUGUST
12, *Sat*. 13.75. acting as infantry. we are pushed for men with British sector				16 *Wed.* German gat hit in hand with a manuel.	
13 SUN.—10*th after Trinity.* Wrote 5 letters. Bomber's coming to bomb 20 Fi Divs				17 *Thurs.* We are covering 20 a day.	
14					

On 18th August the town of Flers was entered by the allies and liberated in every sense. The whole town went crazy throwing garlands of flowers, cheering and waving. Women and children filled the streets offering cider and Calvados to *"Les Tommies."* In return the soldiers handed out chocolate and cigarettes into the clamouring hands of children and their parents. The inhabitants looked half-starved, supplies had been cut off for months after years under German occupation. The seemingly endless convoy trundled slowly through Flers, stopping and starting, inching onwards, through hamlets and villages as they proceeded northward. The Germans were leaving a trail of destruction behind them but that did not concern the locals at this moment in time, they were elated to meet their liberators, glad to be alive and welcomed them literally with open arms. It was an enormous morale boost for everyone, Chic forgot his worries for a few hours, had several drinks and relished the excitement of the moment. This was what it was all about, they were succeeding in their task, fatigue transformed to euphoria.

It took two days for Chic's section of the column to reach Conde-sur-Noireau, about ten miles north of Flers. The flowers kept coming and the cider kept flowing for miles and miles. The convoy was held up constantly, not just by excited children and their families all wanting to thank each chap individually, but also by the unbelievable images of destruction, they were now witnessing the remains of those hard-fought battles. Every twist and turn revealed piles of half incinerated human flesh, indistinguishable from the animal carcasses that shared these gruesome pyres. The column proceeded slowly but surely past these horrific sights with barely a glance, they had to keep moving. As they approached the town of Conde-sur-Noireau, the scene that met their eyes was one of complete devastation, there was nothing left standing. The enemy had taken time before retreating, to systematically destroy every single building in the town. The elation of the last few days was displaced with one huge swathe of shock and disbelief. There were a few citizens wandering aimlessly around in a state of confusion, most had left, many were dead. It was Armageddon.

There was no time to reflect, they kept moving up through the Falaise gap towards the city of Caen again, where the enemy still had a strong foothold. Shells were dropping all around them but the advance troops had managed to drop two bridgeheads across the River Seine and the Eleventh Armoured Division was going strong. The front-line troops were all tired, the 29th Armoured Brigade was pulled out for a rest which meant much work for Chic and his unit in their temporary workshop. Three days of hard graft to get the trucks and armoured vehicles roadworthy, before they set off again. It also started raining and continued to rain incessantly for days and days. Jenni was up ahead with 13FS assisting infantry in its attempt to cross The Seine. He rescued a wounded sapper under mortar fire and directed tanks over one of the newly constructed Bailey bridges, whilst still under fire. Chic feared for his friend's safety, he had been wounded again, this time it was his leg. Sapper Jensen had been recommended for a medal.

On the 29ᵗʰ August 1944 Chic's unit also crossed the River Seine. He pulled the short straw, he was on Johnny's motorcycle, loaded up the hilt, with a STEN *(submachine)* gun over his shoulder. Johnny had a raging temperature and was ordered to passenger one of the Bedford lorries. Progress was painfully slow due to the incessant rain and the constant road blocks. Chic got absolutely drenched as he rode alongside the trucks, in column, behind the tanks and gun carriers. It was still raining cats and dogs when news came through that the allies had taken Amiens, this information was enough to lift all their spirits. Chic wrote;

"Jerry on the run."

The next morning, he found time to write to Joyce before breakfast, he told her about Jenni, the good and the bad news, but that everything was going well. The column continued its laboured progress from dawn until dusk and then all through the night, along the hedge lined lanes. These narrow roads were little more than single tracks in places, with no option but to drive over the mass of rotting carcasses. The enemy was now retreating with great haste on whatever transport it could find, the convoy passed the putrefied corpses of men with their dead horses still attached to carts. The ditches were full of gory debris just left to rot, the stench of decomposing flesh and entrails permeated every inch of the landscape. There was no time to tidy up, the carcasses were no longer being doused with petrol for burning. Fuel was in short supply and haste was considered paramount on the road to victory.

The column snaked its way through the countryside, liberating each village they passed through but without stopping, a few locals appeared from among the ruins to wave them on. There was a lot of confusion, particularly at night, the lower ranks did not have maps apart from the few they had snitched from dead Germans. Everyone followed the lights in front when it was dark and as a result, some units got lost. On the 1ˢ September just before dawn they were stationary due to an incident up ahead. Chic was resting on his still heavily laden motorbike, with a gun at his side. The chaps on the Bren *(gas machine)* gun carriers further up the column, heard German voices on a half-track in front. The occupants were challenged, they abandoned their vehicle and ran off across the fields towards the woods and after being shot at emerged back on the road in front of Chic's unit. They all gave themselves up, except for one bright German spark on a motorcycle, who made a dash for it. He rode straight in front of Chic and went hell for leather to the rear of the column where a static Bren gunner opened fire, he was instantly a gonner. The bike wobbled and veered off the road into the nearest ditch. The Nazi was left there for dead in an unceremonious heap to slowly rot. The following day, Chic wrote in his diary;

"Jerry convoy pulled into our convoy. We fix 'em."

The column remained stationary until dawn when the prisoners were made to walk within the convoy under armed guard. Hundreds more German prisoners were rolling in. Chic didn't have much to do with them, he was ordered to drive the German Pioneer half-track, as they continued on their way.

They were now going hell for leather towards the Belgian border with the French inhabitants in every town, village and hamlet they passed through, becoming more and more enthusiastic. They were showered with gifts, including voluminous amounts of alcohol. Chic and his mates were overwhelmed with the welcome, it would have been churlish to refuse a few drinks. What the squadron did not know was that early on Friday evening their commanding officer Major Bowen, had been killed by friendly fire. His jeep had taken a wrong turn and was attacked by a couple of Spitfires (*British fighter aircraft*) as he was being driven back to Divisional HQ. The squadron now had an acting officer in command, Captain Anderson. This information was held back for a while, it was important that the lower ranks did not lose impetus, not only were they on the offensive but the troops were in jubilant mood. The bad news could wait!

7. BELGIUM.

At 1800 hours precisely on Sunday 3ʳᵈ September, Chic's unit crossed into Belgium just beyond Carvin. The Belgian people were going mad, the streets alive with crowds celebrating; singing, dancing and welcoming their liberators with boundless excitement. It was four years since Britain had declared war on Germany, after the Nazis occupied Holland, Belgium and then France, but now the enemy was on the run. Chic willingly joined in the celebrations, he had never been hugged and kissed so much in his life. The children were a delight and seemed grateful for anything, all he had left to give them was a few hard biscuits. These moments were exactly what they had all been fighting for and they were treated as heroes. The police held back a sea of waving flags, everyone wanted to shake a soldier's hand, kiss them on both cheeks or simply touch them. Pretty young girls were jumping all over the vehicles throwing caution to the wind, while their parents showered the men with gifts of wine and cheese. In return, *"Les Tommies"* threw back whatever they had into the crowd, the world for a few short hours was a happy and positive place. It was time for the division to stock up with supplies, not only food rations but also much needed fuel and ammunition. A huge NAAFI van turned up with some extra delights for the men. Chic bought chocolate and cigarettes with his Monopoly money, he spent all he had.

The next day, Captain Townsend announced to his troops that Major Christopher James Croasdaile Bowen, 63533 RE, had been killed by two Spitfires on the 1ˢᵗ of September 1944. Captain Townsend was now their temporary acting officer in charge. They all thought Townsend a good bloke but Chic and his pals were angry, the major shot down by the RAF, they couldn't even blame the Yanks for that one! The squadron was now to be harboured at Willebroek, the route was yet another obstacle course despite the roads being made as good as possible by the advance parties of the 612 sappers and 13ᵗʰ Field Squadron. Now the engineers were busy building a 120 foot, triple single Bailey bridge across the River Rupel. This was a portable prefabricated structure that was built in sections on site. The bridge was finished and roadworthy by the early hours of Tuesday morning and named *"The Bowen Bridge."* There was still much work to do, the Germans had set floating mines in the river and there were pockets of resistance on the north bank, just south of Antwerp.

While the lads were doing all that, Chic's unit went to Fort Breendonk, a Nazi concentration camp that was in the hands of the Witte *(White)* Brigade, part of the Belgian Secret Army. They were a resistance group formed in Antwerp, set up in retaliation to the hated Zwarte *(Black)* Brigade who collaborated with the Nazis. He was shocked to discover that many of the SS Officers running the camp were indeed Flemish and understood the hatred felt by the Belgian resistance. These vile officers had betrayed their own people, but would now get their comeuppance as prisoners of the Witte Brigade. The camp was empty, the prisoners that were still alive and able to walk were being marched back behind the German frontier by the Nazis. The Witte Brigade certainly had their work cut out at the Breendonk prison camp. The terrible stink hit Chic and his pals before it even came into view. The first thing he saw was a huge funeral pyre, stacked with a mass of half burned emaciated bodies, the Nazis had tried to cover their tracks, but left in a hurry. Within the concrete fortress areas were sectioned off into small rooms, crammed with bunk beds three tiers high, fifty to a room. The filthy, lice ridden straw mattresses were soaked with blood, vomit and excrement. The overpowering stench of urine and faeces hit the senses like a sledge hammer. There were only two small latrines outside, with no washing facilities and one of the cells was set up with a permanent gallows. The barracks was surrounded by a square moat of foul, stinking water, the whole camp was a sea of putrid mud. This really was hell on earth. Chic did not eat his ration that day, just the sight of food made him retch. He gave his sausage pie to Sapper Young who had a cast iron stomach, he could eat anything, anywhere, anytime.

They were very close to enemy lines and the next day the *"Moaning Minnies"* were back. Another bout of heavy shelling showered down upon the HQ camp and the towns folk of Willebroek and Aartselaar. The surprise attack frightened the civilians and some angrily threw their British souvenirs out into the streets. This was soul destroying for the lads, the British went from feted liberators to distrusted occupiers in less than a day, but it was only temporary, the local people quickly came around. Chic kept his head down, there was a lot of work in and after a long day in the garage working on both British and German vehicles, he wrote some letters. Joyce would be worrying if he did not get news to her pretty quickly. Antwerp was now in the hands of the allies, but the enemy was blowing all the bridges as it retreated, from the River Rupel across to the Albert Canal in an attempt to stop the allies moving up into Holland. The Eleventh Armoured Division was at the front. Its sappers had made several attempts at bridging the canal, but all failed and hundreds were killed and injured in the process. They pulled back yet again, the entry into Holland was proving to be a tough nut to crack. Chic was low, he could not get the loss of Major Bowen and the horrors of Breendonk out of his head. Too much thinking was not good, he needed to keep busy.

Chic had just been issued a new motorcycle, it was in very good condition and he was pleased with it. They were on the move again, this time eastwards. The frontline troops were joining them as they had been brought back to rest. That of course meant Chic, Bill and the other mechanics were ridiculously busy again. There was a great deal of repair work in, mainly replacing burst petrol tanks and patching up radiators that had been damaged by mines, shells or machine gun fire. There were countless punctures, bent wheels and missing parts. The next day brought another new experience, the camp at Hasselt was attacked by a Nazi self-propelled bomb a V1 Doodlebug, luckily there were no casualties.

On Monday the unit was sent to Beringen coal mine where they had the chance of steaming hot baths in the pit showers. This was a luxury they had not expected, it was great to soak away all their aches and pains and be kitted out with clean uniforms. Joyce's last letter talked about her best friend Joyce Reed, who was now married to a Texan GI, Creighton Romine and living in Wichita Falls, in the USA, she was three months pregnant. Chic made time to write back to his wife and also wrote a short congratulations note to Joyce and Creighton. The GI had already demobbed and was back working at JC Penny. Chic was very pleased for them, but secretly hoped it would soon be his turn to be a father.

On Tuesday 12ᵗʰ September they moved eastwards again, close to the Dutch border where they were harboured for several days. The garage was inundated with work, Chic was labouring flat out and in a state of exhaustion, when he wasn't fixing stuff, he was asleep. A couple of days later he was sent on his motorbike to Leuven, to repair a truck, and told if he had time he could continue to Brussels. It was a good twenty miles back and the roads were less than perfect, but the truck was an easy fix and the lads were very appreciative. He then rode on to Brussels, where he slept in a proper army bed for the first time since landing in France. He had a fantastic night's sleep and after rising early, with a good breakfast inside him from the garrison canteen, he was back in camp by 0800 hours. He felt much refreshed and after work he strolled down to the ENSA tent to watch Cary Grant in *"Mr Lucky."* It almost felt like being back in Blighty.

The following week was pretty normal apart from getting a new commanding officer, Major Wilson was now in charge. There was just routine work coming in with no pressure, Chic wrote to Joyce and received a letter from his mum. They had been harboured for a whole week and he was beginning to relax. That morning he and Fern were once again outside the camp perimeter working on a breakdown, when totally out of the blue there was an almighty bang. An ammunitions truck had blown up within sight of them, they dived for cover. A series of cracks, bangs and deafening explosions, with clouds of smoke and debris flying in all directions went on for several minutes. Then a deathly silence, Chic popped his head up just as another box of ammo exploded. They waited for a further five minutes of silence, timing it on their watches, it seemed like an eternity. Eventually both men emerged unhurt, but badly shaken. They warily continued working on the truck, aware that they were probably being watched. Where had the mortar come from? That experience was to revisit Chic in his dreams for many years afterwards.

8. HOLLAND.

It was time to move on. The camp was vulnerable to attack so the 29th Armoured Brigade packed up and set out before dawn, with 612 squadron following closely behind. They slept in Belgium and had breakfast in Holland, at the country's most southerly tip near Liege. The boys were still trying to bridge the Albert Canal, but had met stiff fighting at Genenbos just north of Hasselt. The Germans succeeded in cutting the allied forces supply lines that had been dropped in by parachute just days earlier, but in their haste to retreat, the enemy deserted its own precious stores of both ammunition and food. The Nazis were now eating British rations whilst the Dutch civilians, who were already half starved, were desperately scavenging for anything edible. The squadron was being fed on German rations, it was not ideal and supply was short, but it was better than nothing. It started raining again, and boy did it rain! The hail storms came through in violent waves, everyone was cold, wet and filthy dirty, the lads at 612 FS HQ needed a distraction. Neil had been messing about with some matches and singed Sapper Priest's beard while he was asleep. When he woke up he summoned the wrath of God onto Sapper Neil Young, who was quivering in his boots. Chic thought it was hilarious. The next day whilst out on a recce checking for stranded vehicles, he found an abandoned milk saucepan lying at the edge of the road. He was chuffed with his treasure, *"The Jerry pan"* would be perfect for making a brew, on his *"Tommy"* cooker, nothing better than a cuppa when you're at rock bottom. He also picked up a German banknote, five hundred Reichsmark, he put it in his Paybook for safe keeping.

The Nazis were building up strength again and were within touching distance. On yet another cold, wet and miserable morning, a small convoy was returning back to camp from a recce, with Chic bringing up the rear in a German truck they had found abandoned on the road. Suddenly he lost the steering, the rear tyre was punctured. The lads up ahead did not notice he had fallen behind, he couldn't shout or use the hooter the Germans were within earshot. He was scared. He jumped out and frantically started jacking up the wheel, fumbling clumsily from sheer terror. After a few minutes he saw movement in the distance and jumped into the ditch, clenching his fists tightly to stop his hands shaking. As the figure approached he could see it was a priest, he relaxed a little and stuck his head up. The Dutchman spoke perfect English and quietly pointed out where the Germans were patrolling. He reassured Chic that he was not in any immediate danger, made the sign of the cross and took a small object out from his haversack. As he pressed it into Chic's hand he whispered;

"Good luck Tommy."

The priest continued on his way and Chic opened his fist to reveal a large ebony and brass crucifix, he tucked it into his breast pocket. He had now stopped shaking and was able to change the wheel, before long he was driving back to catch up with his mates. They had only just realised he was missing and were planning a search party. They were astonished when he told them the story and showed them the crucifix. Chic told this story many times, believing wholeheartedly that this cross was his lucky charm and he would keep safe from then on in. He believed from that day without doubt, that he had a guardian angel at his shoulder and he would be returning home to his darling wife.

The following day the unit was ordered to move over to make room for infantry. The enemy was now approaching from the coast and attacking on the left flank. After setting up camp further east, there was not much to do in the enormous barn that had been designated as the engineers work shop, so Chic wrote a couple of letters. He also received a lovely long letter and some ciggies from his cousin Molly, but things quickly changed on the 29ᵗʰ of September when he wrote in his diary;

"Getting stuck into jobs that are important."

These important jobs were top secret, the division was refitting, Chic and the other mechanics were working flat out. There was an eerie calm in their sector, the fate of the Eleventh Armoured Division was being discussed by the generals in talks at Antwerp, but it was all hush hush, the lower ranks were only grabbing snippets of rumour. The work now being issued was just routine, they were waiting in the wings for something to happen, but at the same time all badly in need of some R and R. Chic was browned off, even a parcel from his darling wife did not lift his spirits, all the lads felt the same.

Major Wilson decided to lavish a bit of luxury on his men while they were kicking their heels at headquarters. Over a period of just one fortnight he gave orders for every man to have two shower baths and see two or three shows, but in Chic's case that did not quite work out. On Tuesday afternoon he was given a pass to Helmond and tried to get in to see the ENSA show, *"Stars in Battledress,"* but the theatre was full, he was turned away. The town was heaving with troops, every bar, café and picture house was packed to capacity, he called it a day and came back to camp early. The next day he felt even worse, he was so bored he even volunteered for two extra hours of guard duty. He was put on with a corporal who had got hold of a soldier's quiz to pass the time away. He asked Chic for the name of an eminent British woman, Chic replied with a chuckle;

"Jane of the Daily Mirror."

Jane was the invention of cartoonist Norman Pett. She was a voluptuous young lady who featured in a daily strip cartoon in the tabloid newspaper. Chic knew several eminent women: Florence Nightingale, Queen Elizabeth, Boudicea, but Jane was what the lads liked.

He needed something to occupy his mind and began making another brass ornament for Joyce, this time it was a watering can. He received another letter from her, which cheered him up a little and then the news came in that the whole sector was preparing for an assault on Germany. There still wasn't much doing in the workshops, but there was a plan and Chic was ready for action. News quickly came through that their sappers were bridging a wet gap five-hundred feet wide across one of the canals and marshland that separated Holland from Germany. Each and every bridge from west to east, Antwerp to Helmond, had been smashed by the Nazis before they retreated. What the allies did not know, was that there were still strong pockets of resistance and the enemy was building up its forces on the German frontier.

On Sunday Chic went to Helmond again, this time for a proper bath, his first in two months, he relished every moment and made it last as long as possible. When he returned he was given a little mobile generator to take apart. It was an Italian charging engine for batteries and radio equipment, there was not much to it, a simple device that needed an oil change and a good clean up, he soon got it running. He wrote to his mum and Joyce to tell them how well things were going, but in his head he was still well below par. The following Tuesday, dozens of the lads including Chic were given day passes, they all went off to Helmond to see an ENSA show. Jenni was also in town, he and Chic saw each other and waved but they did not get a chance to speak. The town was packed to the gunnels and the atmosphere tense, with a strong presence of military police. The following days continued to drag with nothing much going on, they had been too long in one place. Chic knuckled down to his work despite still being fed up, he wrote more letters and went to the flics again, this time in Gemert, he had already seen the film but it was something to do.

News was now filtering through of the failure by the allies to claim the bridge at Arnhem, with hundreds of British and American troops taken prisoner and hundreds more killed, injured, or stranded. On Sunday 15th October Major Wilson was replaced by the newly promoted Major Anderson, previously 612 Field Squadron's captain, with Captain Crozier appointed as his second in command. All ranks in the squadron knew and respected both these men, they were considered well qualified to lead them back into battle. Chic wrote;

"Now for fireworks."

He was ordered to take a van out in an advancing convoy, but they did not get far, it was too muddy for the armoured division and they were told to return to base camp. The next day they all moved again, this time about eight miles back, it was a huge hit on morale for everyone, they weren't sure what was going on up ahead and the waiting was tedious. Chic was keen to kill time and thought about making a windmill out of spent shell cases. His soldering skills had improved greatly, it would be something to get his teeth into while they were all kicking their heels.

Then Harry Probert, a sergeant from the Army Air Corps visited and spoke to the whole camp about what he had seen and what they were all up against. Sergeant Probert was one of the first paratroopers to drop when Operation Market Garden commenced on the 17ᵗʰ September. He considered himself not only lucky to be alive, but also to be a free man. He was a good speaker, the men hung on to every word he said, they had experienced the tail end of the offensive and had nothing but admiration for soldiers like Sergeant Probert, who had literally been on the front line on many occasions and survived. They understood exactly what he meant when he talked of the weariness, the lack of sleep, the hunger and total exhaustion, the hellish conditions and the constant fear of being captured or shot with no chance of making progress. Chic asked for his autograph, he was an approachable chap and happy to oblige.

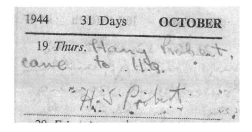

At last some work came in to the garage, a BARV diesel tank needed a decoke and Chic was the best man for the job, he knew his way around these monster engines now. Once he had finished the diesel engine there was nothing to do again. He was not getting on very well with his windmill and after hearing about Harry Probert' experiences in an MTB *(motor torpedo boat),* he decided to make a speed boat instead. He managed to find some pictures in an old magazine and concentrated on drawing up his design, in attempt to drown out the noise of the armour piercing bombs that were dropping very close by.

"Too close for comfort."

Chic concentrated on his speed boat, he was fashioning it from a brass 6PR 7CWT shell case dated 1943. ECC. Lot 704. It was going to be a pen holder with a removable ink well, the process of cutting and soldering was therapeutic and kept his mind occupied. He wrote a couple of letters to Joyce and Mum, telling them he was making a speedboat and it was coming on well.

There was talk of a few men getting four days leave but nothing came of it. Infantry was still suffering heavy casualties and now they had lost their head cook. Corporal Sam Whitaker was back in England with acute appendicitis. His driver, Sapper Edward Stevens *(Stead)* was dragged in to help out in the NAAFI, cooks were in short supply. Chic was pleased to escape that duty, instead he was given general maintenance work over the next couple of days. Every vehicle on site was required to be checked over, underneath a tirade of bombing by the Luftwaffe, they were lucky not to have any casualties at HQ.

Then on 27th October, Captain Crozier reported back on the heavy fighting at Deurne. Chic's best chum Jenni, Sapper Verner Jensen, had been killed by enemy shells whilst picking up mines, he was to be given a military funeral the following day, but Chic was not given leave to attend. He desperately wanted to say good bye to his friend, they had been thick as thieves, since the day they joined up. He wrote to Joyce and his cousin Molly to give them the bad news, he tried to make light of it by telling them he was fine and not in the front line.

Sapper Verner Jensen was a Danish lad, three years younger than Chic and always up for a joke, they quickly became the best of pals. He joined up to get away from home and experience some adventure. His father worked on the boats and brought his family to England when Verner was a baby. It was a hard life and his father died young in the 1930s. His widowed mother ended up struggling in a tiny bed-sit in Brixton, South London. Verner always looked out for his mother, but when she met an older gentleman who wanted to marry her, Verner knew it was time to leave home. He volunteered to join the army when he was eighteen years old and met Percy when they were both on sapper recruit training in Yorkshire, they got on like a house on fire. Sapper Sherwood empathised with Verner and liked his gutsy approach to life, he was a strong lad and a skilled driver. It wasn't long before they both had nicknames, Jenni and Chic were inseparable in the 12th Field Squadron. Later on, when the squadron was given an extra digit and renamed 612th Field Squadron, Jenni was moved to the 13th Field Squadron. From then onwards they did not see much of each other, but they remained friends throughout.

Chic was so miserable, he did not know what to do with himself, his grief for Jenni consumed him. The last time he lost anyone close was Grandpa Charlie, when he was only ten years old. He remembered being sad, but this grief was different. Jenni had been popular among the lads they all felt his loss greatly, but none more than Chic. As he wrote in the diary his pen blotted ink on the page.

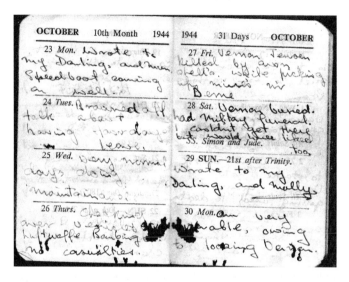

To take their minds off the gravity of the current situation, Sapper Young started a sweepstake. He reckoned the war would be over by midnight on the last day of October, Chic bet him one hundred francs that it would not be, he knew that was definitely a safe bet. The first day of November dawned and the war was still raging, nothing had changed apart from Chic being a tiny bit richer.

Chic and Stan *(Sapper Stanley Groom)* went to visit Jenni's grave, they both took flowers, Chic tried not to cry but he could not help himself. The mounded earth was marked with a simple wooden cross; *"Sapper Jensen V M 5122972. Killed in Action. 27.10.1944."* Jenni's helmet was propped on top. The next day Chic visited again on his own, he rode over on his motorbike and stayed awhile, shed a few tears and spoke quietly to his friend. He had borrowed Johnno's camera and took some photographs, it helped a little he was getting used to the idea that Jenni had gone. Sapper Johnny Rooke *(Johnno)* was also grieving, the three of them had been such great pals back in England. Sapper Jensen was just twenty-one when he died.

Chic threw himself into his work, it was the best medicine for taking his mind off things, despite a blinding headache that he could not shake off. On 5ᵗʰ November severe gale warnings were forecast and on top of that the Jerries bombed Helmond, that was a Guy Fawkes night that Chic would not forget in a hurry. It was bitterly cold, wet and windy, but the 29ᵗʰ Armoured Brigade was put on its feet and ordered to move off with the 612's following. The roads were unstable and could not support the heavy vehicles, a Churchill tank had been lost off the causeway and taken most of the road with it. The idea of using assault bridges was abandoned, the only way to open up the route was to repair the road around the tank with a standard Bailey bridge. The engineers were working flat out. It took over twelve hours to make the road passable for supplies to get through and much had to be carried on foot. Some trucks managed to pass but most failed, it was a miserable business;

"A rum issue."

Chic was put on guard duty on Tuesday, luckily for him it had stopped raining but the wind was biting. Then it started raining again, over the next few days icy rain constantly came down in stair rods. Everything was drenched, they were knee deep in mud, the rain turned to hail and then into snow, the temperature was falling well below zero at night. Chic was working unprotected outside, in, on, but mostly under trucks, his hands were numb and his head throbbed. His back ached with the cold, he was lying on sodden ground for hours at a time and was frozen to the core. It reminded him of Operation Eagle back in Yorkshire. He had thought that was bad, but this was ten times worse, they were fighting for their lives. The next day warmed up by a few degrees but the mud seemed to be alive and growing. Then Chic found out that Corporal Barker had also been killed the previous week at Deurne. He was due to go on guard duty again that night, this time he thought about Jenni, Eddy Barker and all the others who had lost their lives or limbs. He cheered himself up by writing a long letter to his wife.

On 12th November Chic was sent out in a half-track to collect some supplies from stores and took the opportunity to visit Jenni's grave again. He was not one for praying, but he showed Jenni the crucifix and told him the story of the priest and his guardian angel, he hoped Jenni could hear him. When he returned to camp the whole unit was moving into the next field, the vehicles and all the equipment had been slowly sinking into a quagmire of mud. Once they were settled, Chic went to the ration van and picked up a lovely letter from Joyce, just what he needed. He was also given the next day off, but was so cold and exhausted that he stayed dozing in his damp sleeping bag until noon, and then just idled the rest of the day away, apart from writing a few letters. He had a heavy heart and an even heavier head, he was literally itching for a bath, feeling lousy and desperate for a change of clothes. The freezing rain returned, the troops were told that a large offensive was about to begin on all fronts, but the 29th Armoured Brigade was not moving yet, negotiations were taking place to pull them out for a rest. Three days later, infantry including the brigade were pushed into action again, in the middle of a violent thunderstorm. It was not as cold but Chic was despondent, he collected the photographs of Jenni's grave and was pleased to have them. He kept one with him and sent another to Joyce, she had also grown fond of Jenni, in the short time that she had known him.

The following week was intense for all concerned. Just at HQ Chic witnessed a British plane shot down by night fighters, Warboys and Tudor got their legs blown off by trip wires on an enemy mine and twenty other men lost legs or arms. Despite all that Major Anderson reported that the advance was going well. The boys in the front line were more than a little browned off, there were multiple casualties, the rain continued day after day after day, morale was low throughout the whole squadron. On 25th November Chic was sent up to TAC *(Tactical Air Command)* HQ to repair one of the Royal Ordnance Intelligence Officer's scout cars. He was glad to get away for a bit, a change was as good as a rest. It was a small set up with some very clever men in charge of tactics, the ROI engineers were an amiable bunch and knew their stuff, he respected their knowledge and skills as they did his. The scout car was up and running in no time at all, a job well done.

It had now been raining constantly for over a week, making the going was very tough indeed. The Deurne Canal was proving to be a hard nut to crack for the lads, Chic felt for them and thought of his friend. He was having a rough time but nothing like what the boys were going through, day in day out. He was at a loose end again and decided to paint Eli's bike, that cheered Eli up but they were all waiting for something to happen. When were they moving off? Would they be getting a rest? Eventually on the 28ᵗʰ they were packing up ready to move it was still raining, the next day they moved off in column, in torrential rain. Chic was issued an Austin van, it felt strange to drive after what he had been used to and was difficult to steer on the flooded roads, suddenly it veered off into a ditch. He jumped out, the wheels were underwater, the following truck managed to pull him out, but not without some difficulty, it slowed up the convoy. He was not the only one to end up off road, the conditions were dire, with marshland either side of flooded roads and invisible ditches swallowing several casualties. Eventually the convoy arrived at Meterik. Now what?

Chic went to work immediately on squaring up his Austin van, it was badly battered and twisted from his sojourn into a ditch the previous day. It was now December, the rain continued relentlessly, they were all sick of permanently being cold and damp. Now they back in a proper workshop there was plenty of work coming in, everything was being checked over, serviced and smartened up, although stores were desperately short of spare parts. On Sunday he was ordered to passenger Stead who was driving his ration truck to the Brussels garrison on Monday, to pick up much needed supplies. Stead was good company and the mood light hearted, they shared the driving and laughed a lot, it was just what they both needed. During the journey of over one hundred miles there were a few hairy moments, the rough flooded roads were jammed with trucks and lorries constantly going back and forth, endless convoys of troops and equipment. Chic had just been paid and was excited at the thought of buying something for Joyce. The first thing they did was go to the laundry unit and swap their filthy uniforms for clean ones, after a steaming hot shower. While they were in Brussels they did a bit of shopping and had tea at Café Blighty on the Boul du Jardin Botanique, where they met some friendly Belgians who spoke English. Chic bought Joyce a *"Souvenir from Belgium,"* a wooden jewellery box with mistletoe painted on the lid. If only he could kiss her under the mistletoe this Christmas!

They were back in camp by 2100 hours, tired but happy. The next day Chic wrote his cards and packed up a parcel for his wife: a long letter, the brass speedboat, the wooden jewellery box and an army issue greetings card signed;

"To My Darling Wife. All My Love Chic. XXXX,"

It was the 5ᵗʰ of December and if he posted it today, the parcel should arrive at Foxton Post Office, in good time for Christmas.

On Wednesday Bill received a letter from his wife telling him he was the father of an 8lb baby boy, born on 1ˢᵗ December. Chic had not heard from Joyce for over a week and although he was pleased for Bill it made him think about his wife and her miscarriage, he had not been there to comfort her and was worried, why hadn't he heard? The lack of news, along with the rain hammering down and getting into everything, was enough to test the cheeriest of fellows. The next day it was still raining but he received a letter from his darling and was like a dog with two tails. All was well back in Foxton, in Meterik it had started snowing heavily. The camp woke up the following morning to a thick blanket of snow, he wrote to Joyce waxing lyrical about the winter wonderland. By the time he had finished his letters the snow had reverted to ice cold rain, the temperature plummeted and then more snow fell on top of the icy slush. The following Monday Chic and Stead set off to Brussels again. The roads were even more treacherous than before, it took them two hours longer, but after loading up they both went into a night club for a quick afternoon drink before returning back to Meterik. Chic was desperate to have a bath but there was no time in Brussels, although he did manage to get a change of shirt, pants and socks. Two days later he got his wish at the baths in Helmond, it was twenty miles north of Meterik, but worth the drive. Chic was clean again although his uniform wasn't.

On the 15ᵗʰ December it was still raining and the whole squadron was getting ready to move again. It took two days to pack up with the rain hampering every single task, but all the men were going to new billets and looking forward to the chance of a rest over Christmas. News also came in that Glenn Miller's plane had gone missing. Chic was vexed, he and Joyce had danced to the Glenn Miller Band back at Duxford, he loved swing music and Glen Miller was the best. Chic did not have time to dwell on the sad news as events rapidly took over. Two days later the squadron was harboured in Kinrooi with Nazi planes constantly buzzing overhead, they were dropping enemy para-troops. News came in that most had been captured, but it was disconcerting. The Nazis were on the offensive advancing on a forty mile front, none of them were safe. Chic cheered up a little when leave was drawn, at last he was going home, but not for six weeks. He decided not to tell Joyce, after all a great deal could happen between now and the end of January. Little did he know exactly what he was in for.

9. CHRISTMAS 1944.

At 0200 hours on 20th December the Eleventh Armoured Divisional Headquarters at Brussels announced battle stations. The allies were up against twenty-four enemy divisions including ten Panzers and the 6th SS Panzer Army along a stretch of forty miles. Thick fog had penetrated every nook and cranny of the landscape, with almost nil visibility, the only advantage being that the Germans could not see anything either. Chic and his mates were blissfully unaware of this recent enemy action and drove to Breestraat to watch an ENSA show that included a very good Russian dance act, he was impressed. There was not much doing the next day either, so he went off to a café in Kinrooi and wrote a few letters, including a New Year greetings card that he hoped Joyce would receive soon after Christmas.

Meanwhile, Major Anderson and his squadron had been summoned to assemble at Gembloux the next day. Chic arose on the 22nd to be told;

"Be ready to move off by 1100 hours."

They were on the road in column for over five hours. Gembloux was south east of Brussels, about sixty miles from Kinrooi. Chic was driving Stead's ration truck, a two wheel drive Bedford MWD. He tore the bumper off as he hit a flooded crater, there was not time to stop, he would fix it later.

Stead (left). Walt (right).

75

The squadron arrived at their new billet in Gembloux soon after 1600 hours. It was disused sugar factory that had been gutted by the Germans before they deserted the town. Major Anderson called all the men to attention and ordered them to be ready to move at a moment's notice.

The following morning dawned with bright sunshine, a bitterly cold crisp day. Major Anderson had gone on ahead to Namur to receive orders from TAC HQ, where he quickly learned what was required of his squadron. By midnight several units were deployed to relieve the struggling troops out in the field. Chic's unit was on the move again. On Christmas Eve they were travelling in convoy up to Namur towards Luxembourg. On arrival they were instructed to wait, he took the opportunity to write another letter to Joyce. The sky was alive with the spectacle of hundreds of allied aircraft flying eastwards towards Germany, the familiar roar of their own planes was reassuring. Then orders came through to be ready to move off at first light on Christmas Day. There was to be an offensive sortie across the River Meuse, where they would take over defence of the area from the 8ᵗʰ Rifle Brigade. Chic's convoy was behind infantry but it was still dangerous, the Germans were less than one mile away in some places. Driving through the mountains in The Ardennes was a treacherous exercise, it was bitterly cold and the roads were icy with a heavy snowfall on top. At one stage he nearly lost his truck over a cliff, but his driving skills won through. Sapper Sherwood had never travelled abroad before he joined the army, he was fascinated by how the sunshine burned his face, but did not even begin to melt the ice or the snow on the mountains. He was in a surreal world of beauty with menace on Christmas Day in 1944.

There was no opportunity to rest overnight, the convoy kept moving slowly but surely throughout Boxing Day at a snail's pace. Then on the 27ᵗʰ when they were just south of Celles, six enemy Tiger tanks were heading straight for them. The RAF were still out in force and fortunately the Air OP *(operations officer)*, noticed the column of German tanks and half-tracks approaching along the same sunken road that Chic's convoy was on. The officer at Brigade HQ immediately notified his Hawker Typhoons *(rocket fighter bombers)*, they flew in and took out four tanks in the first attack with spectacular accuracy. It was not long before the second attack came through and destroyed the other two tanks within sight of the convoy. Everyone cheered, this was another small but lifesaving victory. It was now obvious the enemy was in retreat, its sinister debris littered the white landscape, but this surreal experience was not over yet.

On 29th December 1944 the beginnings of a thaw had set in, despite a wind chill factor of well below zero. The lads set up a makeshift bath at HQ from an old trough, a water bowser and some corrugated iron with a flame thrower underneath it. The water was boiling when Chic jumped in, it was a moment of ecstasy. The scum on the surface from the previous occupants was half an inch thick, he skimmed some off, it froze instantly as it hit the ground, he was washed and out in a jiffy. After running around naked in the snow to dry off, he put his filthy clothes back on and felt a little better for it. It reminded him of Jenni, who back in Yorkshire talked of the delights of hot saunas and the exhilarating experience of breaking ice on a Danish lake, leaping into the water and then being beaten with birch twigs. Chic laughed at the time, but on this occasion a quick thrashing would have been a welcome warm up.

That night he had no chance to rest, let alone sleep. The extreme cold and unpredictable terrain was putting a strain on the vehicles as well as the men, three jeeps needed new engines. A tarpaulin was set up over a circle of vehicles, including a tractor with a winch on the back. The ground had to be boarded to stop them sinking into the snow, the mechanics were up all night, refitting. It was a race against time, but everything was slow including Chic, his fingers numb to the bone, his face smarting with the cold, but by morning the jeeps were fit for purpose. He had never been so cold, his back ached and he could not feel his feet. He boiled up some water in his *"Jerry Pan"* and melted an OXO cube into it, a savoury delight saved from cousin Molly's food parcel received weeks ago, it was delicious.

After sleeping soundly under his truck on Saturday night, he woke on New Year's Eve to good news, he was issued a forty-eight hour pass to Brussels. He was dead on his feet, but this was just what he needed. A truck load of ten chaps were raring to go to Brussels and Chic was in the queue. They set off after breakfast and arrived before noon, this was his first leave since landing on Juno beach six months earlier, he was determined to enjoy himself. On arrival in the city, dozens of Luftwaffe fighter planes were strafing the streets, but they seemed high and slow, their aim was sporadic at best there were no casualties. The onslaught of enemy fire was not enough to quell the enthusiasm of the crowds including the sappers from 612 Field Squadron, they were all determined to celebrate Hogmanay to the full.

Chic's first stop was the garrison, he picked up a clean uniform at the laundry before going to the newly opened Montgomery Club opposite the palace. It was a large hotel that boasted fantastic facilities, cafes, restaurants, bars, shops, games rooms, a photographic studio, a library, but most importantly, baths. He joined the queue, that luxury of a long soak in a hot bath with clean towels and a steam room, was an experience he would savour for the rest of his life. Now he was clean with underwear and uniform to match. He dropped his dirty uniform back to the laundry before joining another queue at the feeding centre. Once fed and watered he was ready to enjoy his few hours freedom. Along with his Leave Scheme Pass he had been issued a map of Brussels with detailed instructions.

"YOUR FEEDING CENTRE IS SHOWN ON YOUR MEAL TICKET.

You are warned not to enter cafes unless a price list is displayed outside. Your accommodation and meals are free, but purchases from all canteens must be paid for in cash. You must not buy food in civilian restaurants. Do not talk about where your unit is or what it is. Do not discuss equipment, losses or battle experiences. The people of Brussels are very hospitable and will do all they can to make your leave enjoyable. Enjoy yourselves with them but do not tell them anything.

Most cinemas and theatres offer free ENSA shows with English films showing at half price. There are many places of interest; churches, museums, galleries and gardens including: The Mannikin Fountain. Dated 1619. Erected by a wealthy citizen whose child, after being lost for 5 days, was found on this spot.

All cafés must be empty by 2300 hours, curfew midnight until 0500 hours. All brothels are out of bounds. No weapons to be carried. Saluting officers of British and Allied forces will be strictly enforced. The tomb of the Belgian Unknown Warrior at Congress Column will be saluted by all ranks.

Army Issue No 6: Scheme B. 2GHQ/1-12/75M

Gelukkig Nieuwjaar

The lads were back in the garrison by midnight along with a few smuggled beers. They each raised a bottle to welcome in 1945;

"To the end of the war, wishing for peace, good health and happiness."

Chic was fast asleep by quarter past midnight and slept soundly in his army bed. The new year dawned and he felt rested despite a slight hangover, he had got out of the habit of drinking. There were a few more hours to enjoy the cafes and see the sites, despite the still continuous strafing from enemy aircraft. They were not returning to Celles, the squadron had moved down to just outside Dinant. He spent Tuesday night sleeping under canvas in the back of a lorry. The city of Dinant was beautiful, he bought a postcard book too send to Joyce. It was a miracle the citadel remained standing, the scenery was breath taking with snow covered mountains and the vast River Meuse rolling along. The bridge was constantly patrolled by allied soldiers on the look-out for suspicious enemy action. This river was a thorn in the side of the allies, it proved to be a fierce battleground in The Great War and now history was repeating itself.

What he didn't know was that while he was enjoying himself in Brussels, the boys were still building a bridge across the River Lesse at Chanly, under the protection of the 2ⁿᵈ Fife & Forfar Yeomanry and the 8ᵗʰ Rifle Brigade. The bridge was completed first thing on Tuesday morning with little enemy resistance. The lads had returned to camp making it full when Chic arrived back on Wednesday and the mood optimistic. Seven letters were waiting for him, five from his darling, Christmas had arrived at last. Joyce had sent him a photograph and a brown leather 1945 pocket diary signed;

"Best Wishes and Fondest Love. Joyce. Xxxxx"

Chic was in high spirits, it was time for him to have a rest and his leave back to England was now only four weeks away, he could not wait. The next day the unit moved a little further south again to Honnay, where he was put in a civilian billet, what a luxury to sleep in a proper bed with crisp white linen sheets. His hosts were an elderly Walloon couple who spoke little French and no English. Chic wanted to talk with them and tried to learn some French but he was not very successful, they still could not understand each other. But Madame used a spinning wheel and she was delighted when he showed an interest. He was always up for learning a new skill and knew how to engage with people. After his long cold days in the workshop he was pleased to sit by Madame's stove with a small cup of thick Belgian coffee and spin a few yarns, under the supervision of Madame. They could not hold a conversation but actions spoke louder than words.

Throughout that week there was a constant buzzing in the sky from the Nazi V1 self-propelled bombs. The noise unsettled Chic's Belgian hosts they greatly feared being hit. Chic was also worried, he remembered what it was like in Tolworth, early on in the war when London was being blitzed by the Germans. Many stray bombs caused havoc in the suburbs as well as the city, he knew of several incidents where houses were wrecked and people killed. Suddenly the buzzing stopped, to the great relief of the civilians and the soldiers. Chic wrote to his wife on Sunday while the family went to church. It was still snowing and now eight inches deep on the ground, getting around was slow, difficult and cold. On 10th January the squadron was told the enemy were retreating from Chanly and their unit was to follow the 29th Armoured Brigade. It was Annie Sherwood's sixtieth birthday but Chic did not have time to think about his mum, he was packing up in apprehensive mood. What would they be up against next?

There wasn't much to do in Chanly. Chic wrote some letters and received another Christmas parcel this time from his brother Charlie, he was well stocked now for ciggies and a few sweet meats. His new hosts had teenage children, they wanted to take Chic tobogganing, he had never seen so much snow and the kids were good fun, he had a great time. Chic liked the Belgian people, they were very welcoming despite having very little left under German occupation. The enemy systematically destroyed as much as it could when making a hasty retreat, often setting booby traps, but this did not stop the Belgian civilians celebrating liberation, many were hungry, ill and living in dreadful conditions, but they were free. On the 14ᵗʰ of January the unit moved again, this time over one hundred miles north to Neeroeteren. This was good news indeed, as it meant at last everyone could have a well-earned rest with an opportunity for some training and the promise of new kit.

It was now only two weeks to his leave and he spent that time in another civvy billet with the Geelan family, who were even more welcoming than his previous hosts. Lucie Geelan was a similar age to Chic and spoke good English. She and her husband were living with Lucie's Mam and Papa, who were delighted to be free from the Germans and welcomed Chic with great enthusiasm. They enjoyed a bit of fun and were all good sports, Chic fitted in easily with his cheeky charm. He was still eating all his meals back at HQ, but Mam was an excellent cook and always saved him some treats for when he arrived back in the evenings. They played cards and party games sometimes with a bit of singing and taught him some traditional dancing which created a great deal of hilarity, it was almost like being back home. He also had another bath, the third in less than a month and another clean uniform, he did have to drive ten miles north across the Dutch border to Weert with the sound of German bombers in the distance, but they were far enough away not to be a threat. On Friday Mam cooked a celebratory meal in honour of their new friendship, Chic had a very good feed, the best he'd had in months. He wrote to his mother and to Joyce, it was easy this time to give them some good news. In one week, he would be in England with his darling. What he didn't tell them was that Nazi *"Doodle-Bugs"* were frequently passing directly over the house on Rotenserlaan in Neeroeteren *(this address no longer exists,)* but so far they had all kept going and everyone was safe.

The news was also good on the BBC, they were reporting great progress for the allies on all fronts, particularly the Russian side where they were - according to Chic's diary;

"Going like hell, and only one hundred and sixty miles from Berlin."

He wrote to Joyce every other day, he was so looking forward to going home, it looked like the war would be over very soon indeed. There was another heavy snow fall but he had got used to working in the garage in minus temperatures, the snow was better than rain. He was also sent to the doctor for a typhus jab and blissfully unaware of the significance, he was being prepared for more action. The following Thursday the Geelans held a party for him with a great deal of singing and dancing, he had a thoroughly good time. He wrote a final letter to his wife and the day before his expected departure Mam Geelan baked an almond and apple cake to celebrate their friendship. He was overwhelmed with her kindness, he might never see them again, but Lucie wrote her address in his diary and they promised to keep in touch.

10. LEAVE.

It took Chic two days to pack up for his leave, between working and talking with the Geelan family. Eventually on Tuesday 30ᵗʰ January it was time to go. A few other lads were also travelling back to Blighty but despite the long trip ahead they were in jubilant mood, they had some great sing songs in the back of the truck on that first leg of the journey. It was about fifty miles to the military town of Bourg Leopold, where they had their papers checked at the British transit camp. Chic was delighted to be told that he had been given an extra forty-eight hours leave, he didn't ask why! They changed trucks and trundled on through Belgium for another one hundred and fifty miles to the French border, through another check point and down to Dunkirk. It was dark when they arrived at the port where there was yet more checking of papers.

Eventually Chic boarded a troopship bound for Newhaven, it left on the early high tide in pitch darkness. This route across the English Channel was thought to be relatively safe from enemy attack unlike the North Sea that was under constant threat from German U-boats. Regardless of all that, Chic was very pleased to step onto British soil later that morning. By dinner time he was on a London bound train to Victoria Station. There were countless check points, it took a while and several trains to get across London, but at last the Cambridge train pulled into Foxton Station on Wednesday just after 10 pm. It had snowed in England earlier in the week, but after a short spell of rain the snow was washing away to slush, it was mild and miserable but Chic didn't care. He arrived at Addison Cottages at 10,30 pm where his wife was waiting to greet him with a kiss, a cup of tea and Mrs Cheshire had baked another cake. Life was perfect.

Harry Cheshire and his children, Doug and Joyce, all worked in The Burlington Press just a few yards walk from their cottage that came with the job. Harry was the press room overseer and Joyce worked in the bindery. Joyce's elder brother Doug was an apprentice printer but currently serving in the navy on the Russian convoys, they had not heard from him in months. Mr Cheshire was an intense and rather volatile character but he had a keen sense of humour, Chic got on well with him. Every afternoon he ordered an Evening Standard duly delivered by the press van driver, he always read it thoroughly, hungry for reports on the war. The news had been consistently good for several days, Russian troops were thirty miles from Berlin and The Siegfried Line *(the German armoured boundary),* was crumbling. Harry was in a joyous mood and welcomed his new son-in-law into his home with great enthusiasm, he made Chic feel like he had won the war already all by himself. Joyce knew how to get around her father and asked him to persuade the bindery manager to allow her a few days compassionate leave, she was given two days after the weekend.

The press was currently under staffed. Most of the employees lived in the village and nearly all the younger men were now in the forces. Joyce was now promoted from paper folding to casing up, it was heavy work but she became adequately skilled at it. She was then entrusted to gold blocking, this involved being locked in a room with trays of gold leaf where she gilded lettering onto leather-bound books. She was a perfectionist and enjoyed the work, but it was a solitary task and she was gregarious by nature. Meanwhile her previous job was being outsourced to women in the village including her mother, before Edie married she worked as a paper folder in Wisbech for Balding and Mansell, which is how she met Harry.

Joyce did not want to leave her beloved husband on Thursday morning to go to work, but she had no choice and Chic was pleased for the lie in. Mrs Cheshire fried him some eggs for breakfast with dripping toast while he unpacked. Joyce and her father came home at dinner time to one of Edie's vegetable stews with herb dumplings and jam roly-poly. In the afternoon Chic did a few errands for his mother-in-law, while she did her paper folding. Thursday night tea was very welcome with beetroot sandwiches, stewed apples and semolina cakes. Joyce wanted to go to Cambridge straight after tea, they caught the bus from Foxton Station and went to the flics. They missed the beginning of the film but it didn't matter, they watched the beginning at the end and were back home well before curfew. They were ecstatic to be together again, and cherished every moment.

On Friday morning Edie handed Chic some of her son's clothes and demanded that he give her every item of clothing that he possessed. She thought they needed;

"A jolly good boil up."

That evening was bath night, after tea the kitchen was converted into a bathroom, the worktop was lifted on a hinge, to reveal a huge bath. The galvanised electric boiler was already in place from the morning's washing. Cold water was hosed from the indoor tap over the Belfast sink, into the bath, and boiling water was poured from the galvanised bucket, that sat under the electric boiler. A huge bar of Lifebuoy soap sat in a porcelain dish, on the edge of the bath, with four snow white flannels. It was Joyce's turn first, then Edie, then the head of the household and finally Chic. Each time, the soapy scum was ladled off into a separate slops bucket, and the bath topped up with boiling water. Chic was given a huge towel and allowed the use of Mr Cheshire's cut throat razor. There was even an indoor toilet, with Izal medicated toilet paper; Mrs Cheshire liked everything to be hygienic. It was like staying in a luxury hotel. Joyce found him a pair of her brother's pyjamas, and they had a supper of cheese and cream crackers, with hot cocoa made from milk that Chic had collected from Home Farm, that afternoon. Chic could not remember ever being so happy.

On Saturday morning, Harry went out to work on his allotment while his wife went up to the village hall to help clean it ready for the amateur talent night that was showing that evening. At last Chic and Joyce were alone together, they lit a fire in the front parlour, cuddled up and talked for hours. After dinner they went for a walk up to Harston where Chic had been stationed when they first met. There was a constant rumble of army lorries along the Cambridge Road, they both thought the war must be over very soon and then they could begin proper married life together. That evening the whole family went to the talent show, Fred Lowe told a few jokes, Pat Edis sang *"Boots"* just as Harry had done at their wedding and the Royston Town Band played a few dance tunes. On Sunday Joyce was on the organ rota for matins, so Chic went to church with her parents to listen, he was so proud of her. Sunday dinner was delicious, roasted hand of pork, with stuffing, apple sauce, roasted potatoes, sprouts, carrots and gravy, followed by blackcurrant tart and custard. Joyce ironed all Chic's clothes for him in the afternoon while he played dominoes with her father. After tea they set up a game of Monopoly, Joyce joined in but her mother did not want to play because it hindered her knitting.

They were both up with the lark on Monday morning and after breakfast Joyce and Chic made their way down Station Road to catch the bus to Cambridge. It was a damp and drizzly day but they had a wonderful time, shopping, dinner in The British Restaurant for 1/6d and then a walk along the river before going to the pictures to see; *"Double Indemnity"*. The next day they stayed home, it was Edie's turn to go to Cambridge and they liked having the house to themselves. Joyce cooked dinner for them and her father and Chic helped with a few chores, they felt like an old married couple. Joyce went back to work on Wednesday, because Chic was originally leaving on Thursday, he decided to use his extra two days to surprise his parents.

He left for the station soon after Joyce went to work, she ran out the door as the siren sounded, she was always the last one to clock in. Chic arrived in Tolworth by early afternoon, the back door was unlocked but the house deserted. Annie was queueing for her weekly rations at the grocers in Red Lion Road. Just as he was pouring himself a cup of tea, Annie walked through the door, her face lit up when she saw her son. He thought she looked worn out and made her sit down for a cup of char and a natter, they were still talking when Frank arrived home soon after six, he was limping badly. They had all aged but none of them mentioned it. Their other son Charlie appeared soon after with a couple of oranges that had fallen into his lap! He was delighted to see brother but could not stay long, he was needed at home so Chic spent a quiet evening with his parents. Frank wanted to hear all about his experiences while they played cards, Chic was very selective in his subject matter.

The next morning, he was keen to get going and suggested taking his mother to Peggy Brown's for a belated birthday treat. It was a half hour walk because Annie was slow, but they arrived at the cake shop on Claremont Road in plenty of time, his train was not until noon. Annie did not go to Surbiton much and had only ever looked in the window of Miss Brown's pastry shop, there was always a fantastic window display with moving models, she thought it too grand for the likes of her. Chic ordered toasted tea cakes and a pot of tea and told her he thought he would be home very soon, now the war was nearly won. He hoped that he and Joyce could lodge with Annie and Frank in Lenelby Road while he completed his apprenticeship at Fox & Nicholl. Annie hoped so too, it would be nice to have a full house again. Percy bought a platform ticket for his mother and Annie waved her son off on the train before slowly making her way back home.

It took Chic much longer than usual to get back to Foxton, there was a problem with the trains at Kings Cross, a *"Doodle-Bug"* had smashed through the roof on one of the sidings and the station was in chaos. Eventually the Cambridge train arrived and surprisingly, stopped as time tabled at Foxton. As he strolled up Station Road he heard the press siren going to register the end of the working day, they finished half an hour earlier on a Friday. Edie always put the kettle on when the siren went and as he walked into the works yard Joyce appeared at the warehouse door in her scarf, apron and overcoat, it was freezing in the blocking room. They strode together arm in arm back to Addison Cottages where a lovely hot brew was waiting for them along with minestrone soup and the last remains of the Christmas cake. Joyce and Chic only had one more day together, he was expected to report for duty by 2300 hours at Aldershot on Saturday. They went to the flics again on Friday night and attended a tea dance at the Guildhall in Cambridge the following afternoon, after doing more shopping. Then Chic collected his kit bag from the station locker and boarded the London train soon after blackout with Joyce in tears as she waved him off. He was worried about her going on the bus to Foxton in the blackout, but Joyce knew her way around she would be fine.

Chic got back to Aldershot with an hour to spare and at 2330 hours an army truck was driving him and his mates to Newhaven, where they boarded a troopship sailing to Dunkirk. He arrived back in France at 0830 hours on a drizzly Sunday morning and repeated last week's journey in reverse. After his papers were checked at Bourg Leopold he was told to find a truck going in the right direction. It was easy to hitch a lift to Hasselt from a van driver who was on his way to Brussels, but then Chic was left to his own devices. He waved down an Eleventh Armoured Division RASC lorry that was displaying the black bull insignia, it was going to HQ at Neeroeteren, that was lucky! When he checked in to his unit he was pleased that he was still billeted with the lovely Geelan family. He was missing Joyce already and travel weary, but back with friends, a small but reassuring consolation.

11 Sun. Arrived in France about 8.30 AM.

12 Mon. Car to Bourg Leopold. and then to Neerasteveen.

13 Tues. Wrote to my Darling. Fed up.

14 Wed. Fortress on fire crashed. 1 mile away. 5 Crew. safe.

15 Thurs. Am feeling fed up after leave. Wrote to my Darling. b.V.1.

16 Fri. Packing up to move.

17 Sat. Arrived at Overschath. near Nimegean.

18 Sun. Half day. had bath. wrote to my Darling.

19 Mon. Coffee in bed. working in very big garage. wrote to my Darling.

20 Tues. Children injured with hand grenade on canal bank.

21 Wed. Wrote to my Darling. Routine Day.

22 Thurs. Getting truck's ready for move. Wrote to My Darling.

23 Fri. Wrote to my Darling. Packing up to move. arrived at 3.30 AM.

24 Sat. moved 10 miles are now in Reichwald forest. Germany. Everything smashed

11. BELGIUM.

The town was now being bombarded with V1 bombs *(doodle bugs)*. The day after Chic returned one landed very close to the workshop, the car he had been working on was wrecked. He was missing Joyce so much after having seen her and now he was back in the thick of it. He tried to cheer himself up by writing her a letter but it just made him miss her more. On Saint Valentine's Day, everyone in the unit stood and watched as a Flying Fortress *(B17 bomber)* that was engulfed in flames flew directly overhead and crashed just one mile away. The sappers responded quickly and miraculously, all the crew came out in one piece. Antwerp was being bombarded by V1s, many were going astray and hitting towns and villages further afield. The self-propelled rockets were doing their worst, in one day, six of them hit the town, they were back in the war zone and thousands of civilians were being killed or injured throughout the province of Antwerp, the destruction was horrific. There were orders to pack up and be ready to move off, four days after Chic arriving back in Neeroeteren, he was leaving. Chic was sad to say goodbye to the Geelan family and hoped in his heart they would survive the onslaught of the renewed bombing raids. They promised to write.

Rijkesluisstraat — Oirschot.

The arrow points to Madame Maria Corrie Riki's house.

BRIEFKAART
DRUKWERK

Uitg. H. de Croon-v. Heerbeek - Oirschot (N.-Br.)

J v Elzakker
Rijkesluisstraat
A 359
Oirschot
Maria Corrie
Riki

12. HOLLAND.

On Saturday the convoy arrived back in Holland at Oirschot, north west of Helmond and Chic was apprehensive. His new billet was with Madame Maria Corrie Riki, a very kind, motherly lady. Chic was given a half day to settle in and he used the opportunity to take a bath. He had a look around the town and bought some postcards to send to Joyce, one of them showed the house where he was staying. He wrote to his wife every day while he was billeted in Rijkesluisstraat. He had a feeling that things would be bad when they moved on and was keen to let Joyce know he was still alive and kicking. Madame Maria liked to rise early and before Chic was due back in the garage the next morning, she brought him coffee in bed. The coffee was extremely strong and bitter, it was made from acorns, but he didn't mind he felt very spoiled.

The new garage at HQ was enormous, enough to house dozens of vehicles at any one time. They all required a good check over and service, as soon as they were done more were brought in. That same morning some local children were playing down by the canal, they found a spent American hand grenade or so they thought! It was not, they were all rushed to hospital with serious injuries. Chic was very upset by the news and shared it with his landlady when he returned in the evening, but Maria had already heard, it was a small town and she knew the children. The German occupation of Holland had created much hardship, the Dutch people were the first to be overrun and the last to be liberated. Many were near to starvation and angry, but they were resigned to their situation. Madame Maria was delighted to be looking after a British soldier in her house, she made a fuss of him. The next few days were routine, busy but easy work, everything in preparation for the next move, a final spit and polish. The squadron was in Oirschot for less than a week and after packing up on Friday they were ordered to move off at 0330 hours on Saturday morning. That was the last time Chic saw Madame Maria.

25 *Sun.* Raining all day. Sleeping in tents. Canadian and English Barrage going on.

26 *Mon.* Still raining tank's going in. Seen first german civilians.

27 *Tues.* moved to field about 5 miles through Cleves, which was smashed.

28 *Wed.* made Tent 5.5 guns in next field. Too much noise to write letter's.

1 *Thurs March.* Harry Raft + 1. up to 3 troop. 6 shell's fall 200 yards away (Udem)

2 *Fri.* Snowing hard. but any shell's going in by the Dozen.

3 *Sat.* Plane's strafing over line's to hot to be healthy. Wrote to howler

4 *Sun.* We are stationary. but troop's advancing fast. Wrote to my Darling.

5 *Mon.* Flame thrower's going into wood's. about 3 mile away. We are in Siegfried.

6 *Tues.* Plane's over strafing but no one heart. Wrote to my Darling

7 *Wed.* Shell's but we OK. 4 RASC Killed at X Road's.

8 *Thurs.* Wrote to my Darling. two mine's went up.

9 *Fri.* moved from Uden 144 miles to Lanvain. in very nice Billet's.

10 *Sat.* Worried about receiving no letter from my Darling. —

13. GERMANY

Before nightfall on that same day they had travelled seventy miles across the border into Germany and were setting up camp under canvas in the Reichswald Forest. The destruction was total, with nothing left standing, every building razed to the ground. The cold penetrating rain went on for days drenching everything and everyone, making the conditions unimaginably difficult. Underfoot the mud had turned to porridge and it was over a foot deep. The Canadians and British were out in front with the barrage of friendly fire close and relentless, the racket unbearable. There was no relief from the weather or the noise but the good news was that our tanks were going in, the allies were making good progress. On Monday in amongst the chaos Chic saw his first German civilians, just ordinary people, wet, cold and hungry with little possessions waving white flags as they trudged towards and past the convoy. The squadron was on the move again, Cleves had been flattened everything smashed to smithereens. Chic's unit was ordered to set up camp in a field adjacent to the huge BL 5.5-inch *(medium battery)* artillery guns that were towed into position by a tractor. His small tent was just big enough to take three soldiers. The ground was a quagmire and the field so crowded that the guy ropes crisscrossed like cat cradles as the pegs disappeared into the mud. The clatter from the guns was so loud he couldn't think, read, or even write letters, it was impossible to hold a conversation and sleep was out of the question. The barrage went on for hours and hours, the worst Chic had experienced ever.

On the first day of March, Chic, Harry and Pap were sent ten miles along to Udem where 3 Troop were still in the thick of it just east of Goch, they were attached to the 29ᵗʰ Armoured Brigade and being heavily shelled by the enemy. The three sappers took a truck loaded with petrol, oil, water and tools for working on vehicles damaged in the crossfire, some had simply run out of fuel. They were very exposed working so close to the front line, six APBs *(anti-personnel bombs)* dropped just yards away while they were struggling, everything took twice as long. After fixing up several lorries and trucks their supplies were depleted and they had been ordered to return to HQ. The drive back was without incident, but as they passed a notice that marked the breach of The Siegfried Line, the Canadians had got there first and hung some washing up, that gave them a good laugh. Back at camp the day continued into night, they tried to get some rest but it was impossible, especially when it started snowing heavily, the cold, leached into their bones. A small morale boost came from the commanding officers who reported that the allied shelling was gaining ground, the guns were going in a dozen at a time. That was little comfort when Messerschmitts *(Nazi fighter bombers)* were strafing over the lines and squadron HQ was within the line of fire. Four RASC drivers were shelled at the crossroads, all of them injured badly. It was;

"Too hot to be healthy."

Infantry was advancing fast, but HQ was stationary for the time being, Chic wrote to his darling wife. He had temporarily lost faith in his guardian angel and really thought his number could be up. It was now the turn of the flame throwers to go into the woods, they were only half a mile ahead and Chic could hear the blood curdling screams of men caught in the crossfire, in between the massive shelling. They moved up to Siegfried where the weather conditions hindered their progress. Everyone knew the song; *"Hang Out Your Washing on the Siegfried Line,"* here they were again. Chic did not feel much like singing. The enemy strafing was relentless, it made everyone nervous but no one in his section was hurt so far. He wrote another letter to Joyce. On the 7ͭ March they were under heavy shell fire again, then Chic discovered that drivers, Wood and Taylor, the RASCs, had died from their wounds. He was angry and afraid. The following day, two mines went up causing chaos in the camp, they were all on a close call and everyone was exhausted. It was time for their section to be pulled out for a rest.

Mama, Mdme Celine, Pauline, Fernande, Marie, Louise, Emile.

94

14. BELGIUM.

On Friday 9ᵗʰ March 1945 they moved back one hundred and fifty miles to Leuven in Belgium. Every single man was ecstatic to be out of tents and back in civvy billets again. Chic and Harry considered themselves extremely fortunate to be taken in by Mama Kestens: Mama and her daughter Pauline made them very welcome as did the rest of their family, Louise and her husband Emile Simons, Fernande and his wife Marie and Madame Celine. They lived at 36 Albert I Laan, off Gebroeders Tassetstraat in Wijgmaal. Chic had been given time off to settle in but he was distracted, he had not received any letters from Joyce for over a week and thought something may be wrong, but it was just a hiccup, the letters had followed him from pillar to post and the next day he received three from his darling. Everything was fine.

He was back working in the garage doing what he liked best, away from the threat of enemy fire and in comfortable digs with a friendly family. On Monday he was put on double guard duty, at the end of his watch he went to see *"Thin Ice"* at the camp cinema, it was an old film that he had seen at least four times already, but a bit of light comedy with some music and dancing never came amiss and he thought Tyrone Power was a good actor. He wrote to Joyce, to tell her that he had landed on his feet and was in a good place. The following evening, he stayed in his billet and talked with the family, they all spoke a little English and Pauline was fluent. Emile, Louise and Pauline also took him to a dance, it wasn't like any dance he had been to in England, but he enjoyed the company of his hosts. On Thursday Harry and the boys were going to Brussels and persuaded Chic to go with them, but he didn't really enjoy it, he wished he had stayed in the billet. He was fed up and wrote another letter to his wife.

There was plenty of work in the garage, a good thing to make the time passed quickly. The bomb disposal sappers had been sent out to work on booby trapped houses up near Roermond. The Germans had taken time to create as much carnage as possible. On one of the recce's they found civilians tied together in the town square with a trip wire attached to them, the slightest movement could have blown them all sky high. Bomb disposal managed to release them all but not without some injuries, it was abhorrent. There were thousands of civilian casualties and deaths with thousands more in prison camps. The scale of torture and killing carried out by the Nazis was only just beginning to emerge.

Sapper Neil Young also suffered a minor injury, he was taken to the field hospital in Louven and Chic visited him the next day. Johnno was back off leave and had been told he was going to Germany making him anxious. Chic bought him a beer, and they both went to the flics to see *"Pin Up Girl"* to cheer themselves up. Chic thought Carole Landis had a great singing voice, she didn't look too bad either, he enjoyed the film very much. That morning he received a letter from Joyce, she thought she was pregnant again and he was ecstatic. He told Pauline when he got back to the billet, the whole family were delighted for him and they had a little party to celebrate. The weather was lovely, the sun was shining and Chic had a spring in his step, he wrote to his wife. The war would soon be over and he would be with his darling and the baby.

On Friday allied planes appeared overhead, hundreds of them all heading for the Rhine. The same pattern continued all through the next day, planes and gliders filled the sky in their thousands, the spectacle was amazing. Chic had an easy day on Sunday in the garage, everything was great now he was going to be a *"Daddy."* After work he went to see Errol Flynn in *"Dawn Patrol,"* he had seen it before but this time it struck a chord when the subtitles came up;

"When youth rushed into fighting wings, to blaze a trail of heroism."

He loved going to the movies because it was a chance for some escapism, these old war films never showed the reality, the screaming, the squalor, the smell, the chaos.

Monday morning brought a long day in the garage, Chic was working on half-tracks until 2000 hours, he had started before 0730. At the end of his shift he was told to pack his kit bag for the next day, he was being sent down to the 159* Infantry Brigade workshops to help fit new engines in three Bedford lorries. He said hasty goodbyes to the Kestens household, they swapped addresses and promised to write. It took him two days with very little sleep to fit the engines, he was under huge pressure as the brigade was moving off and it needed the lorries. His squadron had already left and Chic was ordered to travel with the brigade in a convoy towards the Rhine. They travelled in darkness throughout the night. After crossing into Germany, he was delivered to his unit at Wesel on Thursday the 29* March 1945.

Chic was in a state of total exhaustion, with only a couple of hours sleep in more than three days. He was ordered to rest and dozed in the lorry cab while the convoy moved forward with astonishing speed. He wrote to his darling wife, his Belgian friend Emile and his mum. News came through that the sappers up ahead were now bridging the Dortmund-Ems canal with no opposition and morale was high. HQ were harboured temporarily on the edge of the Teutoberg Forest when Sapper Wright disappeared, everyone thought he had been captured, the enemy was very close and vigilance was paramount. The next day was April Fool's Day, Wright returned with two German guards under arrest, they had surrendered to him, he was very pleased with himself and feted as a hero for one whole day. The hilarity did not last long however because on Monday morning, infantry was sent out to clear the woods. Chic was in a good position in his truck to watch the whole operation from a relatively safe distance, the lads were up against German NCOs *(Non-Commissioned Officers),* from a nearby training school who were using Panzerfausts *(hand held anti-tank rocket launchers.)* They were causing havoc and it was considered imperative by the officers in command that these blighters be dealt with immediately, in order to pave the way for the allied tanks to move onwards and upwards into Osnabruck. Infantry did a grand job, it was agreed by all that the fighting went very well indeed, everyone was praised for battles well fought despite heavy losses. Chic was relieved once again that he was not in infantry with so many of the boys now dead or missing limbs

News also came through that the Americans had liberated three Nazi POW camps including Ohrdruf, a labour camp near Gotha, where thousands of starving Czech, Yugoslav and Russian prisoners were discovered living alongside hundreds of dead bodies. The corpses had been stripped naked and piled up in sheds, with lime sprinkled over the rotting flesh in an attempt to reduce the stench. A huge funeral pyre constructed in the grounds had a griddle made from railway tracks, the rotting bodies stacked on top were only partially burned, the Nazis had left in a hurry. There were no beds, just blood soaked, lice ridden straw in huts, stables, old bunkers and even tents. The surviving prisoners had little clothing and no sanitation. The SS guards were long gone, they had been brought in from Auschwitz to oversee the forced labour. It was thought they were building a secret subterranean headquarters for

Hitler, to be used in the event of Berlin falling to the allies. This shocking news was hard to take in, little did anyone know how the sight of atrocities was going to increase ten-fold in the very near future. As yet unknown, a few days earlier the Nazis had marched thousands of inmates away from the concentration camps that were at risk of being overrun by the allies, onwards to Buchenwald. Those that were too ill to keep up were shot and left at the roadside.

Chic tried not allow himself to think about anything other than the job in hand. They had advanced nearly fifty miles despite being dive bombed by Stukas *(Junkers Dive Bombers)* and then attacked by Heinkels and Messerschmitts *(fighter aircraft,)* with no sign of support from the RAF. The sappers from 612FS and 13FS bridging the Weser at Stolzenau were bearing the brunt of it, they were continually targeted by the enemy bombers often eight at a time for the whole afternoon until darkness fell. Then the airburst bombs, those *"Moaning Minnies,"* came in throughout the night with the shelling intensifying as dawn broke, they were just over half way across when another wave of attacks came from enemy aircraft. Chic was lucky to be behind the thick of it, thirteen sappers were killed on that day at Stolzenau, four from 612 FS. Dozens more were injured, not to mention all the equipment that had been sunk, blown up, or damaged beyond repair. Eventually by early evening the operation was aborted, both squadrons were moved back, but the dead and injured men had not been evacuated.

At 0800 the following morning the officers from both squadrons and HQ RE, met up to discuss clearance of the site. The whole area had been heavily mortared and sporadic sniping continued with more men suffering injuries. Chic was sent out on his motorbike to see what could be retrieved from the carnage of the previous days. He felt vulnerable, but was keen to do his duty and not be seen to be shirking, he owed it to those fellows who had died. The cratered roads were a nightmare and the stench of death and decay hung in the air even more heavily than usual, it made him gag. He was thinking about Joyce when suddenly the deafening sound of gunfire came from nowhere, his bike veered off sideways and tipped him into the ditch. The bike landed on top of him spewing petrol, a bullet had pierced the fuel tank. Was he shot? The motorbike was a dead weight and he was jammed under it. As he tried to move an agonising pain shot through his left leg. A vision flashed before his eyes of the Nazi biker that was shot dead back in France. If the sniper had another go at him he could be killed outright, or at best burned alive. He was flat on his back, vomiting and then realised he had shit himself, he could not stop gagging. His best bet was to play dead in the hope that the sniper would lose interest, he lay still, desperately trying not to retch or groan and focused his attention on the parcel that arrived yesterday from his mother, a fruitcake, that made him worse, and new clean underpants, they weren't clean anymore!

He was thirsty, but could not reach his water bottle, the dried vomit in his mouth was disgusting. After what seemed like hours he heard a vehicle coming straight for him, the engine sounded familiar and he could hear British voices. The next minute, two faces were peering down at him;

"Are you OK, mate?"

An RAMC *(Royal Army Medical Corps,)* corporal and his driver had also been sent out on reconnaissance, they were on their way back to HQ with three injured sappers. They lifted off the bike and threw it to one side revealing his foot, bent backwards at a disturbing angle. He was pulled up and helped to the jeep, hopping on one leg. They made straight for HQ where Chic reported in before being taken to the dressing station. The medics were overwhelmed with walking wounded, it was a case of waiting patiently in an ever growing queue, he knew he was lucky to be alive. He tried to take his boot off, but gave up. Eventually his turn arrived, his ankle was smashed with the bones sticking through the skin, he vomited again. He was obviously a hospital case, the medic strapped his leg up as best he could and put him on the list for transportation to the hospital at Enschede, over one hundred miles away just beyond the Dutch/German border. Morphine was also running low, Chic had his own supply in his emergency ration kit but in the confusion, he had lost it. He dozed fitfully before being loaded on to a lorry with many who had far worse injuries than him. The journey was slow and painful, every bump resonated through his ankle and up his leg. Some of the lads were moaning, no one slept, one chap did not survive the journey. A few tried a bit of a sing song to cheer themselves along, Chic joined in.

The German roads were jammed with the comings and goings of allied traffic and an astonishing number of German refugees, mainly women and children who straggled along in a never-ending line waving white flags. Some pulled hand carts with their few possessions, they were stopped every now and then at check points and searched. The towns were guarded by armed soldiers, they were unwelcome. Of the civilians

that remained most kept themselves to themselves, but a few came out
and spat at the troops as they drove through, no wine or cider here. It
took all day to reach their destination, but at last they crossed the border
and arrived at Enschede Emergency Hospital. The town of Enschede
had suffered badly throughout the war, not least from allied bombings
but the hospital was fully functioning and in military hands. It was
packed to the gunnels with hundreds of injured patients waiting to be
treated. Chic was sent to X-Ray, he waited in yet another queue, the
results showed several splinters, a fractured ankle that was out of
position and required an operation. Nearly two days after his accident
he was taken down to the operating theatre at 0400 hours, when he
woke up his ankle was in plaster and it felt much more comfortable.

Alf, Bill (front), Percy and Dave. Tolworth 1940.

16. CONVALESCENCE.

The next day Chic was given a walking stick, a clean uniform and his kit bag. He was told to report to the Red Cross van that would drive him another fifty miles back over the German border to Goch where the RAF had recently taken over Laarbruch Airport, he was going home. The flight in a C47 American Dakota transporter to Swindon in Wiltshire only took two and a half hours. He could not believe the speed, it was three hundred and thirty miles that was more than 120 mph, he had nothing but respect for the advances in aviation technology. He spent a comfortable night at Swindon in an army bed and the following day was taken by ambulance to Manchester, then on to a hospital in Warrington, another one hundred and sixty miles. He was glad to get settled, his ankle didn't feel right. The next day, the WRVS *(Women's Royal Voluntary Service)* organised a concert, it was something to do, but pretty awful. On Friday the 13ᵗʰ April his plaster was removed and his ankle X-Rayed again, the bones were not in place. He was booked in for a general anaesthetic the following day. He felt groggy when he woke up with a new plaster and as the anaesthetic wore off, his foot got hotter and hotter. He couldn't sleep and was given another X-Ray, the doctor said the bones were in place and it was just a matter of being patient. Chic was impatient but he put up with it.

It was now a matter of waiting again, he was in bed and bored. He dozed off and dreamed that his friend Jenni was calling out for help but he couldn't find him. He woke with a start when he heard a familiar voice;

"Sherwood, what the hell are you doing here?"

Sergeant Ramsden was standing by his bed. Unknown to Chic, the sergeant had been found injured after their unit moved on and was flown back to England, where he had been in hospital ever since. He did not look a well man, but it was good to see him alive. They had quite a few chats despite the sergeant tiring easily, he slept a great deal. Chic spent the next day reading, his concentration was not good due to the anaesthetic that was still in his system. He had not received any letters since leaving Germany, they had been chasing him from pillar to post but at last, a couple arrived, one from Mum and the other from cousin Molly, but nothing from Joyce. Wednesday 18ᵗʰ April was a lovely sunny day and he was given permission to sit out on the veranda.

101

At last he received a letter from his darling Joyce and read it whilst soaking up the sun, he was beginning to feel better until he read that she had lost another baby. He was devastated. The ENSA lassies and lads were very active up in Warrington and laid on a film at the hospital that afternoon, he went along to take his mind off things. The following day they put on a show and repeated it the day after that. He went to both, they were exactly the same and he lost concentration. Everyone now knew that Chic was in hospital, back in England and parcels were beginning to arrive: his father sent forty cigarettes, underpants from Mum, Joyce sent fruit cake and wrote that she was feeling sad, but physically OK.

Occupational therapy was the order of the day, Chic was making a felt elephant. He was feeling much better and liked the pattern cutting, he was good with a needle and thread. He sneaked off in his wheelchair to find some wool without permission from the nurses and had a bit of fun dodging about, hiding from sister. On Sunday there was an influx of visitors to the hospital, it made a nice change to meet new people and have some female company. Later on, he did a bit of reading and wrote several letters: Joyce, Mum, cousin Molly and his school chums Alf *(Sapper Alfred Rockall)* and Bill *(Able Seaman William Kelly)*. It was back to occupational therapy on Monday morning. Chic finished his elephant, he was very pleased with the way it turned out, a white jumbo with enormous ears and a friendly face, it would have made a perfect gift for his baby, perhaps he should give it to his niece, little Annette.

The days dragged and he was really browned off, he hated lying in bed doing nothing and complained to sister. She told him she would check with the doctors, but she thought he could be up and about very soon. The local people were keen to support their brave soldiers and as a result, enthusiastically organised a huge variety of events. Chic went along to a pianoforte recital by Harriet Cohen, the highly respected Jewish classical pianist. A classical concert would not normally be his cup of tea, but he enjoyed some of the music and admired her talent. News was beginning to filter through of the horrific scenes at Bergen-Belsen, a concentration camp not far from Stolzenau, where Chic was injured, he now knew the source of that terrible stench that hung in the air. Belsen was liberated a week after Chic was flown home, his chums would have seen the horrors first hand. Reports of atrocities at other camps had already been reported in the newspapers. The Buchenwald camps were bad enough, but it seemed there was no end to the horror, with each discovery worse than the last. He thought back to Breendonk, it made him physically sick, he also thought about his chums, Johnno, Stead and all the others still stuck out there somewhere.

When he came back to the ward, he was told his plaster was being reset again, in readiness for fitting a walking iron the next day. The iron was duly fitted, he was told to let it settle and he could try walking after a good night's sleep. This was good news and Chic was in a great mood when he went to see yet another show which this time he enjoyed immensely, especially when he *(as a hospital patient)* was issued a ration of forty cigarettes. On 27ᵗʰ April, three weeks after his accident, he was at last walking again, he needed a stick but there was not much pain. Off he went to an ENSA show that was absolutely first class, he had a good laugh and was in positive mood. It wasn't long before he could walk short distances without a stick and he was able to have a bath. After finishing his elephant in occupational therapy, he decided to make a string belt for Joyce, the macramé teacher only had to show him once how to create the pattern and he finished it in no time. The belt had a smart Bakelite buckle with a wide band of diamond patterned brown string, accented with tiny yellow French knots. He would save this as a gift for his darling when he went on leave.

The newspapers were full of reports about the execution of the Fascist dictator, Mussolini. Italian partisans had captured him near Lake Como whilst he was trying to cross into Switzerland, along with some government officials and his mistress. They were all shot and their corpses hung from trees outside a petrol station in Milan. The Italian crowds rioted, pulled down statues and spat on the dead bodies. Chic wondered where it would all end, the Italians were such an excitable race. On Sunday, May Day was being celebrated in the villages all around Warrington. Some of the fitter patients including Chic, were invited to the festivities, with tea and cake at a beautiful country house with extensive grounds. The WRVS put on a grand spread and everyone had a very nice time. There was dancing around the maypole, a May Queen was crowned and fun and games on the lawn, a traditional village fete. It was great to do something normal, everyone was so kind and appreciative to their lads who had fought for them all this time and now the war would soon be over. Chic had such a good time but he wished his wife could have been there too.

He decided the next day to *"tap"* the doctor for some leave. He used every bit of charm he had and asked if would be able to play football now. The doctor replied;

"Yes, if you are careful."

Percy winked at the nurse;

"That's great, 'cos I couldn't before!"

The doctor smiled and agreed that he was now fit and well enough to travel alone, he could have ten days leave. On Wednesday morning straight after breakfast, he caught a train from Warrington to Kings Cross and arrived at Foxton Station late afternoon. He was tired, his foot throbbed and it was a bit of a walk up to the cottage, but he took it slowly. Edie was sitting in the backyard peeling shallots ready for pickling. She could not believe her eyes when she saw Chic hobbling up the lane and rushed inside to put the kettle on. She gave him a big hug and then ran around to *"The Press"* to tell Joyce. Edie immediately bumped into Mr Jordan, who on hearing the news was delighted to let Joyce go an hour early, he wasn't such a bad old stick!

Joyce was so surprised to see her darling husband, she had been very worried about him, and he, her. She made him sit down and put his foot up, took his leg iron off and fussed over him like a broody hen. She made a good nurse and had her Red Cross Home Nursing Certificate. Her miscarriage was not mentioned. When her father came home, he had already heard the news from Mr Jordan and was beaming from ear to ear, he thought the occasion demanded a bottle of beer or two. They settled down to listen to the news on the radio; Hitler was dead! They all cheered. Chic's foot ached and he was tired, but he was back with his darling wife and her family. Joyce was obliged to go to work on Thursday and Friday, but she came home in her breaks to check that her husband was not doing too much. Her mother set about some celebratory baking, Chic had never eaten so many cakes. By Saturday he was feeling rested so they went to the flics in Cambridge. His foot was throbbing by the end of the day, so they decided to stay home on Sunday, he was having such a lovely time, he didn't write in his diary once.

17. VICTORY IN EUROPE.

Joyce and her father were back at work the following week. Harry Cheshire always had the radio on in his overseer's office, desperate for the latest news. Chic also liked to listen to the radio in the back parlour while Edie busied herself with the household chores. At 3 pm on Tuesday 8ᵗʰ May there was a newsflash. It was Mr Churchill;

"Yesterday morning at 2.41 am, at General Eisenhower's headquarters, General Jodl, the representative of the German High Command and Grand-Admiral Donits, the designated head of the German State, signed the act of unconditional surrender of all German land, sea and air forces in Europe to the Allied Expeditionary Force and simultaneously to the Soviet High Command."

Harry Cheshire leapt from his overseer's chair and pressed the works siren, shouting;

"We've done it, we've bloody done it."

The whole factory gathered round apart from Joyce who ran back to the cottage where Chic and Edie were listening intently;

"Hostilities will end officially at one minute after midnight tonight, but, in the interests of saving lives, the Cease Fire began yesterday to be sounded all along the front."

Mr Churchill went on to say;

"We may allow ourselves a brief period of rejoicing, but let us not forget for a moment, the toils and efforts that lie ahead. Japan, with all her treachery and greed, remains unsubdued. The injury she has inflicted upon Great Britain, the United States and other countries, and her detestable cruelties, call for justice and retribution. We must now devote all our strength and resources to the completion of our tasks both at home and abroad. Advance Britannia!"

"Long live the cause of freedom!"

"God Save the King!"

Joyce and Chic were laughing and hugging each other, but Edie had gone quiet, Douglas her son, was now in the far east and his war was not over yet. Ten minutes later, Harry burst through the door, the factory was closed until Thursday, everyone could celebrate with a day off tomorrow. They celebrated Victory in Europe Day quietly at home. Joyce wanted to go to Cambridge to join in the celebrations, but her father said it would be too rowdy. Chic was also rather reluctant, he was being haunted by nightmares and wanted a quiet life. The date was approaching for Chic and Joyce's first wedding anniversary, their time together so far as husband and wife had been less than a month.
On Saturday when things had calmed down, they went out for dinner in Cambridge and then to the flicks for an early anniversary treat. The *"Pathe News"* was full of the VE Day celebrations in Britain and abroad, the whole population had gone mad. Servicemen and women of all denominations were being courted by thousands of civilians, the streets were packed to bursting with drinking, singing and dancing continuing all day and all night.

Chic was due back at Warrington Hospital on the 14th of May. He said goodbye to his wife as she left for work on Monday morning and was back in Warrington by tea time, thoroughly browned off. The next day he walked around the hospital grounds for a while, but it did not lift his mood, he wrote nine letters. On Wednesday he had a new ankle iron fitted and wrote to Joyce to tell her, it was smaller and a great deal more comfortable. He went to see a film to pass the time but it wasn't very good and he had seen it a dozen times before. Chic was also ordered to go back to occupational therapy, he was marking out another felt elephant when the duty doctor advised matron that he could be moved to Arley Hall. This was a convalescent home for wounded soldiers and Chic was not best pleased, he was missing Joyce and didn't see why he couldn't convalesce at home, not in a home! Arley Hall was pleasant enough with extensive grounds and glorious architecture, but it was no substitute for being with Joyce. She looked after him as well as any nurse.

On Saturday the Red Cross van took Chic and a few of the other walking wounded to Warrington, where they did a bit of shopping and went to the pictures. It was the same film he had seen with Joyce the week before, *"The Man in Grey."* It reminded him even more of his darling, even the Pathe News was the same, he was fed up to his *"back teeth"*. When he returned to the home he wrote a letter to Major Wells requesting a transfer nearer to Cambridge. On Sunday the 20th May their first wedding anniversary, they were apart, Joyce went to church in Foxton and Chic helped the nurses out at Arley Hall, it was better than doing nothing. On Monday, all the patients that were well enough to travel were taken to the Ariel South Naval Training Camp where a continuous supply of popular films was available. First, Sonja Henie in *"Wintertime"*, and then on Tuesday they went back again to see Edward G Robinson in *"Panic"*. Normally Chic would have been impressed, but he was sick to death of making felt elephants and was missing his wife.

On Wednesday he did absolutely nothing, and wrote in his diary;

"Getting TOO MUCH rest."

Thursday livened up a bit with yet another trip to the flics, this time in Warrington to see *"Meet Me in St Louis"* with Judy Garland, the film was good. Nothing happened Sunday, Monday, or Tuesday, apart from stuffing and stitching another felt elephant he could almost do it with his eyes closed. He was doubly browned off and could not wait for the week-end when he would see his family. Even a card from his school mate Bill who was serving on HMS Wayland, did not cheer him up;

Dear Percy.
Got your letter this morning, am sorry to now your fed up, but I am myself. It's a lousy place here. Will write to you later when I get time.

Cherrio Bill.

Midweek, all the patients at Arley Hall were taken to a party at the ICI factory in Lostock. That passed a pleasant few hours and Chic enjoyed the party, but he was looking forward to going home and spent most of Thursday packing, including one felt elephant and the macramé belt.

This time he was going back to Mum and Dad's in Tolworth, he met Joyce at Kings Cross and they both arrived in Tolworth soon after dinner time. Frank was at work, but Annie was waiting with the kettle on, she had made some scones and opened a jar of blackberry and apple jam. She welcomed them both with tears in her eyes and they all had a nice week-end together. The couple went to the pictures at The Regal on Saturday night. The building and its magnificent Wurlitzer organ had been damaged during the blitz, but both were now repaired and the venue was very popular with youngsters, it showed films and held tea dances in the cafeteria. They spent Sunday quietly at home, Annie cooked a special roast dinner, a lovely bit of topside beef with Yorkshire puddings. Brother Charlie was also there with his wife and baby, Chic gave Annette her elephant and Joyce made a big fuss of her. Both Chic and Joyce wanted a family so badly and were sad but did not show it, they all had a great deal to look forward to. Joyce was supposed to be at work at 8 am on Monday morning, they left Tolworth at the crack of dawn on the milk train. Joyce turned up just in time for the 10 am tea break. Mr Jordan tutted and said she would lose two hours pay, Joyce didn't care, it was worth it to spend an extra night with her beloved husband

Chic arrived back at Arley Hall a few hours later and was instantly browned off, with nothing to do except stuff white elephants. The next day was just as boring, apart for another trip to the Ariel South Training Camp. This time the film showing was *"Between Two Worlds,"* that made Chic think, he was in limbo and needed something to happen. The WRVS organised a garden party at Arley Hall on Wednesday and the weather was glorious, the house was packed full with visitors and a good time was had by all. Chic loved a party, nothing like a bit of fun to take your mind off things. He also received a letter from Major Wells. Sapper Sherwood was required to report to the army office at Winwick the following afternoon, to discuss a possible transfer. He immediately wrote to Joyce to tell her the good news. He wasn't sure where he was being sent, but it would definitely be much closer to home. The meeting with Major Wells went very well indeed. Chic told him that he had been married a whole year and hardly seen his wife. In that time she had lost two babies and he needed to be close by. Joyce could not travel up North because she had a full-time job and was only allowed two weeks annual leave in August. The major asked him about his ankle and studied his medical reports. Chic then added that if he had to make one more felt elephant he would go mad. Major Wells sympathised, he himself could not contemplate the thought of spending his days making soft toys. He agreed to give this sapper some leave on compassionate grounds and his medical records would be transferred to Ley Hospital in Cambridge. He would also recommend a posting to Shelford, just a few miles from Foxton. Chic could not believe his ears, he sent Joyce a telegram, he was coming home tomorrow.

18. CAMBRIDGESHIRE.

On Friday 8ₜ June 1945, Chic reported to Winwick with all his gear. It took all day to complete his discharge, a medical, kit inspection and other assorted administrative procedures. Eventually at 1600 hours he was taken by Red Cross van to Manchester where he was told to find an army truck going south, he found one going to Sheffield and then changed again for Peterborough. It was now the middle of the night but there was a 10 tons supply truck on its way to Cambridge. Bill the driver was an amiable chap who welcomed the company, it was good to have someone to talk to on the graveyard shift. Once the delivery was unloaded in Cambridge, Bill was going to Harwich Docks, he didn't mind dropping Chic off in Foxton on the way, he drove him right up to The Burlington Press.

Chic walked into the kitchen at Addison Cottages at 9.45 am on Saturday morning. Joyce cooked him some boiled eggs with toast and dripping, after which he went straight to bed and slept until 3 pm. His arrival home could not have been more timely, it was Joyce's twenty-first birthday in three days. They enjoyed a lovely day together on Sunday and went for a walk in the afternoon up to the clunch pits. While Joyce was at work on Monday, Chic went into Cambridge on the bus and met a couple of mates that were stationed nearby. They had a great time, a few beers and a lot of laughs remembering good times, not bad. Chic bought Joyce a brooch, a wooden sewing box and a birthday card depicting their dream house. He was a sentimental soul at heart and particularly liked the poetic wording:

"Congratulations on Your 21ₜ Birthday
The door of Twenty-One is just ajar,
The gifts of Life are yours, a shining star
Of Hope, for promise there's a gleaming key
To many glorious things, now you are free:
Throughout the days to come may joys abound
And all your efforts with success be crowned."

He signed it;   *Your Ever Loving Husband. Chic.*

XXXXXXXXXXXXXXXXXXXXX

Joyce's birthday was on Tuesday and the girls at The Press had organised a collection. The postman delivered dozens of cards and stacks more arrived by hand. Chic adored his wife, she was so popular. Joyce was thrilled with her sewing box, it was exactly what she wanted. Her mum made a special Victoria sponge with raspberry jam and they ate fresh cucumber sandwiches for tea, harvested that morning by her father before he went to work. It was a beautiful day made even the more special for them all because Chic was back home with them.

On Wednesday morning he was told to report to Ley Hospital in Cambridge, he was registered and given a bed. After another X-Ray he was told the plaster needed changing again, but it was not urgent. There was nothing happening the next day, so Chic went down to Tolworth by train to see his mother for a few hours. The plaster was changed on Friday morning but it felt very uncomfortable. Joyce visited him on Saturday and they walked out for a while in Cambridge. Then on Sunday he was given leave to spend the day at Foxton, but his leg was really playing him up, so Stan Barnes gave Chic a lift back to hospital in the evening, by which time it was very painful.

Monday brought a trip to the dentist. Chic was being measured up for a false tooth and while he was in town, he took himself off to the flics to see *"Key of the Kingdom."* The film was quite good, but he managed to break his foot iron on the cinema stairs, the pain that shot through his leg was agonising, it did not do him any good at all, the skin was swelling above the plaster and his toes were going blue. He was booked in to have the plaster changed on Wednesday, so he went to Foxton by bus on Tuesday to see Joyce, she was worried about him. The following morning the plaster was taken off and Chic was told to rest for a few hours to let the air get to his leg, the swelling quickly went down and his toes returned to their normal colour. Later on that day he got yet another new plaster, this one was fine and his ankle iron had been repaired, he could be discharged. Now he was being transferred to Shelford barracks, only five miles from Foxton.

Once Chic had settled in at the barracks he went off to the dentist again in Cambridge. He had been given week-end leave so decided to travel straight down to Tolworth by train on the Friday to see his parents. He and his father had a long chat, they jokingly compared war wounds and shared a few experiences from their separate wars. Frank was eager to know about the hardship his son had experienced, Chic made light of it. Frank was taken prisoner in France in 1916, after being shot in the leg on the Somme battlefield. The Germans put him to hard labour in Saint Quenten POW camp, where he remained for two years. The prisoners were subjected to a vicious work regime, with inadequate shelter, lack of warm clothing or bedding and a meagre daily ration of one hard biscuit softened in a cup of hot water. After the armistice in 1918, he returned to his family emaciated, but he had survived and gradually regained acceptable good health. His son knew nothing of this, he was born two years later and the war had never been mentioned.

Joyce joined the family on Saturday morning and Annie arranged a little family party in the evening with Charlie, Phyllis and the baby. They went back to Foxton together on Sunday afternoon. The regime was pretty easy going at Shelford, allowing them to see each other on most days and sometimes Chic stayed over at Addison Cottages. At long last he was beginning to feel like he was properly married. He pottered about doing everyday bits and pieces with his wife and helped out on his father-in-law's allotment. He also stopped writing in his diary, there was no need now he was with his darling. On 28ᵗʰ June, Chic had a new false tooth fitted, he thought it extortionately expensive at 30 shillings. *(£1.50)* Joyce thought it looked great, he could smile his lovely smile now without looking like a bruiser. The days drifted by, Chic was doing easy routine maintenance at Shelford and Joyce was working at The Press. They spent their evenings and week-ends together like a normal married couple.

There was a general election on Thursday the 5ᵗʰ July. Joyce and her father met Edie in their dinner break and they walked down together to the polling station at the village hall and voted Conservative, they were very proud of Mr Churchill and his party. Chic was at the barracks and voted for the Labour candidate. Mr Churchill kept his seat down in Essex, but Labour won by a huge majority including the Cambridge seat. Chic did not advertise who he had voted for, he was not up for an argument with his father-in-law or his wife. The next day he was confined to barracks and ordered to attend a lecture. There was a lot of talk about the election and how the Labour government policies would affect the armed forces. He thought back to this time last year in Normandy when he wrote;

> *"Have been working on half-track in front of*
> *infantry……………….SCARED "*

How much he had seen in just one year, he never wanted to experience any of it again. The following week his plaster was removed, he was not in any pain but his calf muscle was wasted and his ankle felt very weak. He was back walking with a stick and told cycling would strengthen the muscle so he borrowed his brother-in-law's push bike for riding back and forth between Foxton and Shelford.

Joyce was still very busy with her village activities. After VE Day, Foxton Parish Council voted in favour of a house to house collection to raise funds for a fancy-dress parade and sports day, in readiness to celebrate when the war would finally be won, in Japan as well as Europe. Her father was on the organising committee, the cause being very close to his heart with his son Douglas still serving in the navy out in the far east. Joyce loved a bit of dressing up and she was also in high demand as a seamstress. The entertainments committee agreed that Joyce should lead the parade, dressed as Britannia, Chic loved being included in all this village activity. It was very different from where he had grown up, he thought he knew most people in Tolworth but in Foxton, everyone knew everyone and most of them liked a bit of fun. What no one knew was when or how the victory in Japan would manifest itself. However, they did not have to wait too long to find out.

On 2ⁿᵈ of August President Truman lunched with the King on HMS Renown in Plymouth. It was the first time the two men had met and the newspapers were full of it. Truman's predecessor Roosevelt, died in April and the new president was proving his worth, he was seen as a good friend to the British people. A few days earlier he attended the Berlin Peace Conference with the Labour Prime Minister, Clement Attlee and the Russian General, Stalin. They discussed much about the way forward with Germany and the destruction of Nazism, but Japan remained a thorn in their sides. The Japanese would not agree to an unconditional ceasefire, despite having a truce with Russia. Truman persuaded Stalin to take up arms again against the Nippon government, to bring the war to a final conclusion. Four days later, the Americans dropped an atomic bomb on Japan. It was Chic's twenty-fifth birthday on the 8ᵗʰ August by which time the radio and newspapers were full of the story.

Colonel Tibbets, the pilot and Captain Parsons, a US Navy ordnance officer were interviewed at length. Captain Parsons said:

"The whole thing was tremendous and awe inspiring. After the missile had been released, I sighed and stood back from the shock. When it came, the men aboard with me gasped; "My God!" What had been Hiroshima was a mountain of smoke like a giant mushroom. A thousand feet above the ground was a mass of dust, boiling, swirling, and extending over most of the city. We watched it for several minutes, and when the tip of the mushroom broke off, there was evidence of fires."

Harry Cheshire and Joyce were jubilant, they hated the Japs but Chic found it all rather depressing. The next day it became public knowledge that Russia had declared war on Japan and invaded Manchuria. He wondered if the carnage would ever end. On the same day America dropped another atom bomb on Japan, this time Nagasaki. Chic did not want to think about it, he was off on nine days leave on Friday and nothing was going to spoil it, he was not expected back in the barracks until Sunday night on 18ᵗʰ August and determined to have a lovely time with his wife in Foxton. He was sitting in the back parlour at 3 Addison Cottages with Joyce and her parents when the Saturday evening news came on the radio, Japan had surrendered. Chic thought he was dreaming, Joyce and her father were going mad. Harry went straight off to summon an emergency committee meeting in the village hall while Edie baked some ginger biscuits.

The following week was frantic. Joyce was busy making costumes for the fancy dress parade and Harry selecting teams for the sports events. There were intense talks in progress between all the allied nations and eventually on Tuesday, President Truman announced that General MacArthur had ordered a ceasefire and Japan had capitulated. It was not until the following evening that the Prime Minister, Mr Attlee, announced on the radio at midnight:

"The last of our enemies is laid low."

Wednesday 15ᵗʰ August 1945 was declared VJ Day *(Victory in Japan,)* the whole British Isles was given two days national holiday in celebration. Foxton Parish Council had one day to finalise the planned fancy-dress parade for Friday, the sporting events on Saturday and the regular village cricket match on Sunday afternoon. Joyce was up half the night finishing her costume, she had left hers until last. Johnny Haines found an old Roman helmet in the props store and Chic was roped in to making a Union Jack shield for Britannia to wield.

On Friday morning, with Chic's help, Jim, Ted and Brian built a makeshift puppet theatre on the pavement outside the church while Johnny Haines painted a large sign for the top;

"PEACE AT LAST"

Everyone assembled outside the village hall at 2 pm, there were dozens of entrants in the fancy dress competition, mostly children. Even Mr How the headmaster came along in his cap and gown despite it being the school holidays. The local newspaper sent a reporter with a photographer who lined them all up for a picture, with Joyce in the middle, resplendent as Britannia. There were costumes and characters from all over the world, an extremely happy gathering, no one dressed as Hitler! After the judging it was time for the puppet show, Punch and Judy hanging Hitler! There was raucous audience participation.

Then it was time for Joyce to climb into Mr Challis's trailer. Normally this was used to collect newspapers from the wholesaler, but today it was attached to the back of his Austin saloon as he proudly led the parade. Joyce escorted by Jim Haynes all dressed up in his mother's clothes, with a fancy hat, a wig, and oodles of lipstick. Ted and Brian also in drag, followed solemnly behind carrying a stuffed effigy of Hitler. Britannia was clapped and cheered as she waved to the crowd. In the next moment, Hitler and his drag queens were hissed and jeered at. The children in their international costumes were all greeted with enthusiastic clapping. After parading up and down Foxton High Street from the Fowlmere Road to Shepreth Bottom and back, the motley crew arrived back at the war memorial in the centre of the village. Britannia led the way into the recreation ground, with Hitler behind, carried by the two torch bearers Ted and Brian. They installed him on top of the bonfire and cast their torches into the pyre to cheers and shouts of:

"Rule Britannia and God Save the King."

Jacket potatoes were thrown onto the fire and dozens of tins of bully beef that some wag in the village had acquired from the RASC stores in Cambridge, were opened and sliced up by the WI ladies. A table was laid out in front of the cricket pavilion, with all manner of relishes: pickled onions and beetroot, piccalilli, sweet chutneys and the most delicious fresh berries straight from the village allotments and gardens, complimented with butter and cream from Home Farm

Saturday brought out the village's competitive spirit with a football match, rounders, tug-o-war, some athletics and numerous novelty races including the egg and spoon. Joyce's father was in his element as one of the referees, Chic helped out with linesman duties. The weather was splendid, the judges lenient and it was all great fun. On Sunday Foxton Cricket Club was playing at home against a neighbouring village, Joyce was behind the scoreboard marking up the runs, Harry was umpire and Edie was in charge of sandwiches, she was the thinnest bread slicer in the village. Chic was not given any duties but was having the most wonderful time with his new family and very aware that he had to be back in Shelford barracks by midnight. He did not want this week to end.

Chic thought now the war was over, he would be able go back to civvy street and settle back into his job at Fox and Nicholl's garage. Thanks to the army he was now a fully qualified A2 mechanic with varied experience under his belt, his wages would definitely go up. He planned to take Joyce down to Tolworth where they would stay with his parents, until they could find a place of their own and bring up a family, just like his brother Charlie was doing, he just had to suffer a bit more army bureaucracy. The next two weeks at Shelford were pleasant enough, the days passed by with routine duties and Chic cycled to Foxton most evenings and week-ends. His ankle was much improved, although it still gave him a bit of gyp at night. He often woke up in a cold sweat having dreamed he was back in the fighting, he would toss and turn and get tangled in the bed clothes. The barracks were full of lads that screamed and shouted in their sleep and once Chic was awake, he found it very difficult to go back off.

19. BEDFORDSHIRE.

On Monday 3ʳᵈ September, Chic was told that he was being sent to
Bedford where his transfer would be arranged. He cycled to Foxton on
Monday night to tell Joyce and Stan very kindly gave him a lift back to
the barracks. First thing Tuesday morning he was on his way to
Bedford, it was only thirty-five miles away but too far to pop back to
Foxton every day. He arrived just before dinner time and the canteen
served up a very palatable cottage pie with beans. It took all afternoon
to go through the various checks, there was an issue with Sapper
Sherwood's *"Soldier's Service and Paybook."* The book had got
soaked through in the Reichswald Forest and much of it was illegible.
The officer in command agreed that Sherwood should be issued a new
certified copy due to accidental mutilation. However, it could take
several weeks for all the necessary information to be gathered and
agreed. Due to all the fuss and bother over his paybook, Chic did not
get his billet sorted until the next morning, when the all best ones had
gone. He found some digs that were adequate, but he was missing Joyce
and extremely fed up. On Thursday there was nothing to do and
frustration had already set in. The working week ended with a lecture
about demobbing and the chance to have shower, that made a very
pleasant change! The week-end loomed, oh how he wished he could be
in Foxton, but he gritted his teeth and went to have a look around
Bedford. The town was packed with troops and appeared to have a huge
variety of entertainment facilities, but Chic knew from experience it
was probably not what it seemed. He went to the pictures and watched a
film that he had seen a dozen times before.

All the troops at the Bedford barracks were expected to attend the
church parade on Sunday morning, the marching and standing left
Chic's ankle throbbing and painful. The country singer; *"Roy Hall"*
came back to the barracks in the afternoon, his rendition of *"Rockabilly
Alligator"* was excellent, but Chic left straight afterwards, he was under
the weather with a heavy head cold and went to bed early, back at his
uncomfortable billet. On Monday morning he reported in sick and the
medical officer signed him off for two days. Chic asked if he could go
on leave because his billet was cold and unwelcoming, he would
recover much quicker at home. The officer said *"no."* Chic was
annoyed and complained of pain in his leg, after a bit of a row he was
allowed to go home on Wednesday, on the understanding that he must
be back by Saturday night. Joyce was very attentive and his mother in-

law prepared all sorts of restorative concoctions to improve his chest. He arrived back in Bedford a happier man.

There was still nothing to do at the barracks apart from routine checks and training. There was a show on at The Corn Exchange in Saint Paul's Square on Sunday night and Chic went with a few of the lads. On Monday he saw another show, it was rubbish. Tuesday, he received a letter from Joyce, she hoped he was over his cold and had the sniffles herself, but also, she felt sick most mornings she could be pregnant again. The news perked Chic up immensely, he went to a dance with the lads and enjoyed the music with a beer while resting his foot. A military parade was planned for Saturday to celebrate thanksgiving and the rehearsals went on all week. Chic was told to get his haircut on Thursday morning and in the afternoon, there was another rehearsal, marching to a band in Saint Paul's Square, he quite enjoyed that. Friday was supposed to be a free day but most of it was spent tidying up in preparation for Saturday's parade.

The next morning thousands of spectators turned up wielding their umbrellas, the heavens had opened with no respite, the parade went ahead in torrential rain. Chic was soaked through to his skin, had a hacking cough and his ankle was giving him serious gyp. So much for thanksgiving;

"Thank you, God!"

Sunday was an easy day, Chic wrote to Joyce and went to The Corn Exchange in the afternoon. The next few days passed by slowly with little to do, he went to see the record officer to chase his paybook, but there was still no sign of it. On Thursday morning he was told he could go on leave until Sunday night, he didn't need telling twice. He was anxious to see how Joyce was and hitched a lift to Cambridge in an old Austin army van, he was back in Foxton in time for Joyce to finish work. She was delighted to see him and seemed to be blooming. Chic spent Friday in front of the fire in the back parlour with the newspaper. Joyce had a practise in the church that evening for the harvest festival, Chic went along to watch the rehearsal. On Saturday they caught the bus to Cambridge, did a bit of shopping and went dancing. Chic's ankle was sore, his wife insisted he get it checked out on his return to Bedford.

The harvest festival service on Sunday morning was delightful, the church bursting with flowers and produce. Every member of the congregation contributed to the display, including Chic who was instructed by Harry to pick half a dozen quinces from the tree in his front garden. Joyce took the dozens of corn dollies that she and Audrey had made with the children at Sunday school and issued one to each child as they entered the church. The Reverend Rowlands welcomed everyone, the children sang *"All Things Bright and Beautiful,"* with Joyce conducting. Chic thought it was all lovely, his wife looked radiant, she was excellent with the little ones and was going to be a great mum. Once the children were dispatched to their parents, Joyce and Edie went home to cook dinner while Harry and Chic walked down to The Black Boy for a pint. Life was good, it was a shame he could only stay until teatime.

Sapper Sherwood went straight over to the medical unit on Monday morning to ask about getting his ankle checked, in the hope of being regraded. After a long wait to collect his medical records and then another long wait to see the doctor, he eventually went in for his examination. He explained that his ankle ached constantly and he frequently could not put his full weight onto it by the end of each day. It played him up big time after all the marching in Thanksgiving Week. The doctor checked Chic's mobility, asked a few questions and rated him L1, he was considered fit enough to run or march for up to five miles and would be put to work on the farm, from tomorrow. Chic complained of pain at night with disturbed sleep, the doctor seemed to think that was normal and prescribed an infra-red heat lamp. Chic was not impressed.

The next morning, he was sent down to the farm for some instruction. He didn't have to do much because George Isaacs was visiting Bedford that afternoon and all those who wanted to hear him speak were given the afternoon off. It appeared by the turn out, that Mr Isaacs was very popular with the troops! He was the new minister for Labour and National Service in the Labour government that Chic had voted for back in July. The government had not done much so far, but he was willing to give them the benefit of the doubt and wanted to know what Mr Isaacs had to say for himself. There was a great deal of pomp and ceremony down in the square, with the mayor, town councillors and a few of the army elite all courting Mr Isaacs and his colleagues. The mayor made a welcome speech, but Isaacs did not respond, suddenly he was whisked away in a fancy car without uttering a single word. Chic was more than a little disheartened, he vowed that he would never vote Labour again, he wished he had listened to his father-in-law.

The next couple of days he did as little on the farm as he could, his ankle ached constantly. He opted for inside jobs where he could at least stand on even ground and rest his foot. The work on the farm was boosted with labour from POWs, Italians mostly, they were pleasant enough and good workers who seemed to know what they were doing. Chic on the other hand, did not have a clue, apart from getting a tractor going when it wouldn't start. After two days he reported in sick, he could not put weight on his ankle, it was swollen and he was ready for an argument. He saw a different doctor this time who was more sympathetic. A medical board interview was booked in for the following week and Chic was given Saturday off to visit Joyce in Foxton. On Sunday he had a very lazy morning and passed away a pleasant afternoon at The Corn Exchange listening to music, watching the dancing and having a few beers. It looked like his complaint had paid off, on Monday morning Sapper Sherwood was transferred to 7ᵗʰ Coy *(Company,)* Royal Engineers, where he was given a job in the admissions centre, he was now able to sit down for at least part of the day. He enjoyed being behind the reception desk, talking to different people and helping them out, he liked his new job very much indeed.

It was time for his medical board appointment. The doctor asked him if he thought he could jump off a lorry travelling at fifteen miles an hour, Chic was definite that he could not, he was subsequently graded B2. In layman's terms this meant he would not be returned to active service, although he may be expected to work abroad, most likely on lines of communication and it was assumed that he should be able to walk or march for up to five miles. Chic was happy with this assessment, he liked his new job and hoped he would be able to stay put until he was demobbed. He wrote to Joyce to tell her the good news, he didn't know when he would be out of the army but he thought it would be soon. The following week, the long awaited paybook arrived, with Chic's up to date service record. His rank was now driver and he was in age and service group:35C. This meant his transfer to the army reserve was complete but he would not be discharged until next July, another nine months to go. He decided to keep that information from Joyce until his next leave, he had no idea when that would be. He also stopped writing in his diary, after all he was writing it for Joyce and at the moment he held a few secrets.

Meanwhile unknown to Chic, Joyce also had a secret. She was suffering complications again with her pregnancy, she had lost a third baby and visited the doctor. He told her that her smoking was not a concern, but her blood pressure was too high and she weighed too much. He said;

"In some women, involuntary abortion becomes a habit."

He explained that as she had already suffered three miscarriages, it was likely her body was not adjusting properly to the child's requirements. He advised in her next pregnancy to take no tiring exercise, experience no excitement and to avoid all infectious diseases, particularly pneumonia and tuberculosis. If she reached the third month without losing the child, she should then go to bed for complete rest for the remainder of her confinement. Joyce was devastated. How was she going to break the news to her dear husband?

S____r's Service Book.

(Sold____ ____ay Book, Army Book 64 (Part II), will be
issued for active service.)

Entrie____ ____ book (other than those connected with the
____ ____dier's Will and insertion of the names of
rela____ ____ be made under the superintendence of an
Officer

Instructions to Soldier.

1. You ____ held **personally responsible** for the safe
custody of ____ ____ok.

2. Y____ ____ **always carry this book** on your person.

3. Y____ ____t produce the book whenever called upon
to do s____ ____mpetent military authority, viz., Officer, War-
rant O____ ____O. or Military Policeman.

4. You must not alter or make any entry in this book
(except as regards your next-of-kin on pages 10 and 11 or
your Will on pages 15 to 20).

5. Should you lose the book, you will report the matter
to your immediate military superior.

6. On your transfer to the Army Reserve this book will be
handed into your Orderly Room for transmission, through the
O. i/c Records, to place of rejoining on mobilization.

7. You will be permitted to retain this book after
discharge, but should you lose the book after discharge it
cannot be replaced.

8. If you are discharged from the Army Reserve, this book
will be forwarded to you by the O. i/c Records.

20. LEAVE.

At the end of October Chic was sent on nine days disembarkation leave from 7ª Company in Bedford. His new posting was in Italy and he needed to tell his wife, face to face. He already knew that she had lost yet another baby, but she had not told him the full story. They both had some devastating news to impart to each other. He arrived in Foxton late on Monday morning with all his kit, just as Joyce and her father were walking home for their dinner break. It was wash day, Edie had prepared a simple meal of mutton soup with potatoes and herb dumplings and there was plenty to go around. Joyce could not wait to get home at tea time to have a long talk with her husband, the afternoon dragged for both of them. After tea, Harry practised on the piano, there was a concert in the village hall the following week and Harry had been given some new song sheets to work through. Edie busied herself with some crochet, she was making dressing table sets to sell at the WI Bazaar in aid of the *"Foxton Forces Homecoming Fund."* The young couple adjourned to the front parlour for a bit of privacy and snuggled up in front of the smouldering coal fire.

Chic was desperate to know how Joyce was. She said she was fine, she was getting used to the miscarriages, they only laid her up for a day or so. He demanded to know exactly what the doctor had said, Joyce left a few things out, she didn't want him to think she could not have children. He had the feeling she was holding something back but did not pursue it, he did not want to upset her any more than necessary. It was time to tell her his news. Joyce knew Chic had been discharged from 7ª Coy, and was excited at the thought of him coming home for good, after a trip up to Halifax on 7ª November. What he had not told her in his letters, was that he was required to serve another nine months in the army reserve. The Eleventh Armoured Division was being disbanded and he was to be posted abroad to the London Division, Royal Engineers 212ª Army Troops Company, in Italy. Joyce burst into tears and blurted out all the stuff she had been worrying about, being pregnant, the doctor's comments, losing the babies, Chic's ankle, would he have to fight? How was she going to rest? Were they ever going to be together? He tried to console her, but they both had a restless night. Joyce did not want to leave the house when she woke up the next morning, but she had already taken too much time off, she got ready for work.

In the evening they talked some more. Joyce was much calmer now and they needed a plan of action. Chic was very worried about his wife and thought it would be a good idea to temporarily take precautions, to prevent Joyce falling pregnant again. They could start a family next year when he was home for good. They needed to make the most of their time together, before he went to Italy. They agreed that he should catch the train down to Tolworth on Wednesday to see his parents and drive back on Thursday on his motorbike. He hoped it could be stored in Harry's shed while he was away. They would have a lovely long weekend together going dancing, shopping and to the flics. Chic would only be in Halifax a couple of days and then they could be together for two whole weeks before he went abroad. Joyce decided to ask for more compassionate leave, she was given two weeks unpaid holiday. Many of the apprentices that had gone to war were returning back to their jobs, Mr Jordan was no longer short staffed. Harry also put a word in, his daughter's happiness was paramount.

Frank and Annie were delighted to see their son although they were concerned about his limp. Frank had a permanent limp from his old war wound and did not want his son to suffer the same discomfort that he endured, day in day out. Chic was not concerned, he was sure his ankle would heal fully, he just needed to rest it. He didn't tell them about Joyce losing all the babies, it would have distressed his mother greatly. When he explained to them about Italy, Annie thought it would be rather exciting and a wonderful opportunity, as long as there was no chance of being shot at. Frank was more reserved in his response but wished his son well. Percy left Tolworth on Thursday afternoon on a full stomach of his favourite kidney and steak pudding. Yes, Annie was always frugal, two parts kidney to one part steak, with more onions than steak, served with cabbage and potatoes. His motorbike was stacked high with two kit bags, quite a weight to manoeuvre but he was an experienced motorcyclist. He took great care across London, past the Hoover Building and up the long, straight Great North Road to Royston and then onwards to Foxton. It was a pleasant ride.

The weekend passed happily, but far too quickly. On Sunday afternoon three young lads came and knocked at the door asking for;

"A penny for the Guy."

Joyce knew all of them, they were her Sunday school pupils, they were sporting a magnificent Guy in their wheelbarrow. Chic remembered doing exactly the same thing when he was a nipper with a guy in his wooden go-cart, that he and Grandpa Charlie built together. He gave the lads sixpence. On Monday night there was a bonfire party at the cement works in Barrington, the girls from The Press were all going with their boyfriends and Joyce wanted to go to, it was only five minutes away, they went on Chic's motorbike straight from work. This was the first Guy Fawkes night to be celebrated for seven years, now the blackout restrictions had been lifted. When they arrived, the yard was full of children brandishing sparklers, they had come straight from school to play apple bobbing and eat jacket potatoes baked in the blazing bonfire, with Guy Fawkes, or was it Hitler, perched on the very top?

The display was due to start at 6.30 pm, each and every person supplied one firework mostly purchased from their village shops. In the morning, Chic had walked across the park to the garage on the Cambridge Road and bought the biggest rocket he could find and a *"Vesuvius"* for Joyce. They were dropped into the cart as the couple walked through the gate. Bob and Claud were in charge of the matches, they had fence posts for the Catherine wheels, rocket launchers and several buckets of water standing by. The firework display was enjoyed immensely by all, the younger children had never seen anything like it in their lives. There were a few moments when Chic had flashbacks to France, Holland and Germany, but he buried his anxiety. He did not want to spoil the evening for Joyce, who was having a wonderful time.

Box Hill, Surrey. 1939.

21. YORKSHIRE.

On Wednesday morning, Chic set off for Shelford with a small kit bag on the back of his motorbike, the bike could be stored at the barracks while he was up north. The sergeant was told Sapper Sherwood was arriving and arranged for him to have a lift with one of the supply trucks as far as Manchester. They travelled all day with a couple of stops on the way, it was a pleasant enough journey. He was glad he was not driving and thankful to be able to rest his clutch foot up on the dash board for much of the time. It was just getting dark when they arrived at the Manchester Depot, Chic stopped for a cuppa and then went off to find a lift up to the Royal Engineers Admissions Camp in Halifax. It was only about thirty miles across the Yorkshire Moors. He told the driver about his training back in 1943, when he and his mate Jenni used to drive the Mark 1 Daimler Dingo scout car, back and forth to the pub in reverse. The driver was a good ten years older than Chic and had never seen active service. He volunteered back in 1939 but was graded C1 at his medical and disappointed that he had not been able to *"do his bit."* Chic told him he was a very lucky man and should count his blessings. He also wondered if his driver could see properly in the dark. When they were in the middle of the moors, there were a few moments when the van nearly left the road, despite the van's lights being on. He wouldn't have fancied travelling with this chap during the blackout years, or up in The Ardennes.

Once he was settled in at the barracks, Chic went off to the NAAFI for something to eat. The camp was full but he could not see any familiar faces. He settled himself down opposite a chap who looked like he had been in the wars and introduced himself, it was not long before they were chatting and laughing together. A few minutes later he felt a pat on his shoulder, it was his chum Eli from the squadron, he was also being sent to Italy. The next two days were spent at lectures, it was easy going but boring. Chic could not wait to get away on Friday night, his embarkation leave began at 1800 hours and two hours later he was on a lorry heading for Cambridge. They drove through the night and arrived in Shelford at half past four on Saturday morning. He had a quick cuppa and then rode his motorcycle to Foxton. Everyone was asleep, he did not have a key so he threw a few stones at Joyce's bedroom window. She crept downstairs and unlocked the front door, they sat in the front parlour and chatted for a couple of hours until her father appeared to make a pot of tea.

The two weeks flew by. The weather was dry and mild for the time of year so they went on several walks, as well as shopping and dancing in Cambridge. Chic's ankle was improving all the time, although he still strapped it up when they went dancing. He did not know what to expect out in Italy, he was being sent to Udine in the Alps. Joyce got the world atlas out, the town was near the Yugoslavian border. Would it be dangerous? Would it be hot? Would it be cold? How long would it take to get there? So many questions, she did not want him to go and he was reluctant to leave his darling wife again for what would be several months and yet another Christmas apart!

Exactly one month before Christmas on Saturday the 24th November Chic walked five miles from Foxton to Shelford Barracks to pick up his lift to Halifax. He was miserable, the weather had turned and winter was on its way. The next day in Yorkshire he was assigned to fire picket duty, it was cold, boring and he was depressed. He decided to write all his letters to family and friends, because he was not sure what was expected of him over the next few days. On Monday morning he was put to work in stores and he liked the work, it was an easy day. Then on Tuesday he had a kit check before being moved to the posting barracks, where had seen Eli a couple of weeks back. Wednesday was the doctor and dentist, vaccinations and a dental check. On Thursday he was sent to work in the cook house, he wasn't so keen on that but afterwards he went to a dance in the gym which cheered him a little. He had to get up before dawn on Friday and go all the way back to Foxton by train, to pick up his monthly rations. He left at first light and didn't get back until 2100 hours. He was only in Foxton for half an hour, just enough time for a cup of tea and some cake with his mother-in-law. He did not see Joyce and was thoroughly browned off, they could at least have given him Saturday with his wife.

Instead, he spent Saturday in Halifax. He went to the flics and then to a dance but his mood did not improve. On Sunday he was moved to Methley, not far from where he had been stationed back in 1943. The camp was very easy going but he would only be there a few days. The next evening, he attended an Old Time Dance, laid on specially by the local girls for the army lads. It was the best night out he had had in years, such good fun with all the galloping up and down, changing partners and waltzing about. The more mistakes he made, the more he laughed and so did everyone else, it was just what he needed. He wrote to Joyce and told her all about it, he thought they could organise something similar in Foxton, when he came home for good. He attended another lecture, this time about Italy and its politics, there was a slide show and it was interesting. Then another dance, this time in the village hall but it was not up to much. It was time to return back to the posting barracks in Halifax, just in time to catch another dance, that was not very good either so he went to bed early.

Sapper Sherwood was put to work in the butchery on Friday and Saturday, he sliced four hundred rashers of bacon, learned how to make sausages with as little meat as possible and stuffed hundreds of pies with bully beef, mushrooms, and potato. It was enough to put anyone off their food, it certainly put him off his. Eli managed to get out of the butchering, due to his religious beliefs, as an observant Jew he was forbidden to eat or handle pork. Also Saturday in the Jewish religion is the sabbath, a day of rest. Chic thought it was all a good wheeze and teased Eli about it, after all, when they were fighting the Hun, the enemy didn't stop for the sabbath on Saturdays or Sundays. Eli took it all in good part and asked him if he would like to go to the tabernacle on Sunday, to meet the Jewish army chaplain. They were both invited to supper, it was the first time Chic had eaten kosher meat, it was very acceptable with some interesting side dishes. The chaplain had a nice way with him, they talked for a long time about the war, their families and their upbringing, the time passed by very pleasantly indeed. Eli and Chic walked back to the barracks together, laughing about some of the tricks Neil Young got up to back in Belgium and Holland. This time last year they were about to go to The Ardennes, neither of them wanted to repeat that experience. They agreed, if they had to be in the army, Italy was probably as good a place as any. They were going on a new adventure.

22. ITALY.

The following week was relaxed. Chic was sent for more inoculations, apparently typhus was rife in Italy. He Blancoed *(Blanco; a green preservative in block form that is mixed with water to paint on canvas)* his kit and polished his brasses, before going to the flics to see Raymond Massey in *"God is My Co-pilot."* On Thursday night he went dancing with the lads, at The Victoria Hall in Halifax, where *"Eric Winstone and his Band"* were playing. This was a great evening, Chic so wished he could have danced with his darling, he knew Joyce loved Eric Winstone's music. Friday morning arrived and it was time to start packing up in readiness to move off. There were several truckloads of sappers travelling down to Dover in convoy, they left Halifax in the dark at 0400 hours and arrived in the dark the same afternoon. It took hours for all the soldiers to board the huge American troop carrier that was docked in Dover harbour. The crew were rather subdued, they had just heard on the radio that General Patton was seriously injured after a car accident in Heidleberg. Chic did not give the news much thought, he was done in. He got settled on his hammock and had a long nap. The weather was unsettled, it had been raining since they left Yorkshire and now the wind was getting up. They missed the early tide and were due to sail on Sunday's second high tide, it was blowing a gale by the time the ship set off, they had a very rough crossing. He remembered his first trip across to France eighteen months ago, a calm crossing with beautiful sunshine but going into the unknown. Today the crossing was horrendous, Chic went up on deck and threw up four times, it seemed to take forever to reach Calais, despite it being a short crossing. He was still woozy when he went ashore, but he quickly recovered. He was going into the unknown again, missing Joyce, but also looking forward to some new experiences.

He slept in Calais on Sunday night with thousands of other soldiers, British, Canadian, and American. He was ordered onto a troop train bound for Dieppe, then another across France and through border control to Switzerland on Tuesday. There were many hold ups, the French railways had been heavily bombed by the enemy and the allies, repairs were ongoing and delays inevitable. The beauty of the Alps took his breath away, the landscape with small villages and fields nestled into snow covered mountains, was magical. The further he went the more spectacular the scenery became. It was Wednesday before his fourth train reached the Italian border, then to Genoa by train again and by truck to the army forwarding camp in Novara, near Milan.

The atmosphere was relaxed and Chic was given the opportunity to rest. It was the week before Christmas and everyone was in party mood, it was also surprisingly chilly but he was used to that. He was not due to leave for Treviso until Friday, so the next day he went for a look around the historic town with a couple of the lads. They could not believe how old everything was, it beat London by centuries. They ate the most delicious rice and beans in a taverna, with bread and gorgonzola cheese, all washed down with some red wine. When they stood up to leave, the chef came out manically waving his arms and shouting in Italian. After a great deal of gesticulation, he pointed to their ciggies. What a coincidence, the exact price of their meal was twenty cigarettes! Chic liked the idea of bartering, his brother had taught him well. In the afternoon they found a local cinema that was showing American films in English. A newsreel came on, General Patton had died from his injuries. Chic thought to himself;

"Not everyone will weep for old blood and guts."

It was two hundred miles to Treviso and it took all day to get there, along war torn, unmade roads. The scenery was amazing, with the mountains towering over them along the whole journey. The truck stopped off for a short break in Verona, another ancient city. It was dark when they arrived at the barracks in the small village of Fregona, just north of Treviso. Chic was saddle sore and pleased to climb into an army bed, he slept like a log. Saturday was spent settling in. This transit camp had only recently been taken over by the allies, there were hundreds of troops waiting to be moved on to towns and cities all over Italy, where they would be required to keep the peace. The camp base was on a small race track owned by the *"Auto Moto Club Treviso,"* the Italian owners resented the presence of the troops, but they cooperated. There had been no racing there since the beginning of the war, but there were some very smart Alfa Romeos and Fiats locked away in the garages. The owners did not want the track to go the same way as Monza, which had been virtually destroyed by the allies after their occupation. They used the track to store tanks, armoured vehicles and all kinds of army surplus, resulting in the track being wrecked. Treviso was one of many Italian towns that suffered badly from allied bombing, but Fregona just a few miles away in the mountains had escaped lightly.

The British officers in charge of the camp were very keen to keep on the right side of the local civilian population. There were riots going on in Trieste and northern Italy in particular, was still volatile after the murder of Mussolini by the communist partisans back in April. On Sunday Chic went into Treviso town to have a look around, the bomb damage was extensive but he was hardened to the destruction now and the civilians seemed friendly enough. He and the lads went to see an Italian musical called; *"Here's to You,"* it was showing at a theatre offering discount to British and American soldiers. The show was a bit too classical for Chic, but it made a pleasant interlude. On Christmas Eve he was ordered to drive his block sergeant into town in a Bedford MWD truck to collect car parts from the base's store depot. They also stocked up with cigarettes, every soldier was issued fifty free ciggies a week. They were a valuable commodity in Italy as Chic had already discovered in Novara. The sergeant bought the maximum allowed, one hundred and twenty-five and advised Chic to do the same.

It turned out the car parts were being donated by the army to the *"Auto Moto Club,"* in return for one day's racing. Many of the camp officers had dabbled in competitive racing before the war and they decided a motor race on Christmas Day would not only entertain the troops, but also be a great bit of fun. Chic, as an experienced mechanic, was enlisted in the pits for checking over the Alfas and Fiats before they went out. He had a smashing time, it was like being back at Brooklands, but this time he had a senior role and was delighted to be given the responsibility. This was the best Christmas Day he had ever spent in his entire life, the only thing missing was his darling wife and he hoped she was having a nice time in Foxton. He worked extremely hard on Christmas Day and loved every minute of it. The adrenalin kept him going from dawn, through until the early hours of Boxing Day, when all the lads who had worked at the track were given a few beers and a slap-up meal in the canteen. He went to bed at 0300 hours and slept late. He woke with a start at 1000 hours, remembered it was his day off, turned over and went straight back to sleep. He eventually roused himself at 1600 hours, he was starving hungry so he spent a pleasant few hours in the NAAFI discussing yesterday's racing.

The next day was spent packing up again, Chic was being sent with a few others to join the 212ᵗʰ Army Troop Company in Udine. They left first thing on Friday morning and arrived in Udine by dinner time, it was below freezing and sunny, it seemed a friendly enough place. Captain Zoller, the acting CO, welcomed all the new recruits in the afternoon and assigned them to their various units. The camp was teeming with troops, not just sappers, they were all waiting for their release papers, most just wanted to get home as quickly as possible, even the officers. Chic met up with a sign writer from Kingston called Bill Mason, he was due to join civvy street very soon. Bill was older than Chic and in group 25 making his discharge imminent. The system for release was based on a combination of age and service, Chic was group 35 and a long way down the list. They swapped addresses for future contact back home in Surrey.

Chic was told to report to the garage on Monday morning. He'd had a kit check and a medical on Saturday and the rest of the week-end off. It was a chance to take a look around the town that had been an important stronghold for the Germans, because it was very close to the Austrian and the Yugoslavian borders. One of the lads, a student of history, talked about Attila the Hun and the Romans. The buildings were impressive, but Udine had also suffered significant allied bomb damage, the locals were suspicious of their new occupiers. Monday in the garage workshop was a very relaxed affair, there was not much going on apart from a lot of chat and banter over endless cups of tea. It was New Year's Eve and Chic thought back to last year when he was on leave in Brussels being strafed on the city streets and yet to face that last violent clash in the Reichswald forest. The year before that in 1943, he was training up in Yorkshire and the worst he had to worry about was a row with Joyce, because he couldn't get leave. So much water under the bridge since then, he could not wait to demob, only a few more months to go. The curfew remained at 2300 but the lads managed to see the New Year in, they all agreed that 1946 would be the best year ever. On the first day of the year, Chic went touring around the beautiful countryside and the following day he did some shop gazing. He wrote to Joyce and told her all about the motor racing, the fabulous scenery, the interesting shops and assured her he was in no danger. There were reports in the newspapers of riots in Trieste and Joyce was fretting.

The London Division of the Royal Engineers was sent to Italy to assist in repair and regeneration. In the north this manifested itself as general building work, to improve facilities for the occupying armies, both British and American, improvements to barracks and hospital facilities, the sprucing up of hotels for use by officers and their families, along with general maintenance and repairs to damaged and decaying buildings within the civilian population. At the end of the month, it was

Captain Zoller's turn to go home, he was replaced by Captain Turtle who was also waiting for his release papers, the atmosphere at the camp was even more relaxed. Everything jogged along without much pressure through January. Each week, a few soldiers were given local leave *(within Italy)* and many went to Rome, it was hardly local, a good four hundred miles away. Chic really fancied that, after all when would he ever get the chance again to come to Italy? At the beginning of February, two of the platoons were transferred from 212ª Coy HQ in Udine to the Vittorio barracks at Mestre, a northern district of Venice. There were just over one hundred men, most of whom were involved in construction and maintenance work. Chic was delighted to go with them, it would give him the chance to explore Venice.

He was very content pottering about in the garage, doing mainly servicing on a wide variety of vehicles including some staff cars, they were a joy to work on and made a great change from trucks and lorries. The lieutenant colonel, a commissioned officer, was not as keen as his men to get back home, there was nothing for him in England. He planned to remain in the army for the foreseeable future. He was enjoying life in Italy, provided with first class accommodation and a staff car at his disposal, a Humber Snipe. He was due to liaise with the Americans down in Rome to discuss supply of building materials and instructed his batman, a corporal, to make the necessary arrangements. They needed a competent mechanic to accompany them on the trip. Sapper Sherwood was an obvious choice, he was always so enthusiastic when working on the Snipe, he thought it a great piece of engineering. Orders arrived to go to the colonel's office immediately, he had no idea why! Perhaps he was up for another dose of *"jankers?"* Had someone seen him doing a bit of bartering in the town?

The colonel asked to see Chic's service book, it said he was suitably qualified, a good tradesman and hard working. How did he like his job as a mechanic? Chic talked of his apprenticeship at the garage, Fox and Nicholl. The colonel was familiar with the name, their *"Sunbeam-Talbot"* was raced at Brooklands and once back in the 1930s, won its class at the 24 hours Le Mans race in France. He then asked if Chic had ever worked on a Humber Snipe? Yes, he had. It was a 4 x 2 heavy utility car with rear wheel drive, that converted manually to four-wheel drive in rough terrain. It had independent front suspension making it more comfortable to drive, but if the suspension went it could be a bugger to fix. His reply was good enough for the colonel.

"Sapper Sherwood, are you any good at map reading?"
"If you mean, can I get from A to B, sir? Yes, I can."

By the time Chic got back to his dormitory, the colonel had already wired through that he was claiming Sapper Sherwood for an essential trip to Rome. He was to report at 0600 hours with two sets of khakis *(hot weather uniform,)* a clean pair of overalls and his kit, they were driving to Rome first thing tomorrow. Chic could not believe his luck, he wrote to Joyce that evening to tell her he was going on an adventure to southern Italy and would write when he could.

The following day was a very early start, Chic was excited, the weather was glorious and he felt like royalty. He was travelling in a four-seater military staff car, preserved for officers of the highest rank. A Humber Snipe with a wooden frame, four passenger doors and rear doors that flipped up and down for the easy loading of luggage. The interior had a folding map table that hung behind the front seats, very useful for navigation and writing purposes. The colonel's batman had requisitioned a few supplies: oil, petrol, water, a camping stove and food for the journey. Sapper Sherwood made sure there was an extensive tool kit on board, to cover most eventualities, and checked the oil and water before they departed. They also packed: a radio, two handguns and some high-brow reading matter, the colonel was an academic. They followed the Adriatic coast through verdant valleys, along hair raising cliff top roads, across fast flowing rivers, past olive groves, vineyards and orchards of lemons, apricots, oranges and peaches. After stopping on the roadside for refreshments, Chic took over the driving. The views were amazing, the sea azure blue, but the roads were diabolical, it took a great deal of concentration to keep the Snipe on the road.

When they arrived in Rimini early afternoon, the sun was still shining and the temperature pleasant. The waves were rolling in gently over a silver sanded beach. It could have been heaven on earth, if it were not for the extensive recent ruins in the town and a huge tented camp holding thousands of Ukrainian POWs and refugees. The reminder of conflict was ever present. Many ancient buildings had been destroyed, another town, another bomb site. The few establishments that remained had been requisitioned by the allied armies for housing troops that were overseeing the reconstruction of the area and repatriating displaced citizens. Chic was delighted to discover that a single room was booked for him in the same hotel as the officers. They all walked into town to get something to eat, the colonel ordered a bottle of red wine called Sangiovese, he translated; *"the blood of Jupiter."* When the bottle arrived he made a toast;

"To Jupiter, King of the Gods."

The wine went down very well indeed and another bottle was ordered. Both officers chose tagliatelle *(pasta)* and coniglio al forno *(roast rabbit.)* Chic ordered the same, the rabbit was delicious. He mentioned that his father kept rabbits for the pot back in Tolworth and his wife made a tasty wild rabbit stew. The colonel told him rabbits were not indigenous to England, but introduced by the Romans, when they invaded the British Isles. They were used as a much needed source of meat for the Roman army. Many scholars thought it was the French Normans, but he was convinced it was the Italian Romans. Chic was all ears, this was going to be an interesting trip. The meal ended with several glasses of Grappa, Chic only had one, it was lethal and he wanted to keep a clear head.

His room was up in the attic, it was small and stuffy but this was the first time he had ever slept in a room on his own. There was a communal wash basin on the downstairs landing and a piss pot in his room next to a narrow iron bed made up with crisp clean and elaborately embroidered white cotton sheets, with a luxurious plump feather pillow. Chic slept deeply. The next morning, after a breakfast of one tiny fried egg and some extremely stringy ham, the threesome took a quick recce on foot around the town, before departing on their way to Rome. Chic was ordered to drive first, the corporal suggested there was some difficult driving coming up later, but if the truth be known, he had a hangover. It reminded Chic of a song about the British Eighth Army who had fought hard and long in Italy;

"We are the D-Day Dodgers, in sunny Italy.
We are the D-Day Dodgers, way out in Italy.
We're always tight, we cannot fight.
What bloody use are we?"

He chuckled to himself, he didn't think anyone had an easy war but he enjoyed a bit of friendly ribbing. Later they would be crossing the Appenine mountains, the roads were treacherous and he was happy to hand over driving responsibility, they were just a tad steeper than the English Pennines! The route to Rome was a difficult one, the roads were not just bad, they were narrow and, in some places non-existent. It reminded Chic of The Ardennes, but without the snow. Then they got a puncture, fortunately not while Chic was driving, but it fell to him to change the wheel, which he did without too much fuss while his companions discussed strategy over a brew. After eight hours of driving, they eventually arrived in the city where the Yanks ruled the roost.

There was an air of disorder hanging over the whole place. The American military had taken over every hotel that was still standing. The streets were seething with GIs with many hostelries and clubs of dubious reputation catering to their needs. The filthy back streets were full of ragged children and wiry youths who looked half starved, always ready to beg or go on errands for a few cigarettes. Chic guarded the Snipe while the officers checked into a large hotel, in the city centre. If the car had been left on the streets, anything removable both inside and out would have been taken within minutes. There were a couple of lads loitering against the hotel wall, Chic gave them a ciggy each and pointed to the car. He ran his index finger along the bonnet, pointed to the boys and mimed polishing the windscreen. How many ciggies to wash the car? They held twenty fingers up, Chic put up ten, they agreed on fifteen. One of them ran around the back of the hotel and came back with two buckets of lukewarm water, some rags and a sponge. Several buckets later the Humber Snipe was cleaner than when they had left Venice. Sapper Sherwood was just chamois leathering the windscreen as the corporal returned, he was impressed by Chic's ingenuity. The car was to be garaged at the army barracks just outside the ancient city, where it would be secure and Chic would have a bed for the night. The two officers were being entertained by their American counterparts the following day and meanwhile it was Sapper Sherwood's responsibility to repair the punctured tyre and make sure the Snipe was ready for the long drive back to Venice, via Florence and Genoa. He was ordered to remain at the barracks until Sunday morning and then return to the hotel at 0900 hours, ready to drive to Saint Peter's Square in the Vatican. It turned out the colonel was a Catholic.

The Vatican remained neutral during the war despite being surrounded by Mussolini's Fascist regime and many rumours of collaboration and corruption. Chic never did understand how a country could just tell an invading army they were neutral and get off scot-free. Switzerland managed it and Belgium tried it, he was sure there must have been a lot of dodgy dealing going on behind closed doors. He parked up in the Piazza San Pietro while the officers ordered *"tre caffee,"* three tiny cups of extremely strong coffee accompanied by a selection of deliciously sweet pastries. The two officers went to look around the Basilica and Michelangelo's Sistine Chapel whilst Sapper Sherwood guarded the Snipe, accompanied by the cooling tinkling sound of the water fountain. The time passed very pleasantly, he watched the crowds and enjoyed some interaction with the local children who clustered around the car. A couple of American soldiers wanted to know who it belonged to? Chic was discreet. They departed late afternoon to a restaurant recommended by the colonel's American colleagues. It was full of GIs and served excellent food, there did not appear to be any shortages here. Chic only had a few glasses of wine, as he was expected to drive the officers back to their hotel. They asked him to drop them off at a cabaret club for officers only. The streets were swarming with drunken Yanks and beautiful young Italian men and women. Both the American and the Italian military police were noticeable by their absence. Chic was pleased to get back to the barracks.

On Monday he drove again, this time the colonel was keen to visit the Colosseum, the Roman Forum and the Pantheon. There was no escape from ancient architecture in Rome, many old ruins and quite a few new ones were around every corner. The poverty and filth distressed him, whole families living on the streets, children with no shoes, gangs of youths roaming wild and hundreds of feral cats and dogs. The officers wanted to retire early, they had not got much sleep the night before and tomorrow morning was an early start. He dropped them off at the hotel for supper and was told to be back in the morning at 0500 hours, ready for the trip to Florence. It was over one hundred and fifty miles and the colonel wanted to arrive by noon. Chic drove to the barracks, the Snipe was pinking a bit and he needed to check the timing on the carburettor, as well as the oil, water and tyre pressures. He topped it up with fuel and wrote a few postcards before he went to bed.

He arose at 0415 having had a good six hours sleep, ready for the day ahead. The drive to Florence was spectacular, the road ran along the ridge of the mountains with hair pin bends, sheer drops and thousands of pot holes. It was both exhilarating and terrifying. Two or three times they came across farmers driving their sheep or goats along the mountain passes, blocking the narrow road and walking at a snail's pace. The corporal drove until it was time for breakfast, a quick brew with some bread, cheese, hard-boiled eggs and oranges. The scenery was breath taking. Chic wanted to take photographs but there was no time, the exhaust did not smell right and he thought the car was still running a bit rich, he needed half an hour to tweak the adjusters. He hoped the chewing gum he squashed around them would do the trick and offered to drive for a couple of hours, to make sure his tuning had worked. The Humber was driving much smoother now, his quick fix had been successful and the colonel noticed.

"That seemed like an easy fix, Chic?"
"Yes Sir, with a little help from the Yanks."
"How so?"
"Chewing gum, Sir. These rough roads throw out the adjusters on the carburettor, that's why she was pinking. I stuck the culprits back in their rightful place."
"Excellent, well done sapper."

The corporal took over the driving as they approached Florence because he was familiar with the territory. There was only one route in across Ponte *(bridge)* Vecchio. The other five bridges had been destroyed by the enemy to halt the incoming of allied troops in 1945. The city was in chaos, street after street of ruins with vehicles blocking the road at every turn. They made straight for the British Embassy where the Humber Snipe and its occupants were directed into a secure zone, a short distance from the building and they were all invited inside.

The building had been evacuated in 1939 and then occupied by the Nazis. The ambassador had only returned a few months earlier and was just getting into the flow of things, there was a great deal to do. The city had suffered riots, bombings and invasion from one faction or another for nearly ten years. The Gestapo confiscated much of the art on public display and stripped the embassy bare of anything valuable. The colonel wanted to see for himself what damage had been done, he was distressed by what he found. He waxed lyrical to his companions about the Medici family and the marvellous paintings, frescoes and sculptures of the Florentine culture. Chic listened and tried to remember some of it, but much went over his head. However, he was impressed when the colonel sketched a very reasonable portrait of the corporal. Chic thought about his friend Harry and wondered where he was now.

They only stayed one night as guests of the ambassador, Chic had never known such luxury, he even had his own bath, but he was dog tired. They left for Pisa the following afternoon, it was only fifty miles and an easy journey, they arrived before dark. The first thing they saw was the leaning tower. Chick knew of the tower and wondered how it could have stood for over seven hundred years and endured several wars without toppling over. He thought to himself;

"Damn clever these Italians, or are they just mad?"

The colonel was keen to see the frescoes in the medieval cathedral before driving on to Genoa. They stayed the night in a very pleasant hostelry on the edge of the city, with a view of the Italian Riviera. Then another early start to reach the port of Genoa in good time for luncheon. Chic waited with the car down at the docks whilst the officers met with officials in the shipping office. The city was a vital link between sea and land, for getting much needed supplies to northern Italy. News was coming through of more riots in Trieste, it was time for them to get back to Udine. It was agreed they should drive overnight to Parma, rest a while and then go on to Venice. The colonel could not pass through Parma without checking out yet another cathedral, so they stayed the night in a luxury hotel and continued on their way the following morning. Chic's ankle was playing him up by the time they arrived back at the Mestre barracks. He hobbled over to the field post office and sent all his postcards, hoping he might put his feet up for a couple of hours.

On their return, the colonel was immediately informed that the whole of 212 Army Troops Coy apart from 3 Platoon, was being mustered in preparation for peace keeping duties. An advance party of sappers were already in residence at *"Caserma Fascista"* on Via Casimiro Donadoni in the centre of Trieste where more violence had broken out. Sapper Sherwood was called to his office and praised for his professionalism. The colonel remarked that he had been a good companion on their important trip to Rome. He could see Chic was limping slightly and asked how his ankle was?

143

"A bit swollen Sir. But nothing a good night's rest won't fix."

He suggested Chic deserved some leave, would he like to learn to ski up in the Italian Alps at Cortina? Chic could not believe his luck, he did not have to think twice. That evening he wrote several pages to Joyce about Rome, Florence, the scenery, the food, the poverty, the cats and how he had eaten so many oranges and apples he was getting fed up with the sight of them. And now he was going skiing for two weeks in Cortina, he would be quite safe and miles away from the unrest Trieste. Life was good, it was such a shame his darling could not be there with him, they could have so much fun together.

The barracks at Udine, were rather depleted when Chic arrived back on Saturday. Three Platoon had been left manning the transit post, it was all very laid back with dozens of lads waiting to go on leave or be demobbed. The transit lorry for Cortina was booked to take Chic and the others on Monday morning to the ski resort. His ankle already felt easier having rested it for a couple of days. All he had to do was collect his windproof camouflage gear from stores, pack his kit bag and go. It was about one hundred miles and a luxury to be driven, although he missed the comfort of the Humber Snipe. There were a good bunch of lads accompanying him, none of them had ever been skiing before, it was going to be great fun.

The army rest camp was based at a luxurious hotel called *"The Grande Albergo Savoia,"* in Cortina D'Ampezzo overlooking Lake Garda, with fantastic views up to the snow covered mountains. Chic was sharing a room with a pleasant chap. There were twenty men in his teaching group, but he got on particularly well with four of the lads. They went on the ski slopes together, learned together, fell over together, laughed together and spent every evening in the hotel bar, enjoying a few drinks together. They were very lucky to be away from the troubles and determined to enjoy themselves. Chic kept his ankle bound up while he was on the slopes, he could not believe how much pressure the skiing put on his knees and his ankle ached constantly. He enjoyed the banter and the larking about but he was not a natural skier. However, by the end of the first week he was proficient enough to enter into a race down the slopes with eight of the lads. Chic *(no: 6,)* was almost the shortest in his group and reckoned that was a disadvantage. Well that's what he said in the bar later when they discussed the competition that Chic came last in. They told him he was talking rubbish, but he just laughed.

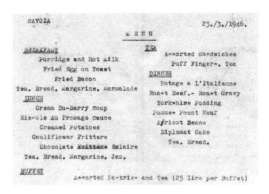

```
SAVOIA                                    23./3./1946.
                        M E N U

BREAKFAST                     TEA
   Porridge and Hot Milk         Assorted Sandwiches
   Fried Egg on Toast               Puff Fingers. Tea
        Fried Bacon           DINNER
Tea. Bread. Margarine. Marmalade      Potage a L'Italienne
LUNCH                         Roast Beef.- Roast Gravy
   Cream Du-Barry Soup            Yorkshire Pudding
Rissole Au Fromage Sauce          Pommes Pount Neuf
   Creamed Potatoes               Apricot Beans
  Cauliflower Fritters            Diplomat Cake
  Chocolate Knitters Eclaire         Tea. Bread.
Tea. Bread. Margarine. Jam.

BUFFET
          Assorted Pastries and Tea (25 lire per Buffet)
```

The Italian hotel staff did their best to make the men feel welcome and tried to please their British taste buds. They served four meals a day, an English breakfast, three-courses for lunch, sandwiches and sweet pastries for afternoon tea and finally a three-course dinner. Soup was served twice daily which was very welcome, there was a chill out on the slopes despite the weather being fine. The evening meal often included great British staples such as roast beef with gravy and Yorkshire pudding and diplomat cake. The Yorkshire puddings were interesting and the vegetables heavily seasoned with garlic, but Chic was not complaining. There was always plenty of delicious Italian bread and tea served with condensed milk and fresh fruit. Chic's palate was easily adjusting to the Italian cuisine although he longed for one of his Mum's proper roast dinner's back home in England.

The second week flew by, he was having such a smashing time he only wrote a couple of postcards and no letters. The weather had changed with several rain showers that melted the snow, it was soft and treacherous but the camaraderie was top notch. Chic took dozens of photographs for Joyce and resolved to bring his wife back to all the places he had seen, and to meet his lovely Belgian friends the Kestens family, who were so kind to him. By the end of the week the snow had almost gone and even the mountain tops were beginning to green up. Chic was now competent on the ski slopes and his ankle much stronger. He did not think it was a sport he would ever take up. He preferred to stick to motorbikes and cars for his adrenalin rush.

Friday the 29th March arrived far too quickly, it was time to go back to Udine. The lads had a good drink on Thursday night and thanked all the hotel staff for making them so welcome. They made a collection for the ski instructors who appreciated their enthusiasm and generosity, they were a good bunch of lads. Chic thought how could they not be enthusiastic, their experience had been out of this world. It certainly beat sleeping in a muddy slit trench, being shelled or facing the Panzers, or in Chic's case fitting jeep engines in deep snow whilst under fire. He was anxious about the future, there was news coming in of more political demonstrations in Trieste and none of them knew what they would be going into next. He arrived back at the transit post to discover that he and the other lads were all expected to follow on to *"Caserma Fascista,"* where the peace keeping troops had been confined to barracks for several days to avoid unnecessary confrontation with the local population.

None of the Royal Engineers were directly involved in peace keeping, they were still assisting repair and regeneration and military working parties were allowed to proceed through the city. But tensions were high, the British soldiers were required to keep their heads down and get on with their work. The sappers frequently co-opted local civilian tradesmen and also Italian POWs, most of whom were cooperative and amenable. Chic only met these chaps in passing and did not come up against too much aggravation whilst carrying out his duties that now largely consisted of collecting and delivering supplies and equipment, with a bit of vehicle maintenance thrown in. The garage was in a secure area where all the military vehicles were kept, in a large courtyard adjacent to the barracks previously occupied by the Italian fascists. The delivery work sometimes took him into volatile areas, but he was streetwise and managed to keep away from any trouble.

It was nearly a year since the Italians had surrendered to the allies and a Victory Parade was being planned in Trieste by the Allied Military Government for Thursday the 2ⁿᵈ May, 1946. They knew there was a strong possibility that this would generate yet more demonstrations by the communist Yugoslavian supporters of Marshall Tito and probably trigger counter protests by Italian activists, but the governing armed forces were not deterred. On May Day news came through of political demonstrations, with violent street fighting and many arrests. A military observer, Captain Henry Thody, reported that;

"Trieste awoke on May Day to the sound of Communist brass bands playing the "International" and the rumbling of 8th RTR (Royal Tank Regiment) Churchills through the streets.
While thousands of pro-Tito demonstrators, carrying massed red flags, filled the Piazza dell Unita, freshly painted Sherman tanks of the 88ᵗʰ US Division, stole some of their thunder as they roared along the water front. They had passed over two Bailey Bridges thrown over the canal specially for the parade by a section of the 220 Field Coy Royal Engineers, men who have built some 65 Bailey Bridges during the Italian campaign.
Later as hundreds of Yugoslav girls dressed in white blouses and blue skirts, marched through the town's main street they were jeered at and spat upon by Italian youths lining the pavement. There were numerous clashes."

The Victory Parade took place the next day to commemorate the surrender in May 1945 of German arms in Italy to Field Marshall Alexander. A salute was taken by Lieutenant General Sir John Harding, commander of the 13 Corps. The troops taking part included, the 6ᵗʰ Armoured Division, the 56ᵗʰ London Division with 212 AT Coy RE and the 88th US Division, with a Desert Air Force fly past and naval detachments. The parade went ahead as planned as a show of force to encourage stability. Chic and his unit were required to march on foot behind the tanks and military regalia. There was no trouble and as military marches go it was not unpleasant, but Chic was anxious. The rise of violence was disturbing and he thought another war could be looming. The Italians were a volatile race and Tito appeared to be very anti-British. Now the Russians, Americans and British were all in disagreement over who should govern Trieste, Italy or Yugoslavia. Where would it end?

Throughout May and June there were dozens of clashes. At the beginning of July, thousands of Yugoslavian protestors crowded the city streets demanding that both the town and port of Trieste should be given back to Yugoslavia. A conference was arranged in Paris for the Foreign Ministers of Britain, America, France and Russia, to discuss demarcation lines and borders surrounding Trieste. Their findings were to be presented to the Security Council of the United Nations at the twenty-one nation Peace Conference planned for the 29th July. The Russians wanted to take even more of Italy than the French, the Americans were claiming a large chunk of Yugoslavian territory with the British only being marginally less greedy. The one thing they did agree on was that the commercial areas that included the city and the port should be free territory, an International Zone. Many Italian and Yugoslavian people were very unhappy about that.

As it turned out, Chic's fear for Trieste's future did not come high up on his list when he was called into the unit captain's office on the 24th July and told that he, Sapper PR Sherwood. 2140769. Rank; Driver. Age/Service Group; 35, had got his release papers. The class "A" soldier's release book, stamped number; 279420 and signed by Major Turtle showed his military conduct as good, his service trade as an A2 vehicle mechanic and an excellent testimonial.

"A willing worker and good tradesman. Sober, clean and smart in appearance. Popular with his comrades."

He was booked to go to the transit post at Udine two days later and then be routed via Villach, Dieppe and Calais when transport became available. On 30th July 1946 he was back in Blighty at Aldershot barracks and could not wait to see his wife. The next day he travelled down to Brighton by train to collect his 202B; 179660, a certificate of transfer to the army reserve effective from the 12th October, when he would be demobbed. Chic was owed several weeks leave and eligible for war gratuity. He needed to get back to Tolworth to make sure he still had a job at Fox and Nicholl and then he would travel up to Foxton. A new episode was beginning, he hoped Joyce would move down to Tolworth, but he had to make sure he could support her first. He caught the train from Brighton to Surbiton and was sitting in the back parlour with his mum at 32 Lenelby Road by tea time.

Mr Fox seated with Chic.

23. SURREY.

The next morning Chic went to see Mr Fox at the garage, who shook his hand vigorously and was very pleased to see his promising apprentice back in one piece looking fit and ready for work, he could start as soon as he liked. Percy *(as Mr Fox called him)* explained that he was now married and going to see his wife in Cambridgeshire, he would confirm his start date once he and Joyce had arranged to move down to Tolworth. Mr Fox showed him around the garage that had changed beyond recognition. The motor work shop was much smaller than he remembered with most of the space was taken over by aeroplane parts that were being assembled and tested for the Hawker Siddeley Aircraft Company in Kingston. The motor racing scene at Brooklands that Mr Fox and Mr Nicholl loved so much had fallen by the wayside while the war was on. Now the garage was locked into aviation contracts with the government, it was mainly doing sheet metal work and assembling for planes such as Spitfires and Hurricanes. Chic was intrigued by this development, it would add another string to his bow.

He travelled up to Foxton that afternoon, it was Friday and he could hear the 4.30 pm siren as he walked up Station Road. The tea was already brewing when he walked into the kitchen at 3 Addison Cottages to squeals of delight from Joyce. Was he back for good? Yes, he really thought he was. Her brother Douglas had also returned home, the Cheshire family was complete and they had a little party to celebrate. The Press was due to shut down for annual staff holidays in the middle of August and after some discussion it was agreed that Joyce should hand in her notice immediately so they could both move to Lenelby Road on Sunday the 18ᵗʰ, thus enabling Chic to start work the next morning.

Joyce only needed one suitcase, there was not much space at her in-law's house and the couple would just have one room to call their own. There was a dance arranged in Foxton Village Hall on Saturday night, Joyce and Chic had a fantastic time, the locals gave them a great send off, it was like getting married all over again. Over the two weeks whilst Joyce was still working at The Press. Chic spent several days fixing up his motorbike that had been stored in his father-in-law's shed It had not been used for months and needed a thorough service, an oil change and a check on the gears and brakes, before giving it a bit of spit and polish. On Sunday morning they set off down to Tolworth, with Joyce riding pillion and arrived in time for Sunday dinner, despite the bike playing up a bit. They unpacked in the afternoon and Joyce thought it would be nice to change the room around a bit to make it her own. Frank and Annie were happy for her to do whatever she wanted, they were so pleased to have their youngest son back home and they liked his wife, Joyce.

On Monday morning, Chic got up early and made sure he was ready for work in plenty of time, he was due to clock in at 8 am and the garage was on the Portsmouth Road, only ten minutes along The Broadway. He left home just after 7.30 am, he did not want to be late on his first day. Joyce stayed indoors and chatted with Annie over a breakfast of toast and dripping. Joyce thought she should get a job, the money would help and she would be bored stiff stuck at home all day. Annie thought she had seen an advert in the window at Woolworths on The Broadway, perhaps Joyce should go and see. Later that morning a letter arrived for PR Sherwood Esq, Joyce put it on the dressing table ready for Chic when he arrived home. He was tired when he got in, he was on another steep learning curve but he thought he was going to enjoy the work. The letter was from the Army Pay Office notifying him that a total of £72 19s 0d would be deposited in his Post Office Savings Account over a period of two months. He was due 65 months war gratuity at 10 shillings per month, totalling £32 10s 0d plus post war credits from January 1942 to June 1946 totalling £40 9s 0d, that was nearly £73. He had already decided to get a motorbike with a bigger engine for when he and Joyce were travelling back and forth to Cambridge. The rest of the money could be put towards a deposit on a house.

The next day was damp and drizzly. Chic walked to work with his father, who was an overseer on the railway and currently working at Tolworth Station. Joyce spent a good hour curling her hair and pressing her serge *"going away"* suit, before putting up her umbrella and stepping out onto the wet pavement. Woolworths was only a short walk, she would not get too wet. The sign was still in the window, shop assistant wanted 4/6d a week. She had been earning 6/- at The Press but beggars can't be choosers, she shook her umbrella and marched in. She went straight to the back of the shop and knocked on the door labelled *"OFFICE."* A face appeared at the tiny window and slid it open. Joyce explained she had come about the advertisement and could she see the manager? After a couple of minutes Mr Bibby opened the door and invited her in. He asked her where she lived and what experience she had. She had worked at The Press for over five years and learned many new skills in that time. She showed him her testimonial from Mr Jordan that said Joyce was hard-working and popular. The manager wanted to know if she was good at handling money and how was her arithmetic? She told him about the charity events she had organised for the Rural Pennies Scheme and all the money she raised. That seemed to be a good enough answer, she could start the following Monday, it was a six day week with Wednesday afternoons off. Joyce could not wait to tell Chic that evening.

Everything jogged along quite nicely, the girls in Woolworths were a cheery bunch and Chic was getting on well at the garage. The happy couple usually went to the flics on a Saturday night after Joyce had finished work and once a month they rode up on the motorbike to Foxton to visit Joyce's parents for Sunday dinner. On Wednesday afternoons Joyce cleaned their room and cooked a special tea for her husband and his parents. Annie was becoming a bit forgetful and Frank was struggling with his angina, he wasn't sure how much longer he could keep working even though he was only fifty-seven. Their other son Charlie helped them out with a few things here and there but their youngest son's rent contribution made all the difference to them managing or not. Charlie wanted his brother to make the leap and buy one of the Sunray houses just like he had. Chic knew this was a good thing to do but he was worried about his parents and how would they manage with no rent coming in? In October Chic was called up to the War Office demobilisation shop at Olympia to return his uniform and get fitted with a brown, double-breasted Burton's pin striped demob suit, a raincoat, shirt, tie, hat, shoes and socks. Joyce went with him and after having their picture taken went dancing at The Hammersmith Palais to celebrate. It was a fantastic feeling to officially be back in civvy street.

Chic wrote regularly to his Belgian friend Emile who with the Kestens family were so kind to him when he was billeted with them back in March 1945. Emile's wife Louise was expecting her first baby in October. Chic and Joyce were delighted for them, despite the sadness of their own lost babies and Emile promised he would write as soon as they had any news. On the 12th October a letter arrived from Belgium, Marie-Louise Fernande Simons was born on the 2nd and died the next day, her funeral had taken place the following Saturday. There was a photograph of the baby and a funeral notice, written in Flemish.

*"This flower was too beautiful to stay on earth.
God wanted to pick her to decorate his paradise."*

Laat de kleinen tot mij komen, want voor dezul-
ken is het Rijk Gods.   Mt. L. 10.

†

TOT ZOET AANDENKEN AAN

Marie - Louise - Fernande SIMONS

dochtertje van

Emile Simons en Marie-Louise Kestens

geboren te Wijgmaal den 2 Oktober 1946,
en aldaar aan de liefde harer ouders ontrukt
den 3 Oktober 1946.

De Engelenmis, gevolgd van de begrafenis, zal
geschieden in de parochiale kerk van Wijgmaal, op
Zaterdag 5 Oktober, te 8 uur.

Vergadering ten sterfh., Albert I Laan 36, om 7.45 u.

Treur niet, Vader, ween niet, Moeder,
Uw kindje is niet dood.
Jezus's heelals Albehoeder
Laat het rusten in zijn schoot.

Zal uw kind zijn stem niet mengien
Bij uw stem, gelijk weleer,
Het zingt nu met het koor der englen
't Drijmaal " Heilig is de Heer. „

Hoor ze staamien " God van vrede „
" Aan het bloedend oudershert,
" Deel uw milden balsem mede,
" Tot verzachting van hun smert.

" Waak, o God, op al hun paden,
" Schenk hun vrede zonder reil,
" Laat ze nu en later baden
" In een oceaan van heil. „

R. I. P.

DRUKKERIJ JOS ROOGAERTS, WIJGMAAL

Joyce was upset and Chic felt very sad for his friends. He wrote back;

"Dear Emile and Louise.
We are so very sorry to hear of your loss and are thinking of you at this
sad time. Please write when you feel able.
             Our condolences and fondest regards. Chic and Joyce."

Chic wanted Joyce to meet all his Belgian friends, Emile and Louise,
Fernande and Marie, Mama and Madame Celine, but especially
Pauline. They were such a kind and loving family and would all be
grieving for the loss of the baby.

Christmas 1946 was a very jolly affair in the Sherwood household
despite it being bitterly cold. Joyce gave Chic a sleeveless pullove
knitted from one of her own jumpers that she had unpicked. Chic gave
Joyce the new edition of; "The Book of Good Housekeeping." She was
thrilled with it, there were so many good ideas that she could copy with
lots of practical information, she could not wait to have her own home
to try them all out. Everyone was invited around to Woodland Way on
the Sunray Estate for Christmas dinner with Chic's brother Charlie, his
wife Phyllis and toddler Annette. There was a coal shortage, but Charlie

always managed to get hold of enough for him and his parents. Joyce and Annie had made Christmas puddings together back in October. Frank supplied sprouts, carrots and spuds from his allotment and Charlie acquired a turkey, they didn't ask where from. Chic supplied the drinks: beer, sherry and ginger wine. Frank peeled all the vegetables while Phyllis and Joyce shared the cooking while Annie played with Annette, she thought the toddler was her own baby. After dinner there was a great deal of hilarity, when they all played consequences. Phyllis made turkey sandwiches for tea with mince pies, Carnation milk and pink blancmange. Then Joyce, Chic, Annie and Frank walked back to Lenelby Road along The Broadway and past all the shops that were in total darkness. The ice made it treacherous under foot, but the walk did them all good, despite Frank and Annie being very slow. Joyce loved Charlie's little house on the Sunray Estate, they really should try and buy one of their own, she was so fed up with living in one room.

The new year brought extreme weather, Chic had never seen so much snow in England, and then there were floods. The country had still not escaped the austerity of the war years, with blackouts, fuel shortages, and fears that food supplies may run out, now even potatoes were being rationed. Factories were closed, both Chic and Joyce were put on shorter working hours, and their wages reduced accordingly. This was not the time to buy a house, it was too risky. By May the weather was much improved and the couple were able to celebrate their third wedding anniversary, together, at last. They went to The Griffin Hotel, for a light supper and a quick drink, before a trip to the flics at the Kingston Odeon, to see *"It's a Wonderful Life"*, with Jimmy Stewart. It certainly was. The following week-end was the Whitsun bank holiday, they rode up to Foxton on Sunday morning and spent two days with Joyce's parents. They visited friends and had a picnic on the green, the weather was glorious, surely the worst of times was coming to an end. They brought Joyce's sewing box back home with them, tied very securely to the back of the bike.

Madame Celine and Pauline Kestens.

Mama Kestens, Chic and Marie Simons.

156

Emile and Chic had exchanged Christmas cards with greetings from all the women folk. Louise was getting on with life after the loss of her baby, despite times being hard. The Kestens family were fortunate in that they still had a proper roof over their heads, many didn't. It was not only Britain suffering shortages, Belgium was in a bad way, the remnants of the German occupation hung heavily. Mama Kestens and Pauline wanted to meet Joyce and in the spring a letter arrived inviting them both to stay with the family in Wygmaal, at the same house where Chic had been billeted back in 1945. Chic suggested to Joyce they could travel to Belgium and France in the summer, but first they needed to sort out a passport. They both went off to get their photograph taken and Joyce completed the application for one passport in the name of Percy Ronald Sherwood, accompanied by his wife Joyce Sherwood nee Cheshire. Joyce was pregnant again but by July her morning sickness had stopped, she had not miscarried and she was optimistic. A holiday was just what she needed. Chic persuaded Mr Fox to let him borrow an old Austin from the garage stores, on condition that he returned it in good working order. Petrol was still rationed, but the garage had a plentiful supply, he would take a few cans with him. They set out at first light on Sunday 17ᵗʰ August to Dover and boarded the aptly named ferry, HMS Twickenham bound for Dunkirk. Joyce had never been further than Yarmouth and she was very excited. She packed a flask of tea and a picnic lunch which they ate whilst on the boat. On landing at Dunkirk, Chic drove straight to Wygmaal, with a couple of stops to top up petrol and water. They arrived before sunset at Albert 1 Laan 36, to a very warm welcome. Emile, Fernande, Madame Celine, Mama, Pauline, Maria and Louise all came out to greet them as they parked up in front of the house. The couple were shown to their room, the same room where Chic had slept in March 1945. Mama had been cooking, they drank wine, played games and laughed late into the evening.

The next day Chic showed Joyce around Wygmaal and they all went for a walk along the canal, there was still evidence of the conflict but the weather was warm and they had a nice time. Chic was surprised how little the town had changed, there was still so much to repair: houses missing rooves and windows, civilians living in cellars with no facilities, shops with nothing to sell, smashed roads and railway lines. The locals seemed resigned to it, they were no longer living in fear and accepted that it would take time to get back to normal. Pauline had been busy planning a sight-seeing itinerary and it was agreed that she and Marie would show their guests around Antwerp on Tuesday, including a trip to the zoo. On Wednesday morning they could drive to Luxembourg and stay in the ancient city of Echternach, returning the following day after a visit to Petit Suisse. Friday, shopping in Brussels and then a long trip to Normandy.

Joyce and Chic were having a marvellous time, they got to see the best of everything with Pauline, their enthusiastic guide who spoke fluent French and English in addition to Flemish. Mama and Madam Celine cooked a slap-up meal on Friday evening and afterwards, they laughed until they cried with some party antics and a bit of traditional dancing.

On Saturday morning, Chic, Joyce, Pauline and Marie set off after some tearful goodbyes with Mama Kestens and Madame Celine. They were going to stay overnight in Lille and arrived early afternoon, giving them time to look around before supper. Pauline told Chic and Joyce about the mixed fortunes of the city, it seemed like everyone had taken a slice of it: Romans, Spanish, Flemish, French, Dutch and the Germans. It was certainly beautiful and did not appear to have suffered too much recent damage, despite it being a vital strategic point in the war. They departed very early on Sunday morning after a breakfast of pastries and took with them a picnic lunch ordered by Pauline from the hotel. After driving through Amiens, Chic suggested they stop on the road for refreshments. He was surprised to see the destruction of the city, he knew Amiens had suffered heavy fighting and been bombed by the allies along with Caen, but to see the devastation was shocking. People thought the London Blitz was bad, but at least the British kept their freedom. The picnic was delicious with pate, cheese, bread, plums and cherries accompanied with wine and bottled water. Chic ate a chunk of bread, a couple of cherries and drank some water, he did not have the stomach for anything else. They arrived in Le Havre quite late. Emile had booked all three rooms in a small hotel close to his mother's house. The hotelier was a personal friend of Madame Simons and welcomed them all with kisses on both cheeks and a glass of Calvados. They were too late for dinner, but were offered some fish soup with bread. They were all travel weary and went straight to bed.

Emile was due to arrive later the next day with Louise and Fernande. He and Louise were going to stay with his mother and Fernande with his wife Marie and the others, at the hotel. Emile was keen to visit the island of Alderney, where his mother had grown up and he had stayed with his grandparents on many occasions. Although the island was owned by the British, Emile's family were strongly rooted in the French way of life. When his father died in the 1930s, his mother moved over to the mainland and settled in Le Havre where she could work and provide for her children. Alderney, the smallest of the Channel Islands, was only a few miles away, just off the Normandy coast. When the Germans invaded France, the British evacuated all Alderney's inhabitants to England because it was too expensive to defend. Emile was pleased his grandparents died before that happened, it would have been too much for them. By the time the Germans reached the island there were no civilians left, the Nazis built four separate camps with forced labour and the whole island became a prison.

Chic thought about revisiting a few places from 1944: Courseulles, Bayeux, Saint Aubin, Flers, Conde, to name but a few, but he had some misgivings. Would it bring back too many bad memories? Joyce understood, they would see how things went. The couple had a quiet time on Monday while the Kestens caught up with family news. They took a pleasant walk along Le Havre harbour and a boat trip around the headland to Honfleur and back, the weather was perfect and the scenery delightful. Emile, Louise and Fernande arrived early evening and all eight of them, including Madame Simons attended a four course dinner at the hotel. They were the only guests and it was an experience to remember, although Chic was still struggling to eat anything. They discussed the holiday itinerary, Pauline suggested they all drive out to St Malo on Wednesday and catch the local ferry across to Saint Anne's on Alderney Island. On Tuesday Chic and Joyce drove to Courseulles, where he had landed on the 14ᵗʰ June 1944. The beach was now free of debris but everything else looked the same, but there was major repair work going on and life appeared to be getting back to normal. They then drove on to Saint Aubin, things looked a little better here, there was a great deal of activity and Chic felt pleased about that.

On Wednesday, all seven of them drove to Cherbourg and caught the passenger ferry to Alderney, Emile's mother did not want to go. Emile was visibly moved by the change in the island, the concrete fortifications, air raid shelters and tunnels, all built by prisoners of war since 1940. Two of the four camps on the island were designated by the German SS as concentration camps. Prisoners were brought over from the mainland and subjected to appalling ill treatment and deprivation, many were literally worked to death. It took Chic back to Breendonk. He suggested they all go for a coffee at a café in Saint Anne's, where they sat outside in the sunshine with a view of the sea. While the others were enjoying their refreshments, Chic went off to the gents *(a hole in the ground,)* and threw up. He did not tell Joyce he had vomited but she noticed he didn't eat much when they returned to the hotel. That night, bad dreams caused him to fall out of bed. Joyce was worried and the others heard the racket, he just laughed it off in the morning and said he had drunk too much Calvados.

The rest of the week was glorious, the friends spent much of their time at the beach, chatting in cafes, walking and sight-seeing. On Friday evening they went to a night club. Joyce had never been anywhere like it before, it was all very dark and moody and not at all like the Foxton hops. The friends were sad their holiday was coming to an end and they all promised to write. Joyce was blooming, the baby was beginning to show and the couple were wished good luck and a healthy baby. Chic told Pauline they would name the baby after her, Paul or Pauline, whatever it may be. On Saturday morning Chic drove down to the ferry at Le Havre and they caught a ferry back to Portsmouth while their friends made their way back to Belgium. They had enjoyed the best holiday, Joyce loved every minute of it, but now they had to make a home in readiness for their new addition, due in February. It was a long crossing from Le Havre, but the weather was fine and it was not too choppy. The four hour drive back to Tolworth was uneventful, they arrived at Lenelby Road, tired but happy. Frank wanted to hear all about it, Annie was not aware they had been away. Chic spent the whole of Sunday working on the Austin, making sure it was in top notch condition before he returned to work the next day.

New Norton motorbike. Foxton 1947.

Joyce was doing well at Woolworths. Mr Bibby noticed she was very quick at working out change and cashing up the till at the end of the day. He asked her if she would like to work in the office and learn book keeping. Joyce was delighted for three reasons; she liked paperwork, she was promised a pay rise at Christmas, but most of all she would be able to work sitting down, which was good for the baby and her legs. Chic was mainly working on vehicles at Fox and Nicholl, although sometimes it was *"all hands on deck"* when a big aeronautical job came in. He was often sent up to Hawker Siddeley in Kingston to collect spare parts and always took the chance to have a look around, despite some areas being out of bounds to anyone who had not signed the Official Secrets Act. He also made regular visits to Mollart Engineering just a mile up the Portsmouth Road at Chessington, to pick up prototype samples for testing. They were a friendly bunch, the six partners originally worked at AC Cars, they set up the company after AC went bust in 1929. They kept close links with Fox and Nicholl with their common interest in high performance cars. Now, as precision engineers, they were designing and manufacturing special purpose machinery for the aerospace industry as well as the motor trade.

Wednesday 19th November was wet and drizzly and Joyce was in a rush to get home at dinner time to show her mother-in-law the newspaper. There was a royal wedding the next day at Westminster Abbey, Princess Elizabeth was marrying her fiancée, Prince Philip Mountbatten and Thursday had been declared a national holiday. Annie was not interested in much these days but she did like hearing about the wedding. Joyce stopped off at Sainsbury's to buy some haslet *(pork meatloaf)* for tea, there was a long queue for the cooked meats counter which delayed her. She was rather distracted as she walked out of the shop and slipped on the wet tiles. There were plenty of people about, a gentleman and his wife helped her up and a porter from the shop brought out a chair. Joyce was shaken, but insisted she was fine, she felt so embarrassed sitting on the pavement in the pouring rain. She was adamant that she could walk home on her own, it was just around the corner in Lenelby Road. When she walked in the back door, the parlour was empty, her mother-in-law was upstairs resting. She made herself a cup of tea with lots of sugar to buck herself up. Joyce usually cleaned and cooked on Wednesday afternoons, but today she made up a hot water bottle and sat by the range.

Chic arrived home at ten past six to find her still sitting there, she was getting stomach cramps. He wanted to call the doctor but Joyce said she was just a bit shaken up. She did not improve and the pains got worse, Chic insisted they go up the hill to Surbiton Cottage Hospital. Joyce reluctantly agreed and gingerly climbed onto the back of the motorbike, the hospital was only five minutes away. After seeing a doctor and several nurses, she was whisked off to Kingston Hospital in an ambulance. Chic was told to go home and return at visiting hours the next evening, he was worried sick. He did not know what to do with himself all day, the couple had intended to travel up to Waterloo by train and soak up the wedding atmosphere, Joyce loved a bit of pageantry. Instead, he fiddled about with his new motorbike and cleaned out Frank's pigeon loft. By the time he arrived at the maternity ward Joyce was sitting up in bed. As soon as she saw him she burst into tears, she had lost the baby, their little girl was stillborn. Chic tried to console his wife, she was sobbing uncontrollably, he also had tears in his eyes and didn't know how to make things better.

He thought of the words Pauline translated for them, when baby Marie-Louise died, he thought of his friend Jenni but mostly he thought of his wife, he was angry. Joyce was kept in hospital for over a week, they would not discharge her until her blood pressure had been regulated. They were not allowed to see the baby and Joyce was distraught, she wanted to get back home to stay with her mother. On discharge, she was given seven days sick leave and after two days at home in Tolworth, Chic escorted her on the train to Foxton and came back the same day. He was grieving too but he kept it all hidden and threw himself into his work at the garage. The following Sunday, Chic went up to Kings Cross to meet Joyce off the Cambridge train and they came back to Tolworth. Joyce was feeling a little better and wanted to get back to work, she needed a distraction. It would start to get busy in the shop soon with Christmas approaching.

Christmas 1947 was not a happy one for Joyce and Chic, but they made the best of it by travelling up to Foxton on the motorbike on Christmas eve, arriving in good time for the midnight carol service in Saint Laurence Church. They had both been given Saturday off, which allowed them four whole days with Joyce's parents and her brother Doug, who had just split up with his girlfriend from before the war. After a huge breakfast, Joyce helped her mother make puff pastry for mince pies and sausage rolls. Harry Cheshire had plucked and tied a large rooster the day before and was now stuffing it with forcemeat.

Christmas dinner was served at one-o-clock sharp, the bird was carved at the table with great aplomb by Harry, while Edie served the most delicious homegrown vegetables, bread sauce and oceans of Bisto gravy. Then the Christmas pudding was brought in with a sprig of holly on top, the head of the household poured over a spoonful of brandy and struck a match, everyone shouted Merry Christmas and tucked in to pudding and custard. Chic got the lucky sixpence, it nearly broke his tooth but he was pleased to have it, he made a secret wish to become a father.

The youngsters all went for a walk after dinner, while Harry did the washing up and Edie prepared a tea of bread and butter, hot sausage rolls, coleslaw made from one of Harry's white cabbages, with salad cream and thick slices of ham from a leg joint that had been curing in Harry's shed for several weeks. Both Harry and Edie were asleep when the youngsters returned, but they quickly roused themselves and thought it was time to enjoy a glass of sherry or brown ale with their refreshments. Chic had never eaten so much in his life, he loved being part of this family. After tea, his father-in-law sat down at the piano and they all had a sing song, lots of tunes from the great war and a few new ones. "Hang out the Washing on the Siegfried Line" was sung with great gusto by Harry, Joyce and Doug who had good singing voices, Chic joined in. Edie was rather shy, she busied herself in the kitchen tidying up and making a pot of tea for suppe to go with cubes of cheese from home farm and her magnificent Christmas cake, that was covered in royal icing and decorated with paper ornaments. Edie knew this Christmas would be very special, she had been saving coupons for months, to celebrate her children being back home, they were a family again.

On Boxing Day, it seemed like the whole village had turned out for a football match on the playing fields behind the village hall. The weather was unseasonably mild, very different to last year, the ground was sodden, it became more of a mud fight than a football game. Chic was put on as a linesman again, although there didn't appear to be many rules. His father-in-law was one of three referees, they all had different opinions and the players were running riot. Doug took the game very seriously and after his team won 5 - 2 against their opponents they all adjourned to *"The Black Boy"* for a pint and some friendly banter. Joyce watched the whole match, shouting encouragement from behind the goal post, she was thrilled her brother's team had won, they were a competitive family. She and Chic walked back to the cottage happy and content only to discover that Edie had laid on another magnificent spread of cold meats, with chutneys and bubble and squeak. Surprisingly, they were very hungry and tucked in enthusiastically. Doug came home about two hours later in a very jovial mood. Edie was rather cross, thinking he was far too full of Christmas spirit, but Harry told her not to complain. He said;

"Leave him be. You don't know what that boy has been through."

Doug never spoke about his service in the navy, not even to his father, but Harry guessed from his own experiences during WW1 that his son may be grappling with some demons.

Sunday arrived far too quickly and it was time to return to Tolworth ready for work on Monday morning. The couple were sent back with several slices of ham for Chic's parents, some jars of piccalilli and a generous portion of Christmas cake. The advantage of living in a rural village like Foxton was that food rations could always be boosted from local, unofficial supplies, dairy produce in particular. There were still shortages, but if you knew enough people, you could get almost anything and the Cheshire family knew everyone. They always had vegetables, preserves and exceptional cakes and pastries to barter with. In contrast, Chic's family struggled despite his mother being a good cook, there was never anything spare at Lenelby Road, although they too had found ways around the rationing largely due to his brother Charlie's flirtation with the black market. Recently Annie appeared to be more confused, she no longer knew how to bake and had become withdrawn. When Joyce and Chic arrived back home, she welcomed Chic with a big hug and asked him who the nice young lady was. Frank made a brew and told them about Christmas at Charlie's house and wanted to know all about their visit to Foxton. Annie said she was tired and took herself up to bed. Frank looked sad.

New Year's Eve came and went with a bit of a party at The Red Lion. Joyce was busy with the January sale at Woolworth's, and Fox and Nicholl's were stacked out with work. Annie became increasingly inactive with Joyce taking over most of the cooking. Frank was now a supervisor on the railway which was less arduous physically but his angina was getting worse, the doctor suggested he should get a motorised bath chair to help not only with his heart, but also the pain in his leg caused by his old war wound. Charlie went straight off to the undertaker in Ewell Road, all the chaps were regular punters with him and they would know someone with an invalid chair going spare. That same afternoon he came back with a tricycle bath chair, purchased for One Guinea. It was not in working order, but didn't look too bad to Chic, he wheeled it down to the garage the following morning and worked on it after hours. Mr Fox let him have a few spares and after a thorough service and a good clean up, it was spick and span and ready for Frank to take on a test drive. He was delighted with his new toy.

The year of 1948 passed by fairly quietly. Food rations were being relaxed and the couple enjoyed a busy social life with lots of works outings and parties. They went to the flics once a week and tea dances at The Regal on wet Sunday afternoons. Chic was learning new skills with his engineering knowledge broadening by the day and Joyce was doing well in the office at Woolworth's. They visited Foxton once a month on a Sunday and took their annual holiday in a chalet at Yarmouth with Joyce's parents. Frank had got a new lease of life now that he was more mobile with his bath chair, but he did suffer frequent chest pain. He was permanently worried about his wife, she was very muddled, some days she didn't know who he was. Annie became increasingly suspicious of Joyce and did not like her cooking in the back parlour, she repeated over and over and over again;

"What is that girl doing in my house."

Chic was worried about them all, but decided it was time for himself and Joyce to move out. They would try and buy a house on the Sunray Estate, just a short walk from work and his parents and close to his brother Charlie in Woodland Way.

In the spring of 1949 their dream came true. Chic was given an excellent reference by Mr Fox in order to obtain a loan from the Lambeth Building Society, although Joyce's earnings were not taken into consideration. They found a little terraced house that was built in 1936 that had been occupied by the same family from new. The owner had recently died and it was now in need of decoration, and available at a good price. It was a leasehold property with leaded light windows, a through lounge, small kitchen, three bedrooms and a bathroom. They used Chic's demob money plus some extra savings totalling £84, as a deposit and made up the shortfall with a low interest loan from Charlie. Joyce's brother-in-law agreed that she could pay off 5/- a week from her wages over three years. She was now earning 9/6d a week as an accounts clerk, it would be a struggle, but she knew she could manage.

Charlie was doing very well for himself as well as still being a milkman, his wife was very frugal and his clandestine betting business was thriving. He had recently purchased his first car with the help of his brother's mechanical knowledge and some skilled haggling. It was a second-hand Austin 8 Tourer with a rather stylish convertible roof, registration DFU 490. Chic borrowed it occasionally in return for free servicing and repairs. The Sherwood brothers made a good team and were always ready to help each other out.

The probate sale dragged on a bit, but eventually the couple were able to pick up the keys to 9 Firdene, their very own home. Joyce could not wait to invite her parents down to see their little house, but first everything needed a good scrub. Chic was still in touch with Emile Simons and the Kestens family in Belgium, Emile's wife Louise, had recently given birth to a healthy baby boy called Gilbert. Joyce and Chic were optimistic that at last they too might become parents. Chic borrowed a van from the garage to move what little belongings they had from Lenelby Road. They could not afford the full set of utility furniture available for fifty pounds, so Frank said they could take everything from their bedroom at Lenelby Road, a double bed, wardrobe, dressing table and one chair with a threadbare rug, plus a few pots and pans to start them off. Both of them cleaned every inch of the house inside and out. Charlie loaned them some house ladders, Chic cleared out the guttering, washed the paintwork and cleaned the windows, everything needed a good lick of paint, but that could wait. Joyce carbolicked *(carbolic antiseptic soap)* the kitchen, then the bathroom, scrubbed all the floorboards and polished them until they shone. She threw out the threadbare rug and the old linoleum in the kitchen and bathroom would have to do for a while. All that mattered was that the house was clean, she dusted and swept every day to keep it that way.

They rode up to Foxton on the motorbike for the Easter weekend to sort out Joyce's belongings and see what household items her parents were willing to part with. They found her mother rather distraught. Doug had a new girlfriend, but she was in the family way and the wedding was being arranged as they spoke. Harry Cheshire was angry with his son for being so stupid, he must face up to his responsibilities by doing the right thing. Joyce also gave Doug a good talking to, she too was angry and jealous, life was very unfair. Doug was a bit sheepish and went off to the pub while Joyce sweet talked her father into giving them a few bits of furniture: a table, a small cupboard, and an easy chair. There was also Joyce's Singer sewing machine, she was very keen to get that back to her little house, along with all her fabric and sewing notions, to start making curtains. Edie presented her daughter with a large suitcase full of bits and bobs that might come in useful and then there were all the wedding gifts from her bottom drawer. They took a few bits back home on the motorbike and Chic arranged to borrow his brother's Austin the following Sunday, to bring back the rest. The weather forecast was good, he and Joyce set out on Sunday morning in the tourer with the roof down. The wind was blowing through their hair, Joyce put a scarf around her head and they both felt like film stars. As always, Edie cooked a magnificent roast dinner with strawberry pie for pudding and rock cakes for tea. Doug and Chic loaded up the car, it was packed to bursting. The couple left Foxton at 6 pm hoping it wouldn't rain, there was a little bit of drizzle as they drove through Richmond, but nothing much. It was dark by the time they arrived at Firdene. They hastily unpacked, then Chic drove back around to Woodland Way where his brother had left the garage door open. He drove straight in, locked up and dropped the key back to Charlie before running home, it was only five minutes away. Joyce had made some cocoa, they tucked into cream crackers and cheese sent back with them by Edie.

There would be no more dancing the light fantastic or going to the flics for a while, they were both eager to get on with the decorating and needed to save every single penny. Frank Sherwood was always making things and taught his son a few carpentry skills when he was a lad. One important lesson that Chic had learned from the army, was that anything was possible if you put your mind to it and thought your way around the problem. He worked tirelessly in all his spare time to modernise the terraced cottage, he built fitted cupboards, hung shelving, painted and wallpapered. His father helped out with the casement windows, they were designed to lift out for ease of painting and Frank was able to sit comfortably at his bench to do a thorough job of stripping down and repainting. Joyce made curtains with matching cushions for the living room and pillow cases out of threadbare sheets. Every Wednesday on her afternoon off, Joyce topped and tailed the bed, removing the bottom sheet, placing the top one to the bottom and adding a clean one for the top, she only possessed three sheets. She then cleaned the house while boiling up the linens on the cooker hob before preparing supper. On Saturday afternoons while Joyce was at work, Chic got stuck in to the renovations: stripping wallpaper, repairing plaster, fixing the plumbing, re enamelling the bath, building kitchen units, the list was endless.

On Sundays they worked together, planning their décor and designing the garden. There was a beautiful laburnum tree in the front garden by the paling fence, but the garden had been neglected. Chic built a crazy paving path to the front door and dug borders either side for Joyce to plant up with standard roses and annuals. They painted the porch and fixed trellis to hang pots of geraniums and begonias. They still could not afford carpets, but after rationing finished they did purchase a three-piece leather lounge suite and were now the owners of two double beds, Joyce's parents could come to stay. The next couple of years flew by, Chic loved DIY and Joyce immersed herself in sewing, knitting, cooking and housework. It was still a struggle to pay all the bills so they decided to get a lodger. Miss Patricia Cutt worked with Joyce at Woolworth's, she would be delighted to lodge in the box room and bring her own furniture. On Wednesday afternoons, they shared the bed stripping and then Pat cleaned her little room, while Joyce cleaned the rest of the house.

The decorating continued. The tiny six foot wide kitchen was given a new electric Jackson 190 Cooking Cabinet that included an oven, grill and a hob with electric rings for ultimate control. Chic also fitted a smart enamel sink and installed a yellow patterned Formica worktop over the base cupboards, with vinyl wallpaper depicting stylised culinary tools, herbs and vegetables in the most contemporary design. The cupboards had red handles and the new linoleum floor complimented the room beautifully, the kitchen was the height of fashion and Joyce was thrilled with it.

Chic made a new ceramic tiled fireplace in the through lounge and papered one wall with giant stylised oak leaves. He also fitted an illuminated wall planter adjacent to the French windows. The bathroom was the last room to be finished, they could not afford a new suite but he panelled in the bath, bought the latest plastic toilet cistern and half tiled the room with black tiles, before painting the walls in bright yellow gloss paint. Frank no longer worked due to ill health but did not like to be idle, he was pleased to cut some art deco style pelmets from plywood for his son to paint and fix. Joyce went to Sherry's in Kingston and bought new curtain material for the whole house, she was in her element, she sat and sewed every Sunday for weeks. Having a lodger made a big difference, they could now afford so much more for their home. The only thing that was missing was a baby, there had been a few false alarms with a couple of early bleeds, Joyce was becoming resigned to the fact that she may never have a child.

Chic kept in touch with his army friends Johnno and Stead, who was now married to Dorothy, a war widow with two children. Both men knew Chic was desperate to be a father, he was great with children and it would be such a shame if the couple remained childless. In March 1952, the King had just died and the whole country was in mourning, everyone needed cheering up. An army reunion was being held at The Guildford Hotel in Leeds for the three R E field squadrons including 612 FS. Johnno, as a born and bred Yorkshire lad would definitely attend and wanted Chic and Stead *(who lived in Barnet)* to go up and stay. Chic had been working hard on the house and Joyce thought it would be a good break for him. He had not attended any reunions, mainly due to lack of funds but also perhaps the reluctance to stir up bad memories, but he would give it a try. Chic met Stead at Kings Cross and they travelled up to Leeds together, arriving in time for a few drinks with Johnno beforehand. Chic and Stead laughed from the moment they left London.

The evening went well. The banter was first class and the food terrible, but that just added to the hilarity, with a few referrals to; *"Two in the Bank Atkinson's"* cooking. There was a minute's silence for those who were lost and Chic thought of his best pal Jenni. Then the beer flowed and flowed late into the night. Chic and Stead woke early on Sunday morning with the worst hangovers in the world, but that did not stop them tucking in to a hearty breakfast of eggs, bacon and black pudding, before making their way back to the railway station. On the journey home they vowed they would get together more often. Chic wanted to meet Dorothy and for Stead to see his little house. They must come for Sunday dinner now that Stead had bought himself a family car, it was only a couple of hours from Barnet to Tolworth.

Things were about to change for Chic. He was doing well at the garage and spent a fair amount of time up at Mollart Engineering. He could often be found talking with the engineers in the tool shop when a new prototype machine was being jigged. He got on particularly well with one of the bosses, Jack Hendra, who asked him if he would like a job in the machine tool shop. Chic was surprised and flattered. He was offered a good salary for a five day week with the chance of overtime on Saturdays at time and a half. Mr Fox did not want Chic to leave, he was a talented mechanic and reliable. He offered him a pay rise, but Chic had already decided it was time to move on, he had been committed to Fox and Nicholl whilst still in the army reserve, but now he was a free man and he needed a change.

After discussing the offer with Joyce, Chic handed his notice in at the garage and started work on Mollart's factory floor as a machine tool fitter on Tuesday 3ʳᵈ June, the day after the spring bank holiday. His clock number was 52. He cycled to work and back on his push bike, the journey was too short for his motorbike, he didn't want to coke up the engine. The couple were saving for when a baby arrived, but as there was no sign of that happening Chic suggested selling his motorbike and buying a car. Petrol rationing was a distant memory, they could now afford to have a bit of fun. Just a month after joining Mollart's, Chic bought a Hillman Minx, DMY 732 from one of the mechanics at Fox and Nicholl. Now the couple could go out whenever they wanted and not have to worry about the weather. The first thing they did was book a holiday to the Isle of Wight with Chic's old school chum Dave Banks and his girlfriend Dora Ferrito. They all travelled down to Southampton in the Minx and caught the ferry across to Ryde. They stayed in a chalet overlooking The Needles and the weather was gorgeous.

By 1953 the house was fully renovated inside and out and it was time to pay attention to the garden. When the houses in Firdene were built, each house had its own garage accessible from a service road behind. The back garden was about ninety feet long and Chic thought he could easily enlarge the garage to include a workshop. The existing building was rather ramshackle and only just big enough to park the Hillman Minx, with no room for working on it. He set about digging out the ground around the existing building to make foundations for a detached brick garage measuring 18 ft x 9ft 6in. The plan was to fit extra wide garage doors with windows to the side and rear, plus a side door for access. The building of the garage commenced. Chic was a competent bricklayer and pulled in the help of his Tolworth chums, to supply reclaimed bricks, windows and a door.

Chic, Harry and Edie Cheshire.

Dave came around most Saturday afternoons and did a bit of navvying while his girlfriend Dora, went shopping along The Broadway for cockles, winkles and whelks from MacFisheries with a crusty bloomer for their tea. She then met Joyce from Woolworth's at 5.30 pm and they walked back to Firdene together. The evening was usually spent playing whist or canasta, accompanied by a few bottles of beer, with port and lemonade for the girls and cheese and biscuits for supper. Once the brickwork was completed, Chic pulled in Alf's help to fit corrugated asbestos sheets on the roof and new oversized, double garage doors. At last his workshop was up and running, he could service the car in comfort, with electric light, power and a cold water tap

It was time to take a break from the building work. Mollart's had a thriving social club: dinner dances, whist drives, sports days, staff outings, there was always something going on. The couple received many visitors over the next few months, Joyce's parents, Stead and his family, Dora and David every Saturday, they were always busy entertaining or visiting friends. Princess Elizabeth was heir to the throne and the coronation was planned for June, just before Joyce's birthday. There was an air of optimism and Joyce in particular was excited, she missed the royal wedding, she was not going to miss the coronation. Chic's brother Charlie had purchased a television especially for the occasion and wanted all the family to join them for a house party, but Joyce wanted to mingle with the London crowds and see the spectacle first hand.

Chic was eager to please his wife and arranged to meet Stead, Dorothy and their boys in Piccadilly at 6 am on Tuesday 2ᵈ June, another national holiday. They caught an early train to Waterloo and walked through the crowds to Piccadilly, it was like being back in Brussels. It was raining but the atmosphere was electric and the crowd good natured, every inch of space was taken up. Miraculously, Chic and Stead spotted each other through the crowds. Joyce and Dorothy got on like a house on fire. They took their own refreshments, egg and cheese sandwiches, apples, biscuits and flasks of tea. The boys Graham and Martin were well-behaved lads, Stead put Martin on his shoulders to see the Queen, Graham shinned up a lamp post. After hours of waiting they got glimpses of the parade through their cardboard periscopes. The colours were magnificent, despite the rain: eight grey horses pulled Elizabeth's golden coach among a sea of red and white. At half past one the crowd started moving towards Buckingham Palace in the hope of seeing their Queen on the balcony. Chic and Joyce decided it was a good time to make their way home, the trains were already packed to bursting. Eventually they arrived indoors at five-o-clock, tired, hungry and happy, this really was the beginning of a new era.

For their annual holiday in July, Chic thought it would be great to go to
a holiday camp with the Stevens family, they booked into Broadreeds at
Selsey for a week. They had so much fun cycling and playing games,
Joyce won the fancy hat competition and Chic the *"Best Beast,"* they
soaked up the sunshine and danced every evening. Most days they all
laughed until they cried with the jokes and antics that Stead and Chic
got up to with the boys. Joyce and Chic also gathered hundreds of
pebbles and shells from the beach to add to their collection from
Yarmouth and the Isle of Wight. Chic had an idea. On their return home
he started work on landscaping the garden, it looked like a building site,
with a huge mound of earth in the middle. The plan was to create a
rockery to conceal the garage. He laid a path with steps leading down
behind a 6 ft retaining wall, which he rendered and studded with the
thousands of shells and pebbles they had gathered from their holidays.
Hardcore and spare slabs left from the crazy paving were used to create
the rock garden, enabling Joyce to spend many happy hours choosing
and arranging the plants, she loved gardening. Chic did not stop there,
now he was building a log store and coal bunker behind the rockery.
Finally, a handsome brick rose pergola was built across the full width
of the garage to disguise the roof. He was very proud of his handiwork
and Joyce thought him very clever.

26. THE BABY.

As the summer drew to a close, Joyce began suffering from morning sickness, she went straight off to the doctor for a pregnancy check. She complained of a bitter taste in her mouth, he told her to stop smoking immediately. After checking her medical notes, the GP advised as much rest as possible, her blood pressure was abnormally high and it was important that she did not become pre-eclamptic. He would keep a very close eye on her and suggested she also go to the dentist, he suspected pyorrhoea. The dentist was very thorough and confirmed the doctor's diagnosis. Joyce was distraught she was always meticulous with her teeth cleaning and proud of her straight white teeth. The dentist explained that pregnant women are much more prone to the disease and it was a dangerous condition for the baby, as the poisons could be absorbed into the bloodstream. He painted her teeth with antiseptic and gave her mouth wash to use daily, if the antiseptic did not work within the month, all her teeth would have to be removed. Joyce reported back to Chic in a tearful state, he comforted her. He would give up smoking too, it was so important to both of them that she should not lose this baby. She was twenty-nine years old, they had been married for nine years and this could be their last chance to become parents. It was difficult giving up smoking, they were both a bit tetchy and Joyce went down with a dreadful cold. She had been working long enough at Woolworth's to benefit from her 30 shillings *(£1.50)* maternity pay. Chic agreed that now they had paid off his brother's loan and he was on a better wage, Joyce should leave Woolworth's immediately. Things would be tight but they would not be spending money on ciggies.

The antiseptic did not work on Joyce's gums and in October she was admitted to Kingston Hospital to have all her teeth removed under local anaesthetic. She was four months pregnant, the second trimester was the optimum time to operate and the dental operation was overseen by an experienced gynaecologist. It was possible that she unknowingly had suffered from pyorrhoea all along, the disease would have contributed to, if not caused, her many miscarriages and the stillbirth. Joyce and Chic felt confident that the doctors knew what they were doing and this time she and the baby would be fine. It was distressing for Joyce to lose her teeth but it was not uncommon. The National Health Service now provided free dentures, unlike when Chic had his false tooth fitted back in 1945. She was kept on an observation ward for two weeks while they monitored her blood pressure and took moulds for her double set of false teeth. Once she was discharged, Joyce was advised to get as much bed rest as possible for the remainder of her confinement. She tried her best, by resting on the bed every afternoon with her knitting and a good book, but there was cooking and cleaning to be done. Pat the lodger helped out by doing all the shopping. She had met a chap called Jack and they were getting married in March. This was good timing with the baby due soon after, but they would miss the rent money.

Friends visited frequently, but there was no entertaining and certainly no dancing. Joyce was advised to put her feet up at every opportunity, her legs and feet were extremely swollen and her varicose veins painful. Chic was always busy working on the car or the house, he spent hours in his workshop, despite the Minx not getting used much. When Dave asked if he could borrow the car for a weekend away with Dora, Chic was happy to lend it. He mentioned this to George at Mollart's, who offered to pay for the loan of the car to visit his wife's family for a few days. This planted a seed that Chic mulled over in his head for several weeks, he did not mention it to Joyce. They drove up to Foxton for Christmas and had a quiet New Year's Eve at Charlie's house in Woodland Way. The baby was due at the end of March and Joyce was doing exactly as she was told, making sure she took at least four hours bed rest every day. Frank Sherwood was now suffering badly with his angina and Annie was very confused. Their boys did not know what to do for the best, it was a hard life for Frank at home with his wife, who on some days could be quite difficult to handle. It was agreed on New Year's Eve that Annie should come and stay with Charlie for a week or two to give Frank a rest. Joyce and Chic would do their share after the baby was born.

Rationing had finally come to an end and Pat the lodger was planning her wedding at the Kingston Registrar Office with a small reception afterwards at Peggy Brown's in Surbiton on the 6ᵗʰ of March. Joyce was making Pat's outfit, a smart cotton day dress with a sleeved bolero. Both Pat and Jack were shy reserved characters and did not want a fuss, just a small gathering of close friends and family, including Joyce and Chic. Joyce enjoyed dressmaking, she had made several maternity outfits for herself, but it meant she was not resting as much as she should. After her six months check, the hospital wanted to see her once a week, her blood pressure was up and her legs swollen. At the beginning of February, she caught the trolley bus as usual from Warren Drive to the hospital. It was a bitterly cold day, it had snowed the week before and the pavements were treacherous but Joyce was very careful.

She arrived in outpatients with a terrible headache and put it down to the cold weather. She did not have to wait long for the nurse to take her blood pressure, it was dangerously high and a doctor was called. He checked her swollen legs and after hearing that she also had a headache, she was immediately admitted into a general ward where she would have to stay for the foreseeable future. She was pre-eclamptic and required permanent bed rest until the baby was born. She did not protest, it was not worth risking the baby, but she needed to let her husband know. The porter wheeled the public telephone along to the ward, to allow her to make a call to Mollart Engineering. The office could not find Chic, but they would get a message to him to visit Joyce that evening, with a few essentials: a nightdress, flannel, soap, tooth powder and a hairbrush.

Chic was outside talking to the storeman about chickens, he kept two in a large hutch behind his hut and most mornings collected at least one egg. Chic wanted to get hens of his own but Joyce wasn't keen, they would make too much mess. When he discovered Joyce had been kept in hospital, he panicked and asked to leave early so that he could cycle home and get to the hospital for evening visiting. It had started snowing again, it was coming down thick and fast on the already icy roads and the wind was getting up. By the time he got to The Toby Jug, he had to get off his bike and walk because the snow was drifting. The weather reminded him of Belgium when he went tobogganing in Chanly, he wondered how the Geelan family were. Then he remembered that terrible Christmas in 1944 when he nearly lost his truck over a cliff in The Ardennes. Now all he wanted to do was get to the hospital to see his wife. It was too risky to take the Hillman out, so after picking up a nighty, a bed jacket and some toiletries he made his way to the bus stop, but everything was at a standstill, he would have to walk. It was only three miles but it took him over two hours, he arrived just in the nick of time before visiting time finished. Joyce was teary, she thought he wasn't coming. Matron turned a blind eye and let him stay for half an hour. He then had the long walk home in the dark. He stopped off at the chippy on the way and ate his rock and chips out of newspaper as he trudged through the snow. He arrived home exhausted just before eleven.

Doctor Roberts orders were compulsory bed rest for Joyce, she was to be kept under constant supervision. The weather improved the next day with just a couple of snow showers, but it was still bitterly cold with no sign of a thaw. Chic knew his wife was in the best place, but she was not due until April, so much could go wrong. Pat rallied round with the household chores while Chic attended the hospital. Joyce was bored and disappointed that she would miss Pat and Jack's wedding. Pat brought her dress in for Joyce to finish off a bit of hand sewing. Dora lived just around the corner from the hospital and popped in every day on her way home from work at Venner's factory in New Malden. She brought in books and sometimes the most delicious Italian ice cream made by her father, Mr Ferrito ran a mobile ice cream business in Kingston. Chic visited every other evening after work, now the snow had gone he could drive to the hospital. He was pleased to see that Joyce was stable but they were not going to let her home, it would be too tempting for her to overdo it again. Her sister-in-law Phyllis visited and told her all about the difficulties of looking after their mother-in-law. Some of the girls from Woolworth's popped in, bringing supplies of knitting patterns and wool for Joyce to make baby clothes and a couple of neighbours visited from Firdene. Joyce did not want her mother to know, she would only worry, she wrote to her parents to say she was fine and getting plenty of rest.

Pat and Jack's wedding went by without a hitch, the weather was cold, wet and miserable but at least it had stopped snowing. Chic did not stay long at the reception, he went straight to the hospital to tell Joyce all about it. The newly-weds were taking a short honeymoon to Brighton and on their return, Pat was moving in with Jack thus enabling Chic to decorate the box room in readiness for the baby. Chic's Grandpa Charlie had made a beautiful white willow cradle for his children back in the 1800s, it had been passed down for his grandsons, Charlie and Percy and then his great grandchild Annette and now it was Chic's turn to take ownership for his baby. The wicker cradle was still in excellent condition apart from needing a thorough clean, but the stand was dilapidated. Chic took the crib into work one Saturday morning and scrounged some mild steel rods and an offcut of sheet metal from stores. Peter from the planning office was also in the tool shop working out a design for his go-cart, a new hobby. The two of them got on with their illicit work and helped each other out with the welding, the crib stand was finished in no time, apart from a lick of paint. Then Chic became engrossed with what Peter was doing, he would like to build his own racing cart. There were never any bosses around on Saturday mornings, they could get paid overtime and work on their hobby projects undisturbed, Chic was very keen to learn what he could from Peter.

Joyce's due date arrived with no sign of the baby coming, she had knitted and sewn so many matinee outfits they would never all be used, now she was making a white woolly poodle. Phyllis had stored her Dunkley coach-built pram in the garage, just in case, but Annette was ten years old now with no signs of her getting a sibling. The time had come to sell it. Chic gave Phyllis a couple of pounds, cleaned it up, oiled it and replaced the tyres. He left it at Woodland Way, it was bad luck to bring a pram into the house before the baby was born. Joyce gave Dora a long shopping list and Chic was sent off to buy a baby bath, a nappy bucket and a rubberised hair mattress with a waterproof sheet. His mother-in-law Edie, had already sent a parcel of cot and pram bedding, flannelette sheets cut down from her own bed, crisp cotton under sheets and six crocheted blankets. The layette was complete but the baby was reluctant to venture out into the world, another week went by with no sign of movement. On Sunday 11ᵗʰ April, Chic was at the hospital for afternoon visiting when Joyce had a few twinges. Matron thought it was just a bit of constipation but she called the midwife in to check, Chic was asked to wait in the corridor as they drew the curtain around her bed.

Five minutes later the midwife came out to tell Chic that his wife was in the early stages of labour. It was far too early to move her to the labour ward and it was best if Chic went home, he could telephone the hospital in the evening to see how Joyce was getting on. It was at this very moment that Chic wished he had a telephone, his brother was connected in 1952 and as a result his betting business was thriving. He drove home and cooked himself eggs on toast, before setting to with a bit of cleaning, he didn't want Joyce and the baby coming home to a dusty house. At six-o-clock he walked around to Woodland Way to tell Charlie and Phyllis the news and use their phone to ring the hospital. Joyce was comfortable but being watched very closely, her labour was progressing slowly, there was no need for him to come in. He gave the hospital Charlie's phone number to be called when they had some news. Charlie suggested Chic stay for supper, they could play cards. Phyllis went into a great deal of detail about how difficult it was looking after Annie, for just three weeks. She was now back home with her husband, but had deteriorated and was even more confused.

Chic was concerned about both his parents, but at the moment his main worry was Joyce. Charlie thrashed him at cards, he walked home at midnight with no news, he knew he was not going to get much sleep. His brother promised he would run straight round if they got a phone call in the night and sure enough at 2 am, Charlie was hammering on Chic's front door. Chic jumped in the Minx and arrived in the labour ward within half an hour. The curtains were around Joyce, Doctor Roberts was with her, she needed forceps and Chic was told to wait outside. They were now very keen to get the baby born quickly, there was a risk that Joyce could have an eclamptic fit. After pacing the floor for only twenty minutes he heard a baby cry, nurse Mullins came out to tell him he was the father of a healthy baby girl and that he could see them both shortly. Joyce needed another procedure to ensure the placenta was fully dispelled and her blood pressure reduced. Chic waited for what seemed like an eternity, but eventually he was allowed in. Joyce was sitting up with the baby in her arms, they were both fine. He cried with joy.

Chic stayed for an hour and then drove home to make himself some breakfast, before driving into work as usual. He was on cloud nine and could not wait to tell his mates he was a *"Daddy"* at last. Joyce was kept in hospital for another three weeks until the medical staff were confident her blood pressure was stable. The baby was doing well and taking the breast, Joyce was an attentive mother. Then she was told that it would be dangerous for her to have any more children. This was a blow but Joyce was preoccupied, her maternal instinct had kicked in beautifully. All that mattered at the moment was that she and Chic had a perfect baby girl, they would call her Jane Pauline. She was keen to get home and into a routine, she had been sitting around doing nothing for far too long.

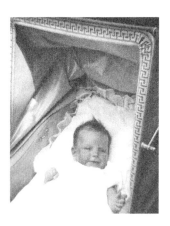

27. SELF-DRIVE CAR HIRE.

Chic suggested to Joyce they should have a telephone connected at home but she was worried about the expense, it was now time for Chic to tell his wife about the idea he had been mulling over since before Christmas. He reminded her about George paying to borrow their car and thought they could start a car hire business to bring in some extra cash. Joyce knew how to do book keeping, they didn't need the car all the time and if it worked out they could buy a second car. Joyce was not sure, she wanted to spend time with the baby. Whilst Joyce was thinking, Chic went off to the post office and ordered a telephone connection, they offered him a party line but he thought it better to pay more for his own individual phone number. By the time Joyce came out of hospital, the telephone was installed in their hallway just by the front door.

Joyce settled very quickly into a routine at home and soon got back into doing her chores between feeding the baby, she enjoyed having the house to herself now that Pat had moved out. Chic came home every dinner time and Joyce rested every afternoon while the baby slept. Her mother came to stay for a couple of weeks, she fussed about doing all the cooking and laundry while her daughter regained her strength and by the end of May Joyce was back to normal, scrubbing floors and doing her own washing, ironing and cooking. The baby was christened at Saint George's Church in Hamilton Avenue on the 4ᵗʰ July. Her godparents were Uncle Charlie, Auntie Phyllis and her mother Joyce. The christening was attended by family and friends, Edie and Harry, Frank and Annie and Dora and David. They were celebrating back at the house when a congratulations telegram arrived from Joyce Romine in Texas, she had two sons of her own and was thrilled for her friend.

There was still a great deal to be done in the garden during the summer. They were not taking a holiday this year and Chic had put the word about that his car was available to be hired for a competitive fee. George was keen to take up the offer and a couple of other colleagues and Chic was very pleased with the cash he received from his lowkey car hire operation. By October, the baby was thriving and Joyce was in better health, it was time to think about starting up a business. Brother Charlie recommended his excellent accountant Mr Clutterbuck, who lived in Malvern Road, Surbiton. Joyce and Chic went to see him, he thought Chic's business idea a sound one, particularly as Chic could carry out all his own servicing and car maintenance. Joyce was well qualified to manage the office with her book keeping skills and organisational abilities. The rates on their garage and some of the house bills could be offset against any profit, their biggest expense would be insurance and motor car tax. Mr Clutterbuck was insistent that the car hire insurance be fully comprehensive and water tight, Joyce agreed, she liked everything to be above board. It just so happened that Phyllis's brother-in-law Tony, was an insurance broker, he was happy to take on Sherwood Self-Drive Car Hire as a business account.

Joyce had a great respect for authority and always abided by the rules and regulations, but Chic was a sceptic. He was taught from a young age by his grandpa that those in authority could not always be trusted. He believed in keeping his head down and doing what he thought to be right, even if it meant bending the rules. Chic's experiences from the war confirmed this view, he served under some excellent officers, but there were many who were not up to the job. The same applied in civilian life, those who professed to be respectable pillars of the community were often up to no good behind closed doors. His brother's clandestine betting business showed this up only too well, Chic was wary. When the proposal forms for hirer driving insurance arrived, he could not believe his eyes, the terms and conditions stated that no vehicle could be let on hire or driven by:

"Foreigners. Students. Actors/Actresses. Music Hall Artistes. Dance Band Leaders/Members. Theatre, Cinema or Music Hall Proprietors. Members of the Theatrical or Variety Profession. Film Producers. Members in Cinema or the Film Trade. Publicans/Employees on Licensed Premises. Bookmakers, Turf Accountants or their Agents. Jockeys. Persons connected with Racing. Air Pilots. Members of the Army, Navy or Air Force."

This lengthy list of supposed ne'er do wells wiped out most of his customers, including his own brother. Joyce thought he was fretting about nothing, they would find plenty of clients by word of mouth, their next-door neighbour was already interested and he was a very respectable bank clerk. She enquired about advertising in The Evening Standard, The Surrey Comet and Kelly's Directory. It was a costly exercise, but the bookings for their newly acquired 1938 Morris 10 that replaced the Hillman Minx steadily filled their diary. Within months Chic could afford to purchase a second-hand 1946 Morris 8 for £275 from Mr Long who lived in Mansfield Road, Hook. The diary was full

125 Mansfield Road,
Hook.
Surrey.

To Mr Perry Sherwood,

Received the sum of
two hundred and Seventy five
pounds, (£275), in payment
for Morris 8. No LMX 779.

Life was busy. Joyce used the dining table as a desk at the front end of the lounge while baby Jane played with her dolls in a playpen at the back. Chic came home from Mollart's every lunchtime and in the evenings, he did vital maintenance and servicing on the cars. They were always spotless, if Chic did not have time to clean them Joyce did. Their first year of trading had its problems, with some minor mishaps and a couple of breakdowns. At the height of the holiday season in 1955, a customer was driving to Cornwall in the Morris when it broke down on the New Direct Road near Ilchester in Somerset. RAC cover was included in the hire cost and Joyce received a phone call on Monday morning to say that an RAC patrol officer had reported that the clutch was burnt out. The client was frustrated and so was Chic, when Joyce told him the news. The family were now booked in overnight at The Mermaid Hotel in Yeovil while a replacement was found. Chic rang the hotel and agreed to pay for the client to hire another car chargeable to Sherwood Car Hire.

He needed to go down to Somerset to sort out the problem. He went back to work and explained to Jack Hendra who agreed he could take a day's holiday in lieu. He then rang Mr Fox to see if there was a pick-up truck available, there was, he collected it on his way home from work. On Tuesday morning at dawn, he set off with a spare set of Morris keys to Somerset, Ilchester was at least an hour beyond Stonehenge. Yeovil was his first stop, to collect the keys. The customer had already left but Chic wanted to see what the hotel was like, he was probably going to have to pay for that as well. He found the Morris sitting on the side of the road just outside the village of Ilchester. He started it up, it was stuck in gear and he was furious, this was the result of bad driving. Then he thought back to when he was on the Yorkshire Moors trying to fix the Dingo on his back in a sea of mud. His thoughts jumped again to The Ardennes, when he was fitting jeep engines at night in below zero temperatures with the risk of being killed. His current situation was just a nuisance, he calmed down.

He winched the car up on to the pickup and steadily made his way back to Tolworth, parked it up in his garage and delivered the truck back to Fox and Nicholl's. A new clutch meant taking the gear box out which was a major job, but he had source the spare parts first and he needed the car up and running in ten days' time. It was booked out to be collected on Friday night and this meant working all over the week-end with loss of overtime. The following week the garage light was on well into the small hours every single night and he finished the job on Friday morning at 2 am. When the bill came in for the hotel and the alternative car hire, Joyce thought Chic could claim on the insurance, but Tony advised them not to claim. The expenses could be offset against the business and this would be the cheapest option in the long run. Chic was not sure he agreed, but he went along with it. The company car insurance for that year was £76.14. 2d, the total cost of repairs and carriage came to £114.11.0d, most of which was due to the incompetence of one customer. Their takings for the whole year totalled £348.10.0d with insurance and repairs of £190, over half their profit. This did not warm Chic to the world of insurance.

At this time, the Sherwood family were the only car owners in Firdene, they always parked one in the garage and the other out the front when the need arose, which was not that often as they were booked out most of the time. Joyce did not have a driving licence, which posed a problem if one of the cars needed moving whilst her husband was at work. Chic started teaching her, there were some arguments but the tension never lasted long and there was always much laughter. Chic had great respect for his *"Darling,"* they made an excellent team. By the time their baby daughter was nearly two years old, the Morris 10 had been sold to a private buyer and Chic bought a new green Ford Popular, registration 331 APB at a cost of £424.10.6d including £138.17.0d Purchase Tax. The business was going well despite a loss showing on the books, their accountant was very adept at offsetting the profit. The couple enjoyed running their own business and taking responsibility for themselves, their separate skills complimented each other.

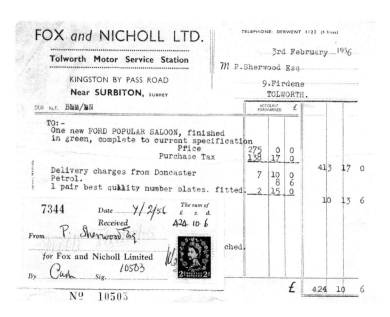

FOX and NICHOLL LTD.

TELEPHONE: DERWENT 1122 (4 lines)

Tolworth Motor Service Station

KINGSTON BY PASS ROAD
Near SURBITON, SURREY

3rd February 1956

M P.Sherwood Esq

9.Firdene
TOLWORTH.

OUR REF. BMM/MN

	ACCOUNT FORWARDED £					
TO:- One new FORD POPULAR SALOON, finished in green, complete to current specification						
Price		275	0	0		
Purchase Tax		138	17	0		
					413	17 0
Delivery charges from Doncaster		7	10	0		
Petrol.			8	6		
1 pair best quality number plates. fitted.		2	15	0		
					10	13 6
					£	424 10 6

7344   Date *4/2/56*
Received
From *P. Sherwood Esq*

The sum of
£   s.   d.
424 10 6

ched.

for Fox and Nicholl Limited
By *Cash*   Sig. *10503*

Nº 10503

Frank Sherwood had not been well for a very long time, his stomach never fully recovered after his experience as a POW in WW1. His old war wound made him lame and that, combined with angina, aggravated by the stress of looking after Annie had taken its toll. When he died aged sixty-seven, his body was laid out in the front parlour at Lenelby Road. Chic remembered his friend Jenni and cried for his father, he knew he had been in constant pain;

"Well Dad, you are out of your pain now."

Annie was seventy-one years old when her husband died, she repeatedly asked who that dead man was in her front room, it was distressing for them all. Annie Plant had moved to her rented house fifty years earlier with her father and little brother Sid. She met and married her husband there, had her children there, but now she would have to move. It was Chic's turn to look after his mother while his brother found somewhere safe for her to live. Joyce was willing to help take care of her mother-in-law, she could still run the business, although she was worried about the effect on the baby. Annie thought Jane was her own child, she played with her, sang her songs, or just sat and watched her. Joyce could not leave them alone together, Annie was unpredictable and had started roaming. One blessing was that both Annie and Jane were good sleepers giving Joyce and Chic a chance to relax for an hour or so before they retired at night. They were always dog tired when they eventually got into bed and both slept soundly, usually right through to the alarm clock waking them at 6 am.

One particular night Joyce woke with a start, nature called and as she went to the bathroom, she saw the light on in the baby's room, she went to look, the baby had gone and Annie was not in her bed. She rushed downstairs, there was no sign of either of them and the pram was not in the front porch. She called Chic who still half asleep wondered what all the commotion was. His mother had taken their baby girl, Joyce was beside herself. He threw his coat on over his pyjamas and frantically searched outside, perhaps Annie had gone to Charlie's in Woodland Way. After waking his brother and searching for nearly half an hour, it was time to call the police. Joyce dialled 999, an operator answered immediately and put her through to the duty sergeant at Surbiton Police Station on the Ewell Road. He would send a constable out on a bicycle immediately to check the surrounding roads, they didn't think Mrs Sherwood would have gone far. Joyce waited by the phone, Chic got dressed and went out searching again all over the Sunray Estate but within the hour there was a knock at the door. Joyce opened it to see a police constable standing behind her mother-in-law, he was holding a bicycle and her pram, with the baby inside fast asleep. They had been found walking along The Broadway.

When questioned, Annie told the constable she was taking her daughter home to Lenelby Road, but Annie was dressed only in a nighty and the baby had no blankets. Joyce grabbed Jane and the policeman led the old lady inside, she protested a little, but eventually agreed to go back to bed and Joyce locked the bedroom door. The constable suggested ringing the family doctor, he thought Mrs Sherwood (*Annie*) should be given a sedative. By the time the GP arrived Chic was home and Charlie had turned up on his way to work at Job's Dairy, he started his milk round at 4.30 am. Joyce was distraught, she didn't want Annie in her house and neither did Phyllis, something had to be done quickly. Annie was now refusing to come out of her bedroom, the doctor asked her a few questions while Charlie, Chic and Joyce all chipped in with their version of events. The GP had a quiet word with the constable and suggested taking Annie immediately to Long Grove Mental Hospital, in his car. The police constable parked his bike in the front garden, radioed back to his sergeant and escorted Mrs Sherwood with the doctor to hospital, where she would be assessed.

Chic went to work having had no sleep, he was grieving for his father, anxious about his mother and worried for Joyce and the baby. It wasn't the first time he had gone to work without sleep and it was good to be busy, it stopped him thinking. Mollart Engineering always had plenty of work in, the Suez crisis was keeping their order books full from British Aerospace and Chic's day job was a welcome distraction from all his responsibilities at home. The world was unsettled again, it took him back to his time in Trieste, surely there could not be another war! He would have liked to resign from his full-time job as supervisor in the machine tools workshop, but the world was too volatile at the moment with the Suez Crisis, he needed to wait. There was also an annoying side effect that affected his business directly, petrol rationing had returned. As business vehicles, each car was eligible to more coupons than a private one but there were still not enough. Chic begged and borrowed where he could, he frequented Fox and Nicholl more often, and his brother Charlie always knew how to get hold of a few extra gallons.

Annie never came out of hospital, her sons visited regularly for the first few months, but she no longer recognised them and gradually the visits became less and less. Joyce and Phyllis made up parcels of clothes for her and delivered homemade cake, fruit and toffees, Annie loved toffees. As the illness progressed she was often heavily sedated. It was a sad day when Annie died two years after her husband, but both Percy and Charlie thought it a blessed release, she was a tormented soul at the end. They arranged her burial in the same plot at Surbiton Cemetery as her husband Frank and her father Charlie Plant, Chic's grandpa.

Left to right seated. Sappers: Stead, Chic, Johnno, Corporal Sam Whitaker.

189

That same year Chic and Stead attended another army reunion up in Yorkshire, Johnny Rooke was there and Sam Whitaker, but Chic did not enjoy this event as much as the last. It was good to see the old faces and laugh over a few funny moments, but he didn't see much point in looking back he wanted to look forward. Many of his pals had claimed their medals, Joyce wanted Chic to claim his but he wanted no part of it. He saw no glory in his service, many did more and too many were dead. What use are medals if you are dead? His father Frank never wanted his medals from WW1 and Chic would not claim his. That was the last army reunion he attended.

The remainder of the 1950s brought good times for Chic and his family. Rationing was a faint memory and the business was thriving. He was also in full time work as a highly respected precision engineer. There was always plenty of banter in the tool shop at Mollart's, George Dent was a great joker and Chic was always happy to join in. They lived near to each other and both went home for their dinner breaks, George on his bike and Chic quite often by car when he had one available. When the weather was fine the staff from the Ministry of Defence buildings behind The Toby Jug would eat their sandwiches outside. George who fancied himself as a bit of a *"Norman Wisdom,"* loved an audience and one lunchtime as he was cycling in front of Chic on the service road, he suddenly stopped and pretended to fall off his bike. Chic jumped out of the car, George winked and they promptly started a mock fight with shouting and fists flying all in the name of comedy. The civil servants loved it and Chic thought it hilarious. When he arrived back at work in the afternoon, the story was all round the factory, they laughed about it for weeks and did it again and again.

Ken Scutt, Peter Pollard, George Dent, Chic, Keith Howard.

Joyce loved her role running the office at home, it blended perfectly with childcare and gave her time to carry out domestic chores including a great deal of dressmaking. Their previous lodger Pat, still lived locally and was always available for babysitting if they wanted to attend any of the numerous functions not only at Mollart's, but also Venner's where their friends Dora and David both worked. Chic was often included in the Fox and Nicholl staff outings such as coach trips to Brighton, he knew all the lads and he was good fun to be around. He was also invited to Mr Fox's retirement party, this talented and skilled mechanical engineer who designed, built and raced Talbots before the war, would be missed. Chic had a lot to thank him for, his life would have been very different if Mr Fox had not taken a chance on him as a grocer's delivery boy who made a nuisance of himself in the garage workshops.

The garage was sold to Berkeley Square Garages and renamed Bye Pass Motors, they continued as Ford dealers and in 1958 Sherwood Car Hire was able on the advice of the accountant, to purchase two cars. On the 21st March, Chic took delivery of 147 FPD, a new Richmond Blue Ford Popular with blue upholstery at a total cost of £455.6.4d, which included factory delivery charges of £8.6.0d and 8/4d for two gallons of petrol. On the 19th November in the same year, Bye Pass Motors also sold him a used 100E 1958 Ford Anglia saloon in white with red upholstery for £510.0.0d. The registration was 611 PMH and the car came with luxury fittings, a heater and screen washer. This was a shop demonstration model and it was a bargain because the garage was dropping the Ford dealership and moving over to Triumph.

They were beginning to reap some benefit from running the business and Jane was at Knolmead Infants School, giving Joyce more time. She did a lot more baking and Chic bought her a red and white A 700 Kenwood Chef electric food mixer for her birthday. It had a glass mixing bowl, liquidiser, juice extractor, mincer, grater and shredder and cost £41.14.3d including purchase tax. It matched the kitchen perfectly and Joyce was delighted with her extravagant gift, the first thing she did was make a Victoria sponge for the cake competition at the school fete and she won first prize. There was some discussion among the judges due to one competitor claiming that Joyce had cheated because she did not mix the cake by hand, but the complaint was overruled. What neither Chic or Joyce anticipated when they set up the car hire business, was the reaction of some neighbours who objected to any cars being parked in Firdene. They were always very careful to park one in the garage, one at the front and one down by the service road around the corner, but this still triggered complaints from a minority. Chic did not have a business licence for the premises, he could have been shut down if anyone reported him to the council. There were constant niggly issues to resolve, but Chic was not a quitter.

Just as the new decade emerged, the self-drive business suffered two irritating blows. In January the Anglia was hired out for a week to a new customer who lived on The Sunray Estate, he was driving to Scotland to visit family. It was a much easier journey now the M1 was fully open, with no traffic jams and no speed limit. He collected the car on Saturday morning and planned to drive up to Glasgow that evening. The telephone rang just as Joyce and Chic were going to bed, there had been an accident. The driver was at Watford Gap Service Station, he was not hurt but the Anglia was stuck under a lorry and the police were in attendance. Chic was furious, it was quite foggy out, this chap must have been driving too fast. There were no lights on the motorway and the visibility would have been dreadful. Now, he was going to have to liaise with the police and his insurance company to get the car towed back and repaired, before it was booked out again in two weeks time and prayed it was not going to be a right off. It turned out the Anglia could be fixed, but not without a lot of aggravation and arguments with the insurance broker.

As soon as that was resolved, another client hired the Popular for a weekend to go to a wedding. Whilst he was driving back to Tolworth on the Sunday morning from Kensal Green in North London, a Jaguar car appeared from the opposite direction, driving erratically and at very high speed. As it approached the car swerved from side to side and lost control, hitting the rear offside mudguard of the Popular. The driver of the Jaguar slowed down at the corner of Langler Road, where he and his passenger turned around to see what damage had been done before speeding off and disappearing from view. The customer was canny enough to get a witness statement from Mr Tonner who lived in Mortimer Road, but that gave cold comfort to Chic. This was in effect a hit and run and involved a hefty insurance claim, his premiums with the Equity Insurance Association were about to go sky high.

Chic habitually worked overtime at Mollart's on Saturday mornings, the extra pay was not to be sneezed at and most of the time he was able to work on his own projects, along with Peter, Ray and Dougy, who were all mad keen on building and racing their own go-karts. Peter knew a chap who owned some land opposite The Hogsmill Tavern at Worcester Park, and the chalk stream valley was perfect for laying a short circular track to test the karts. The landowner was interested in motor racing and encouraged the boys to mark out a dirt track, with a fast first turn and run off, a long straight and then an S bend, before arriving back at the start. There was a natural bank that offered protection, with hay bales scattered intermittently around the circuit. The boys including Chic, spent all their spare time building the karts and testing them at the track on Sunday mornings. They were extremely basic, the frames were welded from mild steel with a low flat chassis, rear engine and an A frame seat. There was a brake, accelerator and column steering wheel with no protection, the aim was to tune the engine to go as fast as possible. Chic would set off early on a Sunday with his sandwiches and flask of tea, he preferred testing and working on the karts to the actual racing, but his mate Ray was competitive, they made a good team.

By 1960 the club was thriving, it was all amateur with no insurance required and the club members all participated enthusiastically. They took it in turns to drive and marshal the races, the yellow safety flags were in prolific use, a single wave to slow down and a double wave to stop. One chap who loved his job a bit too much, would jump up and down as he waved the karts through on a staggered start. Family and friends came along to watch and sometimes take part at the special meets on bank holiday weekends. The crowd parked on the bank, brought picnics and set up their deck chairs, right on the tracks edge. One day, *"Cliff Michelmore"* turned up with a film crew from Thames Television, it was a real thrill to be on the TV, Jane and Dougy's daughter Jackie were filmed racing around the track. The large clubhouse had a licensed bar and a snooker table and the social committee organised treasure hunts and car rallies, it was all great fun. The track became so popular it started attracting professional drivers and commercially built karts, the small amateur enterprise was becoming big business. That is when Chic began to lose interest. Suddenly there were dozens of rules and regulations, compulsory insurance, safety checks, the RAC deemed the first bend too fast and ordered the track to be altered, Chic was frustrated. He hated interference from authority, but also realised he needed to spend more time on his own business.

9 Firdene 1960

28. MOVING HOUSE.

It was time to look for somewhere else to live, where his business could be totally above board, a house with an office and parking for several cars would be the perfect solution. They started looking in the spring of 1961, Chic had been thinking for a while that he could now afford to pack in his full-time job, but he needed proof of his salary to acquire a mortgage, building societies did not like customers who were self-employed. He thought he could afford to borrow another £1,000. It just so happened that his sister-in-law Phyllis, had a brother who was a mortgage broker. Bernard advised Chic to stay in full employment until he had secured a loan on a property and made at least six months repayments, the search for the perfect house was on. His brother Charlie recommended Ellis, Copp & Co, Estate Agents based in Ewell High Street. They were helping him purchase commercial premises in Epsom where he was planning to open a betting shop. The Betting and Gaming Act passed in 1960 now allowed him to apply for a licence with the Racecourse Betting Control Board. On 1ˢᵗ May 1961 it became legal for all registered bookmakers to publicly take bets. Charlie's shop was one of hundreds that popped up on high streets all over England that year, no more skulking around the back streets to meet punters and settle debts. It was Charlie's plan to also get a mortgage whilst still working as a milkman before embarking on his fulltime career as a turf accountant.

The agent thought 9 Firdene was *"beautifully maintained"* and would sell easily, they were given sole agency rights and found a buyer almost immediately with an offer of £3,400, but Chic and Joyce could not find anything suitable within their price range. Their budget was £4,500, they could only afford an extra mortgage of £1,000 and needed a local property with business use and land for parking. The hunt went on through a freezing cold winter, there was snow on the ground for months. Chic was meticulous about making sure his vehicles were fully topped up with antifreeze. De-icing and warming up the engines took twice as long in this weather, he was getting up an hour earlier on the days the cars were booked out to make sure all was ship shape before he went to work. The couple looked at many tumbledown Victorian houses needing mountains of work, a nursery school with cavernous rooms that would have cost a fortune to heat, a redundant doctor's surgery with antiquated plumbing and a rectory that needed a new roof and was in the final stages of decay, with snow inside the house. They thought they would never find anything, but then a twist of fate turned in their favour. Tony the insurance broker was getting divorced, he owned a house in Beaconsfield Road, Surbiton and it was licenced for business use. The price was £4,750 with an option to purchase the service road that ran behind the house from King Charles Road up to Birchington Road. The house was advertised as;

"An older style family residence previously owned by a builder who has so improved and modernised this property that it would put many post-war houses to shame."

"You will not be enamoured by the exterior appearance, but upon entering the property you will walk into a beautiful reception room with light oak panelling and feature fireplace with fitted oak bureau. From there a further door leads in to the main accommodation which comprises a superb lounge made for parties."

Ellis, Copp and Co waxed lyrical for several paragraphs about the loggia, the dining room, kitchen with solid fuel Raeburn, walk-in larder, interestingly shaped bedrooms with a mass of expensive built in furniture, luxurious bathroom with heated towel rail, two toilets, ring main wiring, tasteful modern décor and most importantly, two large brick garages. Finally;

"Could well suit a professional man,
as the property enjoys a bold corner position."

They were already stretched to their limit and could not afford to buy the service road, but the yard with the garages stretched behind the house next door and gave potential to park six or seven cars. They agreed the full asking price of £4,500 plus £250 for fixtures and fittings.

They had another buyer for Firdene, but were £350 over their budget, the house was perfect, Joyce loved it and Chic thought it was worth the risk. On the 12ᵗʰ January 1962 Joyce caught the 406 bus to Ewell village and gave a £500 cheque to the estate agent in the High Street, a deposit to secure the purchase of the house. The snow lingered but the couple were excited about their new venture, they exchanged contracts in March and moved in one month later just after their daughter's eighth birthday in time for Easter. The repayments were due to commence in June at more than £13 per month, the cost of one week's self-drive car hire in the high season, they would have to make this work.

The family spent the Easter holiday getting settled into their new home, it was more than double the size of Firdene. The enormous lounge had a fashionable grey patterned carpet with white venetian blinds, fluted wooden window seats, wall lights and a gas fire set in a black tiled fireplace. Their red boucle winged lounge suite, purchased with Chic's small inheritance from his mother back in 1956 looked just the part. The square farmhouse kitchen was cosy, with a solid fuel Rayburn and the previous owners had left a few buckets of coke in the coal bunker. The constant bubbling of the coffee percolator, brought back from their trip to Belgium in 1947 provided a delicious aroma. It reminded Chic of his friends Emile and Pauline, they had lost touch. There was a new gas cooker, an enormous fridge freezer and a heavy-duty washing machine including mangle next to the old butler sink. The walk-in larder under the stair well provided extensive storage. Their dining table sat in the middle of the kitchen and Joyce only half filled the cupboards.

All the other rooms had bare floorboards, they were draughty and unwelcoming, but the study despite having no carpet was inviting. The perfect office to welcome customers, with oak panelled walls, a delightful brick fireplace and most importantly a large built in wooden desk complete with a telephone and brass lamp. They took over the existing telephone number, Elmbridge 3303, put the bookings diary on the desk and were ready for business immediately. Chic went to see Bill Mason who still lived in Kingston and had a thriving sign writing business. The reminisced a little about their time in Italy and within two weeks there was a smart sign hanging next to the front door.

There were four bedrooms upstairs, with no carpets or curtains. The sash windows were twice the size of their little windows at Firdene, but the long curtains just about reached across in the main bedroom as a temporary measure. The back bedroom had been used to rear a family of kittens and it stank to high heaven, even after Joyce had scrubbed and bleached it. They opened the window and kept the door shut for several days but still it lingered, eventually a soaking of vinegar did the trick, although Chic thought the vinegar smell was almost as bad, eventually it dissipated. Jane was put in the smallest room, which only had one window with a blanket as a temporary curtain. All the bedrooms had fitted wardrobes and dressing tables, the storage was voluminous but most remained empty.

Chic wore himself to the bone. The business was thriving, he was still working full time at Mollart's and as well as servicing the cars, he was discovering all sorts of problems with the house, dodgy electrics, ancient plumbing, wet rot and questions about the ownership of the original brick wall on the rear boundary. In addition to this he decided to extend the garage. It was a major undertaking while all these other issues constantly needed his attention and the financial pressure of the hefty mortgage made him anxious.

He was working eighteen hours a day, but not sleeping well, the nightmares from his army days returned. He would toss and turn and often scream out in the middle of the night, hurling himself over and taking the bed clothes with him. Joyce was also losing sleep, she was weary but more worried about her husband who was depressed. The holiday season was upon them and every waking moment was spent making sure the cars were fit for purpose. On Saturday 21ˢᵗ July a regular customer collected the Ford Anglia De Luxe for two weeks at a cost of £27.10.0d, the family were driving to Pembrokeshire for their annual holiday. On their return Chic noticed the offside rear brake light was smashed and a dent in the bumper, the customer said it had happened while they were at the beach and it must have been someone in the car park. Joyce withheld their deposit, but that did not cover the cost of repair and it was not worth claiming on the insurance, Sherwood Car Hire absorbed the expense. Chic needed to make the car roadworthy immediately because it was booked out that same afternoon. He rang Willment's, the Ford dealer in Twickenham but they could not get a spare glass until Monday morning.

Bob, a colleague from Mollart's, was due to hire the Anglia. He was an amenable chap and was just taking his mother out for day trips. Chic offered him a £5 discount if he could bring the car back on Monday morning to have a new glass fitted, Bob agreed. Chic was waiting at Willment's spares department when they opened at 8 am, only to be told the spares delivery was not expected until nine. He spent the time chatting with the staff and looking around the showroom, they had a new Consul in stock, it would make a great chauffeur car He arrived back home just after 9.45 am, Bob was already there enjoying a cup of tea with Joyce at the kitchen table. It took just five minutes to fix the light, Bob was all set to drive his mother to Kew Gardens and Chic should have been at work. He got back to Mollart's just before eleven and bumped straight into Ken Mollart;

"Where the hell have you been, Chic? Keith and Ken are waiting for you in the drawing office."

Chic rushed down to the office, Keith the chief designer was writing on the drawing, the measurements were out by several thou, *(thousands of one inch)* on a drill for the jet blade milling machine, it would have to be retooled. That was no problem for Chic he could do that in a jiffy. He went back to the tool shop and duly shaved 16 thou. off the drill end just as Mr Mollart walked back in with Keith. The boss demanded to know why he was so late for work and Chic answered back without thinking;

"You are not the only one with a business to run! I had a car to fix."

The boss was not best pleased, but Chic was an excellent precision engineer and he did not want to lose him. He told him to work through his dinner break and if it happened again he would be put on a disciplinary. Chic got on with his work and kept his head down.

He had already taken his annual leave earlier in the year and spent it working on the house. Now it was peak holiday time and he was under pressure to keep all the vehicles running smoothly. Every weekend was frantic, the cars had to be checked over, oil, water, cleaned inside and out, sometimes he worked all night on a Friday to ensure the cars were roadworthy and ready for hire on the Saturday. He had been thinking for a while that he should diversify by offering a chauffeur service, the self-drive cars were always needing maintenance and repair due to neglect and abuse by more than a few customers, who it seemed to Chic, needed to learn how to drive properly. The number of tyres he got through was ridiculous, he was one of Ralph Dark's best customers. A new venture would be risky, it meant acquiring a bigger car and leaving Mollart's. Joyce thought they should wait, they had only just started paying their enormous mortgage and he knew deep down that his wife was right, he would bide his time. What he did not tell Joyce was that he was suffering from intermittent chest pain. He thought about his father Frank, who ended up in a bath chair when he was not that much older than Chic, who had just had his forty-second birthday.

After a profitable summer, things started to wind down in October, Chic and Joyce were able to have a rest and enjoy some socialising. Joyce went to the Whist Drives every Tuesday evening at Mollart's social club, while Chic baby sat. Jane was now eight years old and attending Saint Matthews Junior Girls School in Broomfield Road. It was only around the corner and she could walk to school and back on her own. Chic went to the club for a couple of drinks after work most Fridays, where he enjoyed the company of several pals, Ray, Dougy, John and Joe. Their friends Dora and David visited every Saturday afternoon and stayed for the evening, just as they had done at Firdene. Chic was often out in the garage working, but he usually managed to finish up before tea time, he never missed the seafood suppers. In November Joyce began preparing for Christmas, her parents were going to stay for a whole week, now that her father was retired. The couple bought a fashionable grey marbled Formica furniture suite, a table and chairs with sideboard for the kitchen and a matching bar with stools and coffee table for the lounge. This blended perfectly with the grey carpet.

Joyce, Dora Ferrito, Chic and Dave Banks. Xmas 1962.

The first winter at Beaconsfield Road was going to be hard, December was icy cold. Joyce's parents arrived by train into Kings Cross in the afternoon on Saturday the 22ⁿᵈ and Chic drove Joyce and Jane up to meet them. They took afternoon tea at Lyons Corner House before driving along Oxford Street and Regent Street to see the Christmas lights, it was magical. The house was freezing when they arrived back home, the only warm spot was in the kitchen where Marla the cat was curled up in front of the now red-hot Rayburn, Joyce popped five large potatoes in to bake for their supper. She had prepared the open fires in the lounge, dining room and office in readiness for their return and Chic soon had them all roaring nicely, although it took a while for the heat to build up. Their old wooden table was now in the dining room on top of a square of carpet they had bought as an offcut from Addisons on the old Ewell Road, it helped to block the drafts. Paperchains made by Joyce and Jane were draped across the ceiling and the bay window, with tin foil twirlers spinning from the light fitting to the heat of the fire. They wanted this first Christmas in their new home to be a memorable one.

On Sunday morning they all tucked in to a huge fried breakfast and afterwards, Edie wanted to go to church. She liked the singing especially at Christmas so Joyce and Jane went with her to matins at

201

Saint Matthew's. While the women were at church Harry and Chic went off to Worcester Park to collect a Christmas tree that Chic had ordered the previous week from The Plough. One of the regulars was a woodman on the Old Malden estate and he was doing a roaring trade. They stayed for a beer and then drove home with the tree strapped on the roof rack. Joyce was cooking roast beef when they returned. They busied themselves with stabilising the tree trunk between some bricks in a bucket, it was difficult to keep the tree upright even though it was only four feet high, but after nearly an hour the tree was installed in the lounge in readiness for the fairy lights. Chic checked they were all working, but once hung on the tree they refused to light up. He twisted and pushed every single bulb and it was almost the last one that had come loose. After lunch and much more twiddling the tree was aglow.

On Christmas Eve Chic went to work, there was not much to do and he had an easy day. Jane decorated the tree with tinsel and baubles, while Joyce arranged her artificial flowers, poinsettia, Christmas rose, holly and mistletoe. Her father hung paper lanterns and twirlers from the lounge ceiling. A whole ham was braising slowly in the Rayburn and Edie was in her element making flaky pastry for mince pies and sausage rolls, the house was a hive of activity with Nat King Cole singing *"Chestnuts roasting on an open fire"* on the radio. When Chic arrived home, Joyce was stuffing the capon and covering it in a lattice of streaky bacon, it was put in the Rayburn to cook slowly overnight. They settled down to a supper of ham with boiled potatoes and piccalilli and a couple of alcoholic beverages. Joyce had to finish hemming some pyjamas for Santa, who was due in a couple of hours. Christmas Day was perfect, they rose very early to the smell of a roasting bird. Santa brought Jane a Bako building set, a walkie talkie doll and a pair of spiky pyjamas, the elf that made them had forgotten to remove the dressmaking pins before he wrapped them up!

They sat down to a three course dinner at 1 pm: half a grapefruit with a glace cherry, then capon with all the trimmings, washed down with a bottle of German Liebfraumilch, followed by Edie's Christmas pudding and mince pies. What a feast! Harry got the lucky sixpence and gave it to Jane to make a secret wish. They were all done just in time for *"The Queens Speech"* on the television at 3 pm. Afterwards, Harry and Edie dozed while Jane watched *"Billy Smart's Circus"* and Joyce and Chic tidied up in the kitchen. Then it was time for a tea: beef, ham, chicken, sausage rolls, cheese, celery and nibbles, with trifle, mince pies and Christmas cake. They were all bursting at the seams when they sat down as a family to watch Eamonn Andrews present *"Christmas Night with the Stars,"* a variety show featuring The Billy Cotton Band, Russ Conway, the Black and White Minstrels and many popular programs like Dixon of Dock Green and Steptoe and Son.

On Boxing day morning, Chic and Harry took Jane for a walk across to the park where there was a feisty game of football going on. It was bitterly cold and as they made their way back for lunch it started snowing. Joyce and Edie had prepared another feast, by the time they got down from the table the snow was beginning to settle and Jane wanted to play snowballs. Chic took her into the garden, they didn't stay out there long as it was rapidly becoming a blizzard. Bing Crosby was singing *"I'm Dreaming of a White Christmas"* on the radio and Chic had a flash back to his Christmas in The Ardennes. He was also worried about his car that was out on hire, he hoped the customer would be sensible and not drive in these conditions. On Thursday morning they woke to four inches of snow and the telephone lines were down. Chic was due to go to work and decided to walk, but before doing that he cleared the snow away from the back gates. The Anglia was booked out from Saturday until New Year's Day and he needed to check it was running OK. The snow lingered, Harry cleared a pathway out the front and watched as a couple of cars slid sideways down King Charles Road. The milkman in his electric float failed to get up the hill, he delivered the milk to Alexandra Drive on foot. The news on the radio reported train and bus cancellations, people were being told to leave their cars at home. There was not much going on at work, none of the bosses came in, so Chic left at dinner time and made his way home. He passed a couple of abandoned vehicles covered in snow on the by-pass. As he walked down Red Lion Road, he bumped into so many acquaintances that it took him over an hour to walk just one mile, by which time it was snowing again.

The telephone was still not working on Friday so Chic walked to work again and came home early. The roads were so treacherous he really did not want his best Anglia going out, his customer was a local man from Elgar Avenue, he decided to walk around to the house and discuss the problem. The matter was resolved in just a few minutes, the family were intending to visit relations up north but it was even worse up there, they had already decided to cancel but were worried about losing their deposit. That was the last thing Chic was thinking of, he agreed to return their deposit in full, the customer was happy and so was he. Joyce's parents were supposed to be going home on Saturday, but the newspapers showed photographs of Cambridgeshire with snow drifts six feet deep. Even if Chic could get them up to Kings Cross, they didn't know what they would meet the other end at Foxton Station, so it was decided they should stay until after New Year.

The weather did not improve over the next few days, more snow fell snow on top of already deep snow on the ground. The Popular was returned back in one piece on Sunday, albeit a day late, there was no extra charge. Joyce and Chic were planning a party for Tuesday night, after all the estate agent had said this house was made for parties. Chic walked to work on Monday and Tuesday while Joyce and her mother cleaned the house and prepared all manner of delicacies for Hogmanay, including cheese and silver onion sputniks *(cocktail sticks stuck in an orange)* and asparagus rolls *(tinned asparagus wrapped in brown bread and butter,)* plus the last of the leftovers from Christmas and of course an assorted range of desserts including Christmas cake. Chic ordered a barrel of beer from the off licence in Alexandra Drive and three bottles of cream sherry which they supplied on tap. Guests had been asked to bring their own tipple, but just in case there was a well-stocked bar of spirits and mixers and two dozen bottles of Babycham, a very popular drink with the ladies. It snowed a little on New Year's Eve, but not enough to put off the guests, friends, family and colleagues from Mollart's, there were at least twenty people. They played party games and danced to the radio, a good time was had by all.

Seated left to right: Jack Helen and Heather Stirling.

At midnight they sang *"Auld Lang Syne"* and everyone wished each other a Happy New Year with a great deal of kissing, then Chic disappeared. The partying continued with the singing of some good old Scottish songs and about twenty minutes later Chic reappeared with four strangers. He had blacked his face with coal and taken a glass of whisky, a slice of fruit cake and a lump of coal, over to the Park

204

Superintendent's house across the road in Alexandra Rec. Jack Stirling was on nodding acquaintance with Chic and as a Scotsman, recognised the tradition of first footing immediately. He welcomed the dark stranger into his house and introduced his wife Helen and their daughters, Heather and Pat, they were all from Aberdeenshire and missing the high jinks of Hogmanay. They were thrilled to be included in Chic's New Year celebrations and readily accepted his invitation to join the party. The entered through the front door of course, to ensure good luck for all. The party wound down about two in the morning, everyone had to go to work the next day. Chic went to bed and set his alarm for seven while Joyce did a bit of tidying downstairs. It had a been a great party and a positive start to 1963.

There was not much work done in the tool shop on Wednesday and everyone looked a bit worse for wear, but they had a good laugh about what they had got up to. The weather did not improve much over the next week, with more heavy snow the roads were now like ice rinks. Harry was keen to get home and Chic agreed that he should drive his in-laws to Foxton on Sunday because Joyce was worried about them walking up from the station, if they went by train. She stayed at home with Jane, who was due back to school on Monday. They set out late on Sunday morning, the A1 was not too bad at all with only a few treacherous patches of ice, but Foxton village was buried under a wall of snow. The Press employees had cleared a pathway past Addison Cottages and their neighbour Mr Sizer had lit a fire in the back parlour to give them a warm welcome. Chic stayed for a cup of tea and then went on his way. The journey home was more difficult, it got much colder at dusk and the windscreen wipers kept freezing, he had to stop four times between Baldock and Richmond to clear the ice away and was very pleased to get home to a warm kitchen and a supper of jacket potatoes and corned beef.

January was bitterly cold with even more snow and everything remaining frozen solid until the last few days, when a thaw set in. Joyce then discovered that the outside toilet had sprung a leak, there was water everywhere. This was the last thing Chic needed when he got home from work on Monday night, it took him several hours to make a temporary repair. He vowed there and then that when the weather was warmer he would give each appliance its own personal stop cock. He was weary, everything took so much longer in the winter, the snow was a nuisance and the cold was no good for his chest pains, they had returned and were more frequent. Joyce noticed, she suggested a visit to the doctor, but he refused saying he did not have time. Then a customer returned the Popular complaining it had clutch problems. The car was the oldest in the fleet but it had not long since had a new clutch. Chic was angry and exhausted.

On Sunday morning, Joyce was up first and she took her husband a cup of tea, he was still fast asleep. When he eventually woke he thought he might have a bout of the flu, he ached all over, had stabbing pains in his chest and the worst headache since July 1944 when 612 FS had just crossed the River Caen and Sergeant King was killed at Cuverville. He appeared to be delirious, so Joyce rang for the doctor who arrived within the hour. He took his temperature, blood pressure and listened to his chest, it was not flu he diagnosed hypertension and nervous exhaustion. Chic was to have complete bed rest for at least a week. He wrote out a medical certificate for seven days and prescribed tablets to calm the nerves. Chic slept more or less constantly for four days and remained in bed for another two. He was worrying about everything and thought the house was unlucky, his guardian angel was noticeably absent.

29. SPAIN.

Joyce was extremely worried about her husband, but coped admirably with the business while he was ill. She cleaned the cars, their friend Dave came over to help out and fortunately nothing mechanical went wrong while Chic was out of action. The following Monday, he was booked in to see Doctor Gooding at the Cottage Hospital for an ECG, he was suffering from angina as well as hypertension with depression and given another week off work, with more tablets to take. The doctor prescribed a jolly good holiday and Joyce agreed, perhaps they could go abroad. Her friends at the Mollart's Whist Drive were talking about a chap called Martin Rooke who lived in Epsom somewhere. He organised holidays for railway workers and was now offering airline package holidays from Gatwick Airport to the Costa Brava. He filled a Caravelle *(jet airline)* from London to Barcelona and back, once a week throughout the holiday season. The plane carried eighty passengers who were then coached to a few select resorts, including Loret de Mar where the Hotel Dex was a very popular choice. Bookings had to be made in person, with all passengers present and his travel agency was close to Victoria Railway Station, an easy train journey from Surbiton.

Chic, Joyce and Jane rose before dawn on a very cold Sunday morning in March and caught the early train to Victoria. The holiday reservations were issued on a first come first serve basis and they wanted to travel the last two weeks in September when the car hire season would be winding down and the Spanish sun not too hot. When they arrived at the shop, the queue was already down the street and around the corner. They had to wait over an hour, but got exactly what they wanted and paid their deposit. Now all they needed to do was renew their passport and put Jane's name on it as a minor. As the days got warmer Chic improved, he was off the anti-depressants and back at work. It was easier to maintain the cars in mild weather although Chic would have liked a bit more sunshine. Joyce felt bad that they were not holidaying with her parents this year, so Chic suggested going to Bournemouth for a long week-end in August. Their friend Vi who worked with Dora had recently inherited some money, handed in her notice and bought a guest house with her husband Johnny. Chic, Joyce and Jane drove down in the Popular. Harry and Edie travelled by train and were already at the guest house when they arrived. The Cheshires were staying for a week at a cost of eight guineas all in. Vi's regime was run with military precision, it was like being back in the army:

breakfast at nine, evening meal at six, Sunday *(lunch only)*, at 1 pm sharp and if they wanted early tea it was an extra 4d. The rooms had hot and cold water and the beds, interior sprung mattresses with a shared toilet on every floor. There was only one bathroom and its use, was not encouraged. The house was just a short walk from the sea and the shops and the weather glorious, they spent all day on the beach, with picnic lunches. Chic and Jane built a racing car in the sand and swam in the

sea, while Joyce sat in the sun with her parents. Harry was quite adventurous, it was so hot he rolled his trousers up above his knees and took his tie off. The sun was burning his bald patch so Edie knotted a handkerchief for him to wear on his head while he dozed in the sunshine. Joyce thought how well they both looked, it was good to spend some time with her parents. On their return, Chic felt rested but was still not quite up to scratch.

It was not long before the day of their foreign holiday arrived, it was the first time Joyce and Jane had flown and Chic hoped it would be more comfortable than his flight home from Germany in the army Dakota back in 1945. Dave drove them to the airport. They arrived far too early but eventually were checked in and given boarding passes. After miles of corridors, it was a short bus ride across the runway to the plane where they queued on the steps while the passengers ahead were shown to their seats. After the safety talk and seatbelts were fastened, the air hostess brought around boiled sweets and the duty-free trolley, gin and tonic for Joyce, whisky for Chic and Jane was allowed Coca-Cola, a very special treat. After about one hour into the flight, a problem developed with one of the engines, the pilot announced that all passengers should fasten their seat belts, they were making an unscheduled landing at Perpignon airport. The descent was bumpy and the landing erratic but they were on *"terra firma."*

They were escorted off the plane to a reception area where free food and drink was provided for all. Chic took Jane outside to get some fresh air, the heat was searing, it took him straight back to Normandy. He noticed a scorpion scuttling across the dusty runway and pointed it out to Jane, they were on foreign territory. The engine could not be fixed immediately, but two coaches were organised to take the holidaymakers to their destinations in Spain, it was dark when they arrived. The journey over the Pyrenees was hair raising, the Spanish driver obviously knew the mountain roads well and drove accordingly, Joyce was terrified, Jane was asleep and Chic thought about his time in Italy. They were glad to arrive at the Hotel Dex, the room was pleasant enough with three single beds, a balcony overlooking the sea and a bathroom. Eugene their courier, met them in the bar and showed them around the restaurant, the pool and the silver sanded beach, it was paradise.

The holiday was very good medicine for the whole family, they made new friends, the sun shone continually and the sea was warm. They went on a boat trip to Callella, took a coach trip into the mountains for a barbecue and watched flamenco dancing in a night club. They were full board, but the hotel food was rather strange, they ate a few meals in local restaurants where the shell fish was amazing. The markets were full of exotic fruit and vegetables, it was even better than Italy, there was so much choice. Chic was fascinated by the architecture, and how the Spanish builders appeared to just plonk one storey on top of another. The Hotel Dex was brand new and they were adding another level, it looked like an afterthought. Hotels were popping up everywhere, much of Lloret de Mar was a building site but it did not spoil their enjoyment, Chic was interested in all of it. Everything shut down at noon for siesta, the shops closed, the builders put down their tools and the locals all disappeared inside. Then mid-afternoon the town started to wake, the shops stayed open until 10 pm, the clubs and restaurants until the early hours. They did not want the holiday to come to an end but all too soon they were boarding a coach to Barcelona airport, where they flew home on another Caravelle that was running two hours late. Thankfully, this time both engines remained fully functional and Dave was waiting for them at the barrier when they landed.

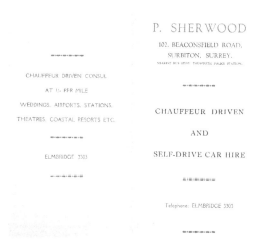

CHAUFFEUR DRIVEN CONSUL

AT 1/- PER MILE

WEDDINGS. AIRPORTS. STATIONS.

THEATRES. COASTAL RESORTS ETC.

ELMBRIDGE 3303

P. SHERWOOD

102, BEACONSFIELD ROAD,
SURBITON, SURREY.
NEAREST BUS STOP: TOLWORTH POLICE STATION.

CHAUFFEUR DRIVEN

AND

SELF-DRIVE CAR HIRE

Telephone: ELMBRIDGE 3303

The Ford Consul, two Anglias and the Popular.

30. CHAUFFEUR DRIVEN CAR HIRE.

Now they had settled in to their new home and Chic was feeling better, it was time for a meeting with their accountant. Mr Clutterbuck had retired but Peter who was still mad keen on go-karting, knew someone from the factory where he sourced the little kart engines. Chic was still dabbling with go-karts but he could not really spare the time, although that would change if he left Mollart's. Don Hamilton was a newly qualified accountant with a young family, who had just become a director in this small engine manufacturing business. He was keen to take on more clients and offered very competitive rates as well as being willing to visit the house for consultations. Joyce finished the books for the year end April 1963 and Chic delivered them to Don before they went on holiday. He had the prepared accounts and arrived with the paperwork ready for discussion on the tax implications and the way forward. The business was making a healthy profit and it would make sense to invest in some more vehicles. Chic presented Don with his idea for chauffeur driven car hire, alongside the self-drive. He told him about his experience in Italy with the colonel, his love of driving, his skills as a mechanic and his desire to be independent by working in the business full time. They discussed the cost of buying a new Ford Consul, the tariff, tax deductible expenses, mortgage repayments and the loss of Chic's wages. It all seemed feasible if they could raise enough cash to buy the Consul. It was agreed that Chic and Joyce should book an appointment with the bank manager at Barclays, up on the Ewell Road.

The bank agreed to provide P R Sherwood Esquire a business loan to purchase a Ford Consul and Chic went straight down to Willment's to see what they had got. There was an ex-showroom model available at a knock down price, it was black with a red interior. Chic haggled with them and managed to get more discount for cash, he was very pleased with his new acquisition. He now owned a Ford Popular De Luxe, two Ford Anglia De Luxes and a Standard Vanguard available for self-drive hire throughout the year at a maximum daily rate of £2.5.0d, £2.10.0d and £3.5.0d in the high season. All cars were fitted with heaters. There was a surcharge for hiring at weekends and bank holiday and a returnable £10 cash insurance deposit was required for all bookings. The chauffeur driven Ford Consul was charged at 1/- per mile and available for weddings, airports, stations, theatres, coastal resorts, etc.

FORD POPULAR DE LUXE

	1 Day	2 Days	3 Days	4 Days	5 Days	6 Days	7 Days
NOV. DEC. JAN. FEB. MAR.	£1.5.0	£2.10.0	£3.10.0	£4.5.0	£5.0.0	£5.10.0	£6.0.0
APRIL	£1.10.0	£3.0.0	£4.5.0	£5.0.0	£5.15.0	£6.10.0	£7.0.0
MAY	£1.15.0	£3.10.0	£5.0.0	£6.0.0	£6.10.0	£7.0.0	£7.10.0
JUNE	£2.0.0	£4.0.0	£5.10.0	£6.10.0	£7.10.0	£8.10.0	£9.10.0
JULY	£2.5.0	£4.10.0	£6.0.0	£7.10.0	£9.0.0	£10.10.0	£11.10.0
AUG.	£2.5.0	£4.10.0	£6.5.0	£7.15.0	£9.5.0	£10.15.0	£12.0.0
SEPT.	£2.0.0	£4.0.0	£5.10.0	£6.10.0	£7.10.0	£8.10.0	£9.10.0
OCT.	£1.10.0	£3.0.0	£4.5.0	£5.0.0	£5.15.0	£6.10.0	£7.0.0

FORD ANGLIA DE LUXE

	1 Day	2 Days	3 Days	4 Days	5 Days	6 Days	7 Days
NOV. DEC. JAN. FEB. MAR.	£1.10.0	£3.0.0	£4.5.0	£5.0.0	£5.15.0	£6.10.0	£7.0.0
APRIL	£1.15.0	£3.10.0	£4.15.0	£5.10.0	£6.10.0	£7.5.0	£8.0.0
MAY	£2.0.0	£4.0.0	£5.5.0	£6.5.0	£7.0.0	£7.15.0	£8.10.0
JUNE	£2.5.0	£4.10.0	£6.0.0	£7.10.0	£9.0.0	£9.15.0	£10.10.0
JULY	£2.10.0	£5.0.0	£7.0.0	£8.15.0	£10.10.0	£12.0.0	£13.10.0
AUG.	£2.10.0	£5.0.0	£7.5.0	£9.0.0	£10.15.0	£12.5.0	£14.0.0
SEPT.	£2.5.0	£4.10.0	£6.0.0	£7.10.0	£9.0.0	£9.15.0	£10.10.0
OCT.	£1.15.0	£3.10.0	£4.15.0	£5.10.0	£6.10.0	£7.5.0	£8.0.0

STANDARD VANGUARD

	1 Day	2 Days	3 Days	4 Days	5 Days	6 Days	7 Days
NOV. DEC. JAN. FEB. MAR.	£2.0.0	£4.0.0	£5.5.0	£6.5.0	£7.5.0	£8.5.0	£9.0.0
APRIL	£2.5.0	£4.10.0	£5.15.0	£7.0.0	£8.0.0	£9.0.0	£10.0.0
MAY	£2.10.0	£4.15.0	£6.5.0	£7.10.0	£9.0.0	£10.0.0	£11.0.0
JUNE	£2.15.0	£5.5.0	£7.5.0	£9.0.0	£10.10.0	£12.0.0	£13.10.0
JULY	£3.0.0	£5.10.0	£7.15.0	£9.15.0	£11.15.0	£13.15.0	£15.15.0
AUG.	£3.5.0	£5.15.0	£8.5.0	£10.10.0	£12.10.0	£14.10.0	£16.10.0
SEPT.	£2.15.0	£5.5.0	£7.5.0	£9.0.0	£10.10.0	£12.0.0	£13.10.0
OCT.	£2.5.0	£4.10.0	£5.15.0	£7.0.0	£8.0.0	£9.0.0	£10.0.0

SATURDAY & SUNDAY only: 5/- per day extra.

BANK HOLIDAYS: £3 surcharge, minimum hire one week.

ALL RATES ARE FOR UNLIMITED MILEAGE AND INCLUDE INSURANCE.

Driving Licence must be shown. Hirer must be over 21 and under 60 yrs, with 12 months regular driving experience and must pay a £10 cash Insurance deposit which will be refunded on safe return of vehicle.

When available, cars may be collected on evening previous to hire at no extra cost.

ALL CARS HAVE   FITTED HEATERS

They were already taking chauffeur bookings for the build up to Christmas, mainly to London hotels and theatres with a few trips to Heathrow and Gatwick airport. It was time for Chic to hand in his notice at work, he left at the end of November. He was given a good send off in the club bar, but would still see all his chums as he and Joyce were keen to remain members of the social club and the Surbiton Sports Club where all the karting enthusiasts hung out.

December arrived and there was much to do. They stocked up on maps, directories and worked out prices for popular venues. They needed headed notepaper, business cards and invoice books. Printed matter was expensive, they chose Knapp Drewitt who also owned The Surrey Comet. The advertising and printing costs amounted to almost as much as the licensing of all the cars and five times more than the cost of the telephone. Chic ran a stand pipe down to the yard so he could wash the cars easily and sorted out the garage. Only four cars could be fitted in if he was working on one, but that was not a problem as usually at least one was booked out and there was always plenty of space to park in Beaconsfield and King Charles Road, particularly when he was late back. He often did not get home until the small hours and he didn't like crashing about with the back gates in the middle of the night. It was a real luxury to have a lie in some mornings and he often caught up on some sleep by napping on the lounge window seat in the afternoons. It was a glorious place to snooze when the sun was shining through the picture windows. When he was not driving he was working on the cars, how did he ever do all this and work at Mollart's as well?

After one unfortunate experience when a prostitute tried to get a free lift by masquerading as a client, he made a rule that customers were required to book both ways, if he did not take them to London he would not bring them back, to ensure he knew exactly who he was meeting. There were also the Black Cabbies *(London taxi drivers)* who were angry over the relaxed laws allowing mini cab firms to tout their business both within and outside the law. Chic did his best to steer clear of all trouble, but sometimes it was unavoidable. He drew on his experiences in Italy and always kept his wits about him.

Joyce wanted her parents to visit at Christmas again. Neither of them could drive and they did not have a telephone, it was considered an unnecessary gadget that would never catch on, so she regularly corresponded by letter with her mother. On Sunday the 15th December the telephone rang early in the morning while Joyce was making tea, Chic was asleep he had not got to bed until gone 3 am. The operator asked if she would accept a reverse charges telephone call from Mrs Looker her parent's next-door neighbour. Ruth explained that Edie was sitting next to her but did not wish to speak on the telephone. Harry had died in the night and the doctor was due to visit shortly. Joyce was shocked and responded instantly by telling them she would drive to Foxton as soon as she had organised herself. She woke Chic.

The Vanguard was not booked out, she thought she could drive up there with Jane and stay a couple of days. He wasn't very happy about her driving on her own with the possibility of snow, but there was no choice he had chauffeuring commitments. He jumped out of bed, quickly dressed into his overalls and went outside to check the Vanguard: oil, water, windscreen wash, tyres, all was good. By 10.30 Joyce and Jane were on their way to Cambridgeshire. They had done that journey dozens of times, but Joyce had never driven on her own before. The journey passed without incident and they arrived in Foxton just before 2 pm. She parked outside The Press, her mother was so pleased to see them, the doctor had just left, he thought Harry had suffered a heart attack.

Chic telephoned Ruth at 6 pm to check Joyce had arrived safely, she ran to fetch her. Joyce was upset, her mother was in shock and the doctor had given her a sedative. They were waiting for an ambulance to take her father to the mortuary where the coroner would carry out a post mortem the following day and they were expecting the vicar after evensong. She really hoped the funeral could be arranged before Christmas. The vicar was very kind, he knew Harry and Edie very well and offered to carry out Harry's remembrance service in St Laurence Church free of charge. It was the least he could do, Harry was a member of the church choir and could always be relied upon to step in when a substitute organist was needed. Joyce's mother wanted Eden Lilley in Cambridge to arrange the funeral. Joyce rang them first thing on Monday morning and they agreed to send out a representative that same afternoon. By the time the undertaker arrived, the coroner had finished the post mortem, Harry suffered a retroperitoneal haemorrhage caused by an aneurism of the abdominal aorta, there was no need for an inquest.

Edie wanted Harry to be laid out in the front parlour, he was brought back to the cottage on Tuesday afternoon. While Joyce drove to Cambridge to register the death on Wednesday, a long line of mourners visited Edie and Harry at the cottage, including Doug and his family who were staying with the Condors in Caxton Lane. The church service was arranged for 11 am on Thursday morning with a gathering back at the cottage before the cremation in Cambridge later on. Chic caught the early train up to Foxton to attend the funeral and stay overnight. The family walked to the church just as they had done when Joyce and Chic got married, he remembered that happy day, with the sunshine and a life to look forward to. Today it was cold with drizzle turning to sleet. He also thought of his friend Jenni again, strange how the weather triggered so many memories.

The Vanguard was needed back by tea time on Friday, it was booked out over Christmas. Joyce wanted Edie to come back with them, it took her a little while to tidy up the house and pack her suitcase but they were on the road before dinner time. They stopped at a nice Italian Restaurant on the Great North Road near Elstree. One of Chic's customers had told him that it was frequented by actors from the film studios, who Joyce thought was marvellous, but there were none there today. They all ordered the same; pollo alla cacciatiora with patate arrosto, *(chicken and potatoes.)* Chic enjoyed the chicken despite the tomato sauce being rather strong, Joyce ate most of hers, but there was

214

too much garlic. Edie and Jane barely ate two mouthfuls between them, although Jane polished off all the bread sticks that were arranged in a glass on the table. They had ice cream for pudding, Chic paid the bill and they were soon on their way and back home indoors by half past three. He went straight out to the yard to prepare the Vanguard ready for collection, while Joyce settled Edie upstairs and cooked beans on toast for tea. He had a chauffeur booking at 7 pm to drive four people to a dinner dance at The Bridge House on Reigate Hill, with a return booked for 1 am. It would probably be past two before he got to bed and he had a busy weekend following, it being the last before Christmas.

Christmas was spent quietly. Chic was driving, he could charge double time on Christmas Day. He had four chauffeuring jobs, two in the morning, one local and one to Guildford and then the returns, one around tea time and Guildford at 9 pm. Christmas dinner was fitted in between and it was all quite relaxed. He finished his day's work by ten-o-clock when he opened a bottle of barley wine as a night cap with a hot mince pie. He had earned nearly nine pounds in just one day plus a good tip, but he was in reflective mood, with Joyce and her mother grieving. He thought about Grandpa Plant who before Chic was born worked as a wherryman on the Surbiton Ferry at the weekends, to boost his income as a basketmaker. He would come home from a day's rowing, ferrying the rich folk back and forth and throw gold sovereigns onto the table. He often got more in tips on a Sunday, than he could earn in a whole week as a basketmaker. He told his grandsons stories of the goings on, particularly with the theatrical and literary folk, who were the best tippers. Chic also remembered Grandpa's advice;

> *"If you are honest to yourself,*
> *and know your place, you can be happy."*

There was no New Year's Eve party this year, it was Harry's birthday on the 2ⁿᵈ, he would have been seventy-two and none of them felt like celebrating. Jack Stirling popped over with his wife Helen and daughter Heather for a drop of whisky just before midnight but they were all asleep by 1 am. Edie was very low, she saw no joy in anything and had even stopped knitting. She stayed while the weather remained dreary, but the sunshine came out in the middle of the month and she wanted to go home. There was no work on mid-week, so Chic offered to drive her back to Foxton, to make sure everything was working properly. He didn't say anything but he put his tool box in the boot, it was highly likely there could be a frozen pipe or two with the cottage being left unheated for so long. Joyce stayed in Tolworth, she needed to be there for Jane, when she got home from school. Mr and Mrs Sizer had done a grand job keeping an eye on the cottage, there was a lovely fire burning in the back parlour when they arrived, but the cold tap in the kitchen was dripping. Edie told Chic not to worry about it, the landlord would sort it out. She plugged in her electric bed pan, to warm up on the kitchen table, she wanted to air the bed, but still had no electricity upstairs. She was happier now she was back home; Chic left her to it.

By 1965 everything had settled down. The business was going well, the self-drive car hire was popular with customers returning year on year to hire their holiday transport, although more and more people were purchasing their own family cars. Chic wanted to celebrate his twenty-first wedding anniversary with his wife, family and friends at *"The Bridge House"*, on Reigate Hill. He and Joyce, treated nine guests to a marvellous four course, evening meal on Thursday the 20ᵗʰ May. The service was impeccable and the atmosphere jovial, he gave a toast, to his wife and daughter, he was the luckiest man in the world. The bill amounted to £17 19s 6d, he gave them two £10 notes and told the waiter to keep the change. He knew how much a good tip was appreciated.

Chic thought the way forward was definitely chauffeuring. He was not competing with the mini cab business he would offer an upmarket service, a professional, uniformed chauffeur wearing a peaked cap in an affordable vehicle. In 1967 after discussion with the accountant he sold one of the Anglia's for £230 and the Consul for £185. He put the money towards two C registration Ford Zephyrs, to enable him to provide two matching cars for weddings and funerals. This of course required him to find a couple of drivers to help him out on busy

216

weekends. No one was safe from his persuasion: Jack Roberts the mobile green grocer, Len Tidy the meter reader, Bob a client and colleague from Mollart's, the list went on. There were other chauffeur businesses popping up in the area and Chic made sure he got to know them all: Oakes, Harding, Day and Ribbins, to name but a few.

Jack Roberts and Chic. 1970s.

The following year, the self-drive business was closed down and Chic sold the two remaining Anglias for £250 each and bought another second-hand black Zephyr, MYU 966 D with the proceeds, his fleet was complete, three matching Fords.

Once all the self-drive cars had gone much of Chic's work was evenings and week-ends, leaving him spare time to embark on some home improvements. He had already rebuilt and extended the garage to hold three cars as well as two in the yard. It was time to come inside the house and make a few alterations before central heating was fitted. The first thing was to get rid of the panelled interior doors downstairs and fit fully glazed ones to bring in natural light. Chic also thought he could add a frosted picture window between the dining room and the lounge and in the hallway. The dividing wall was load bearing, but that did not

217

daunt Chic, he ordered an RSJ and set about knocking out a few bricks with the help of his old school mate Alf Rockall. They fitted the beam, opened up the hole, 8 feet wide by 3 feet high and Alf made a bespoke hardwood frame before Chic ordered the fluted Pilkington glass from Hill Aldam in Red Lion Road. The hallway was easier, that just needed the largest sheet of glass available, to bring light flooding in from the glazed front door.

Brian Broadhurst was a heating engineer who lived in Chessington, Chic trusted him and his men to do a good job, although he was not the cheapest. The house was turned upside down with plumbers working in every room, first upstairs and then downstairs. Every chap had a radio and they all listened to different stations, it was like Piccadilly Circus for several weeks. Chic was busy building and decorating while the work continued, it nearly drove Joyce mad, she took hostage in the kitchen despite the constant flow of men walking back and forth to the gas boiler now housed in what had been the coal shed, shortly to become the utility room. Then on an extremely cold spring day the heating was turned on, the house was as warm as toast like the height of summer, no more woolly bed socks, no more ice on the inside of the windows, the disruption was worth every penny. The lounge window seat was now heated from below, the perfect place for Chic to nap when he had been working late the night before.

In 1967 Bye Pass Motors was compulsory purchased by the Ministry of Transport for essential road development. Chic was sad to see the old place being knocked down, but thought the new road plans for the A3 would be a great improvement, the new underpass promised to remove all the congestion on The Toby Jug roundabout. He had bought most of his cars from Mr Fox, but when Berkeley Square Garages took over they moved away from Ford to Triumph. Chic bought the cream and tan Standard Vanguard off them for use as a larger self-drive hire car, but it had some niggly glitches, he got rid of it and stuck to Ford after that. He watched with interest as the building was demolished, it seemed such a shame that all the 1920s fixtures and fittings were being destroyed. He often popped in to chat to the workmen, he knew most of them and usually returned home with some treasure, a chrome door handle or a light fitting or two. He was refurbishing the kitchen and the art deco glass light shade he had just scrounged was perfect for hanging over the kitchen table.

Now they had central heating, the Rayburn was superfluous. They went off to the Ideal Home Exhibition to look at kitchens. Leisure had just brought out a split-level gas cooker and hob divided by a stainless-steel work top with integral Formica cupboards underneath, but it was too big to fit in the fireplace. Chic had a solution, he knocked down the left pier and fitted an RSJ, providing more than enough room. He was now confident with structural work and embarked on a huge picture window running the whole width of the kitchen. Then he decided to recess the old fridge freezer into the wall to save space and Alf built some extra cupboards while Chic modernised all the existing doors by laminating them with Formica to match the oven, it was a long slow job.

The couple enjoyed a varied social life and still found time to have holidays with friends, although not always for a whole two weeks, it was difficult to leave the business for more than a few days. After Jack Stirling retired, the family moved back to Aberdeenshire, Joyce, Chic and Jane went to stay in their rambling granite house for a couple of weeks in May. Their trusted friend Bob was willing to use his holiday from Mollart's to hold the fort while they drove up to Scotland. Nancy the cleaning lady took bookings and cooked his meals, Bob was enjoying the responsibility, most of the clients were pleasant and appreciative, until …..

One evening, a young lady who resided at The Hotel Antionette in Surbiton had booked a car to go to Shepherd Market in Kensington, wait and return. Bob picked her up at 8 pm and dropped her off at the booked address where she asked him to wait outside for one hour. She then appeared and asked him to drive less than a mile away, where she asked him to wait again and then for a third time. On her return she wanted to go to a Soho nightclub and after twenty minutes or so, she invited Bob in for drinks. He did not feel he could refuse, he only wanted a small beer, he was not a drinker. The club was sleazy, filled with smoke and scantily clad girls were dancing on the stage. It was 5 am when they arrived back in Surbiton. Bob worked out the price but she did not want to pay, she offered her body instead, he was terrified. He told her he would get the sack if he did not collect the fare and she reluctantly paid up. Chic drove this lady many times and was worried that Bob would panic if he knew beforehand what was involved. It was too good an earner to pass up, she always offered her body to Chic and he always said no, he did not know where she had been and anyway he would never be unfaithful to his darling wife.

Joe and Maureen Hall with Joyce and Chic. 1982.

Chic and Joyce had developed a taste for the good life, they worked hard and deserved it. Their clients included the great and the good from all walks of life, Chic was learning a great deal about how the other half lived and discovering new venues and experiences all the time. After watching *"Come Dancing"* on the TV, they were learning ballroom dancing at Claygate Village Hall and loved a bit of Latin American music, Pepe Jaramello was a particular favourite. At Christmas, New Year, birthdays and anniversaries, there would always be a celebration of some sort, often at the house with dancing, eating and drinking but especially laughter. On these occasions, when Chic thought it was time for the party to end, he would appear in his pyjamas with a night cap and candle, much to the amusement of the guests and his wife. He and Joyce were slightly incompatible in that she was a night owl and would often stay up long after Chic had gone to bed.

Chic in pyjamas, with Joyce, Bob & Joan Wakefield.

They now had several new friends from the dancing classes including Nora, a widowed lady who helped run the club. She and Joyce became great friends and attended evening classes at Hollyfield Road School to learn contract bridge, they became a formidable team and won many

220

competitions. Nora volunteered at Esher Cancer Research and invited Joyce along, where she made even more friends who also became customers, Sherwood Car Hire had an increasing circle of contacts. Chic far preferred this way of working, he did not think much of the Chamber of Commerce, Freemasons or Rotary Club. He liked to make his own way in business without the help of pompous pen pushers full of their own self-importance, although he was not averse to driving them and taking their money. Frank Sinatra had just released a new record, *"I Did it my Way,"* and Chic agreed whole heartedly.

Glenna, Chic, Joyce, Joe, Norah, Maureen. Claygate Dance Club.

One memorable holiday in April, was Majorca. They were staying in a four star hotel and met Stan and Doris who lived in Banstead. They owned an apartment in Spain which they visited on a regular basis, but also liked to holiday at different resorts around the Mediterranean. Stan was a retired bank manager and bought the apartment as an investment, this gave Chic an idea. When they returned home, he went to see his brother Charlie who now lived in a large house on Epsom Downs and still owned two houses on the Sunray Estate, as well as his betting shop in Epsom. Charlie and Phyllis enjoyed going abroad, how about they go halves and buy an apartment in Spain.

Joyce was not so keen on the idea, her mother had just been told by her landlord at The Press, that she would have to vacate the house she had lived in all her married life. She was offered a small cottage in Caxton Lane but Edie did not want to move anywhere. Joyce suggested buying a little semi-detached bungalow that was for sale in Foxton High Street, they were in a position to increase their mortgage and Edie could pay them rent. Chic listened to the plan, but first wanted to join his brother on a recce to the Costa del Sol to see what properties were available for purchase. They returned rather disillusioned, property was cheap but management costs were high. They also discovered that dealing with Spanish bureaucracy was a minefield and sterling restrictions would thwart their liking for paying with cash. By the time Joyce met them at Gatwick they had decided to shelve the idea. Joyce immediately began the process of purchasing Grey Gables for her mother, it was a simple transaction, Edie knew the owner who had moved away and her sister lived next door with her husband, they proved to be very kind and friendly neighbours. She moved in at the end of July and Joyce took Jane to stay for a week in the holidays to help Edie get her settled.

Joyce Romine kept in touch by letter from Texas and came to England every few years to visit her mother in Melbourne, Cambridgeshire. Chic always met her from the airport and drove her back to Tolworth, where she would stay for a few days at the beginning and end of each trip. Her husband Creighton did not like to travel, but this time she was bringing her youngest son Lee, he was just about to start medical school to train as a dentist and had never been to England. On this occasion, Joyce went with Chic to the airport, they arrived in plenty of time and went up onto the roof to watch the plane land. Joyce was always pleased to see her friend, they talked about old times and were terrible gigglers. Chic thoroughly enjoyed planning an itinerary, they ate at *"The Bridge House,"* saw Bruce Forsyth at *"The Talk of the Town,"* and went shopping at the Portobello Market in Notting Hill.

The Mansion House in the city was a regular destination for Sherwood Car Hire, Chic was on first name terms with all the doormen. He took a chance and drove his American guests up to the front door, George was on duty and it was all very quiet, Chic dropped him a handsome tip and George pointed to a private parking space. Lee, Joyce and Chic were lucky enough to be shown around the Lord Mayor of London's official residence, a magnificent eighteenth century building. Chic had seen it all before but his guests were amazed and delighted, this was a rare treat. They also visited the Kennedy Memorial at Runnymede and looked around St George's Chapel at Windsor Castle when the Queen was in residence, they could not have asked for a better guide.

All this had to be fitted in between chauffeuring work, it was quite exhausting. On the night they were going to *"The Talk of the Town,"* Chic was booked to take a regular client a local head mistress to Paddington Station, to catch a train at 9 am. He got her there in plenty of time, but was too early for his meet at London Heathrow so he parked up and went to the cafeteria. He dropped the cup and spilled hot coffee all over his shirt and tie and down his trousers. He managed to clean himself up in the men's public toilets, he was soaking wet but his suit jacket would cover it. He did not like using these facilities, there was always at least one dubious character loitering in the wash room, he preferred to steer well clear of any possible misunderstanding. He then rang Joyce from a pay phone on the station concourse to see if she had any flight information, the plane from Hamburg was on time. He was meeting an account customer, the director of a magazine company. Chic liked him, he was a personable chap and always appreciative. The traffic was worse than usual, by the time he parked up at Terminal 1 he was late. He ran in to the barrier but there was no sign of his client, he went to the enquiries desk, all passengers had collected their luggage. He found a phone box and rang Joyce who had been pacing the floor waiting for him to ring. The client had telephoned to find out where Chic was, he could not wait and had jumped in a black cab. Chic was annoyed, all that effort, a lost fare and bad feeling from one of his best customers. The golden rule;

"You are only as good as your last job."

He drove home exhausted and needed a very long nap on the window seat to recover for the evening. One consolation, Bob was driving them up to town and back, Chic would be able to relax and have a few drinks, Bruce Forsyth was superb with his guest Sammy Davis Junior, the whole show was outstanding.

Something that did irritate Chic to the extreme, was being treated differently to his drivers. He believed he gave the best service, but Bob, Jack and Len nearly always got bigger tips. He tested out this plan on a few occasions when meeting business clients flying in from Europe and America. One evening on a dark and dreary November night he was booked for an airport meet, they were friends of a regular client, a comedy actress who lived in Kingston Hill. The meet went well, but the driving difficult, the weather was atrocious, with rain turning to sleet. The passengers made polite conversation, Chic introduced himself as Ron. They asked if he had any more jobs after them, he said not, despite his boss Mr Sherwood wanting him to work later. They then asked if Mr Sherwood was a good employer. Ron replied;

"He's a moody so and so."

Chic thought it all a bit of a joke, but they gave him a £5 tip. He felt guilty afterwards and owned up the next time he drove the actress. She thought it hilarious.

"So Chic, what do I owe you? Or should I call you Ron?"

He replied,
"Just call me Sir Percy."

She also gave him a whopping tip.

Airport meets were often fraught with complications, many clients wandered about instead of waiting at the designated meeting point. It could be particularly tricky meeting strangers at the airport. Either Chic or Joyce would always ring flight enquiries before leaving home to check landing times and then it was a case of waiting at the appropriate barrier with a name sign, it could be a very long wait with no means of contact. On one occasion a man approached him and said he was the said customer, he only had hand luggage which he kept at his side and asked where he was booked to be taken. When Chic told him, the gentleman said his plans had changed and he needed to go straight into the West End of London. The booking was on account and Chic was obliged to do as asked, when they arrived in Conduit Street the chap leapt out of the car and did a runner. Chic felt very stupid, from that day on he always checked the name on the luggage before escorting a client to his vehicle.

The 1960s was a decade of optimism and Chic was caught up in it. When Apollo 11 landed on the moon in the summer of sixty-nine he watched every single moment that was televised. It was only thirty years since the outbreak of WW2, how the world had changed and he along with it. He was managing his angina, with exercise and half an aspirin a day. The driving did not help his spine, he often suffered from back pain, but he took a daily dose of cod liver oil to grease his joints, put a board under his mattress and frequently hung like a bat from the garage rafters to stretch himself out. He still suffered from short bouts of depression but believed he could physically work his way through it, knocking down a wall was always good therapy. On one occasion when Joyce went into Surbiton Cottage hospital for a week to have an operation on her varicose veins, Chic decided to surprise her. There was not much work on and Chic was at a loose end. York stone fireplaces were all the rage, he decided to modernise the landing bannisters that

224

had been panelled in by the previous owner. He ripped the whole thing out, ordered two chunky teak beams, some spaceframe and a cubic yard of York stone bricks. He then proceeded to build a double brick wall just three bricks high and inserted the spaceframe every 6 feet to support the rail. By the time Joyce came out of hospital, Alf had helped Chic fit a chunky, teakwood rail and he was busy varnishing it. She thought it looked rather good, Chic wanted to start on the lounge fireplace, she readily agreed.

By 1970 he had the bit between his teeth and was constantly working on the house when not driving or servicing the cars and his love of knocking down walls came to the fore again. He went to Galleon Fireplaces to discuss the making of an asymmetric fireplace for housing a living gas fire. The result was a huge York stone and quarry tiled hearth that ran half the length of the lounge. An L shaped steel hood was fitted over yet another RSJ that replaced one of the fireplace piers, the extended hearth was the perfect place to stand the television. The finished result was the height of fashion fit to feature in any home design magazine.

His love of Spanish architecture inspired him to be even more ambitious, he wanted to knock out the frosted glass window that he fitted ten years earlier and create a walk-through brick archway between the lounge and the dining room, stretching for thirty-seven feet. The kitchen door had already been removed and now the lounge doorway was redundant he bricked it up to include an exposed brick port hole. The dining room fireplace was given a makeover with an ornamental fire grate and both rooms were wallpapered with anaglypta and painted white. New white and gold paisley carpet was laid throughout, modern leather sofas and chairs were purchased from Bentalls, along with a large dining room suite called Toledo, it all looked magnificent. Spain had come to Tolworth.

31. THE DAIMLER MAJESTIC.

Day's, the florist on the Ewell Road regularly recommended Sherwood Car Hire to their customers when they were getting married. Next door was a branch of Frederick Paine the undertakers, with rear premises for parking their limousines in Beaconsfield Road. Chic got to know the manager very well, he was occasionally asked to help out with a saloon car for a funeral and sometimes stepped in as a coffin bearer. He found these occasions oddly enjoyable, the banter behind the scenes was often hilarious, it appeared that the morbidity of their work brought out an irreverent sense of humour in them all. When Chic was converting the brick coal hole into a utility room he wanted a slab of marble to fit over the sink. He went along to the undertakers to see if the stone mason might have some offcuts and was invited to the yard at the rear of the manager's house in Kingston. This chap was also rather keen on DIY and very proud of his house, he wanted to show Chic around. The master bedroom had a whole wall of fitted wardrobes. The mahogany doors were coffin lids with brass handles and trim from the undertaker's stock, all considered perks of the job. It really tickled Chic, it was another story to tell his customers.

Chic was again in need a project. The wedding business was proving lucrative but he was competing with companies like Dawnier Motors in Stoneleigh, who had bigger and better cars. It appeared that brides now wanted to travel to the altar in style and their fiancées were willing to pay a premium price. After all the bride's parents were still footing most of the wedding bill and the young seemed to have plenty of cash to splash around. He still worked with Frederick Paine and the manager told him that Dawnier were selling one of their limousines because the engine needed some attention, it was smoking badly. The black car was previously owned by the Queen, it had very sound bodywork with a grey leather and walnut interior. In January 1973 Chic paid £450 for his Daimler Majestic limousine, it just needed a bit of tweaking in time for his daughter's wedding in August. He was back in his element again and down the garage every spare moment, he decided to take the engine out and give it a de-coke. He could not believe the quality of the parts and praised the workmanship, even the seals were engineered from steel, most cars just had rubber seals. It was a joy to work on, Joyce had trouble getting him in for meals, he was obsessed. They now had a wall telephone in the kitchen where Joyce kept the desk diary, Chic wanted an extension telephone connected in the garage. He had a transistor radio, an electric kettle, tea, coffee and biscuits. It was his second home.

The wedding planning took up much of Joyce's time over the next few months with some input from Chic. It could not have been more different to their wartime wedding in May 1944. Chic thought Oatlands Park in Weybridge a good venue, where they celebrated their silver wedding anniversary in 1969, it was a residential temperance hotel run by Quakers. The ballroom seated seventy-five people, the food was excellent, the facilities grand and if you wanted to consume alcohol you brought your own, they did not charge corkage. The service was at Saint Mary's in Long Ditton, a pretty church with a quaint lychgate. What Chic did not know was that many of his Sherwood ancestors had been baptised, married and buried there.

Edie was now rather frail and spending much more time in Surbiton. She was prone to being a little superstitious and did not approve of Jane making her own wedding dress. She told her;

"Every stitch will be a stitch of sorrow."

Jane was embroidering her dress and the marriage was obviously doomed in Edie's eyes, but they all took her prediction with a pinch of salt. After all, Joyce made her own wedding dress and she had not suffered too badly. Chic liked and trusted Jane's fiancée, as soon as he came of age he was recruited as a part-time chauffeur. It was very part time as Ken worked very long hours in London, but it was helpful to have him on standby.

On the day of the wedding Jack was booked to drive Chic and his daughter in the Daimler, its first job. The sun was shining, the limousine was parked out the front in Beaconsfield Road and all the neighbours came out to wave them off. As they drove slowly along, more people came out of their houses, Jane felt like a princess and Chic was extremely proud. Even the undertakers at the end of the road stood on their forecourt and waved. After the reception some guests were invited back to the house for a party, the garden was festooned with lights, there were sausages cooking on a BBQ in the yard and the house was full of music. The newlyweds did not want to miss the party, they came back too before driving home to their maisonette in Kent. They were flying to Minorca the following day for two weeks. Chic remembered his honeymoon, five days in Tolworth and a weekend in

Foxton, before leaving his wife for army life back in Aldershot, two weeks before D-Day, he didn't wish that on anyone.

Chic was very kind to his mother-in-law, but having her living with them did put a strain on him and Joyce. The business was often stressful and they could not escape it, one reason why Chic loved his garage so much. Small things began to niggle him, he was irritated when the council painted zig-zag lines on the zebra crossing right across his yard gates, preventing him parking and making it difficult to manoeuvre the cars in and out. He now had three Ford Zephyrs and the Daimler and was now unable to park on King Charles Road. The new seatbelt laws were also a damn nuisance, just days after he fitted them in the front seats of the Zephyrs, one of his customers got caught in the strap and twisted her ankle. It was ridiculous to expect a professional driver to *"belt up"* each time he got in and out of the car. Edie's bungalow had also become a burden, every time they went back to Foxton there was too much to do, it was no longer a pleasant day out. He knew he needed a holiday.

Both Joyce and Jane had visited Joyce in America over the last couple of years for an extended break. Chic would have loved to go to the USA, but he could not afford to take more than two weeks off and the flights were too expensive to go for a short break. He decided to take pot luck at the airport. He packed a suitcase and with a wallet full of dollars he asked Joyce to drive him to Gatwick. He told her he would ring when he was fixed up. Joyce was happy to hold the fort in his absence, but worried for his safety. General booking enquiries often had information on available flights, he asked for a cheap return flight to somewhere sunny. There was a flight later that afternoon to Dubrovnik in Yugoslavia but no suitable return, but he could fly back from the capital Zagreb in ten days' time, it was about three hundred and fifty miles north. Chic collected his tickets and exchanged a few dollars for Yugoslavian Dinar. He kept most of them back, he had read that communist countries liked trading with American dollars. He bought a map, a phrase book and made his way to the telephone kiosk, to tell Joyce he was flying to Yugoslavia and give her his return flight details. She told him to be very careful, he laughed and told her he loved her.

32. YUGOSLAVIA.

The adventure had begun. President Tito had recently relaxed the rules on tourism, Yugoslavia was a communist country and Chic was looking forward to a new experience and some sunshine. On arrival in Dubrovnik he booked in to a luxury hotel for one night, although the term *"luxury"* was rather debatable, but the receptionist did speak English. He gathered up a few brochures and went to his room to plan his itinerary. The following morning he asked the hotel staff to book him into a hotel near Zagreb airport for one night, a week on Tuesday, he was flying back to England on Wednesday afternoon. He then went for a walk around the city, ate lunch in a taverna and chatted to some English tourists who were on a package holiday. They were going to the island of Korcula the next day to visit Lumbarda, a coastal village with glorious sandy beaches. He asked where they were staying and what time they were catching the coach, they were boarding at 8 am. He thought he might tag along and see if there were any spaces. He settled his hotel bill and arrived in good time for the coach, the driver was standing outside smoking a cigarette and he spoke broken English. It did not take Chic long to persuade the driver to let him board the coach, after he showed him a few Dinar. The tour guide spoke excellent English and was curious not to find P Sherwood on her passenger list, but there were spare seats and he was welcome to join them. It was only one hours drive to the ferry, where all passengers disembarked and were told to meet back by 6 pm. Chic grabbed his suitcase and jumped on the boat, the Adriatic was azure blue, just like the Italian Riviera that he visited thirty years ago.

On arriving in Korcula, the first thing he did was find a bar to see if he could get a bed for the night. The town was full of small hostelries and most offered bed and breakfast, the first one was a shared room, the second had a drunken landlord, but the third was managed by a very pleasant Croatian lady and her daughter Ana who spoke excellent English. She asked Chic why he was travelling alone, he showed her a photograph of his wife and daughter and explained he was making his way to Zagreb to go back home to England. He would like to stay two nights because he wished to spend a day at Lumbarda. They showed him to a very basic but clean room with a small double bed, a bedside table with jug and bowl for washing and one chair. The toilets were outside. He settled himself in and asked the best place to go to eat. He arrived back after supper to find the hostelry overflowing with locals, he joined them in a glass of wine before retiring to bed. The next morning, he woke early, breakfast was a delightful mix of bread, cheese, tomatoes and fruit with strong coffee. His hosts told him there was a bus to the beach at Lombarda, it was only a twenty minute journey and the return ticket was a couple of dinar. Ana said;

"Have a good day"

Chic spent a glorious day at the beach, swimming and sun bathing, he made sure he put plenty of sun cream on, the sun was deceptively strong. He ate freshly caught fish on the beach and chatted with a few locals to see where he should go next and how he should get there.

On Thursday morning he said goodbye to his lovely hosts who sent him on his way with a picnic and kisses on both cheeks. This time he caught the ferry to Split, it was nearly a four hour trip but the sea was calm and there were stunning views along the Adriatic coastline. He really did wish Joyce could be with him now, she would love it. He thought about all the adventures he had in Italy after the war without his darling wife, and then their trip to Europe in 1947. Joyce was not an adventurer, she liked to plan ahead and on this occasion she would be an anxious travel companion. Chic's first sight of Split was the magnificent waterside marina that seemed to go on for miles, it appeared to be wealthy, private yachts jostled with fishing boats and there was a naval presence, it reminded him of Trieste. Chic decided the best policy was to check into a hotel and asked for recommendations at the ferry masters office. He was pointed towards the old town, if he walked that way he would pass several establishments. The route took him through a huge bustling market, there was produce he had never seen before, fruit, vegetables and herbs, he was fascinated. The high walls of the old town sheltered narrow streets with tiny cafes, bars and shops selling souvenirs. He stopped to browse and bought Joyce a leather purse. He asked again for somewhere to stay, there was a small hotel at the end of the street. It looked rather shabby from the outside but on entry it seemed pleasant enough, they had a double room available and Chic took it.

He spent the afternoon exploring the city including Diocletian's Palace, where he tagged along with an American group who were on a guided tour. He got talking to one friendly couple from Texas, he told them about his friend Joyce who married a GI. They were on a whistle stop tour and tomorrow they were off to Zadar to see the Roman Forum. Chic asked if there were any spaces on the coach, they introduced him to the tour guide and after a brief discussion and several dinar changing hands, Chic was booked on the coach to Zadar leaving at ten the next morning. The road took them through beautiful countryside with the sea to the west and mountains to the east, the fertile valleys housed small farms, orchards and vineyards creating a verdant patchwork much the same as he had seen in Italy. The people looked poor and worn down by hard work, with skin like leather from exposure to the sun, but they usually had a smile, they were a friendly race. Chic was not that interested in the Roman ruins, he had seen plenty back in 1946 and took the opportunity to tap the guide on her local knowledge. She knew of a "tiristicne kmetije" *(farmhouse that offered bed and breakfast)* at Murvika on the way to Novigrad, they could drop him off on route.

The family were delightful, there were four children aged seven to sixteen and they all helped on the farm, growing tomatoes, zucchini and thousands of beans. They kept goats and cows and served their own cheese for breakfast with the biggest tomatoes he had ever seen in his life. They made him very welcome and showed him on a map that he must visit the lakes at Plitvice on his way to Zagreb. It was now Saturday and he had time to take it easy, he decided to stay for at least one more night. Josip, the eldest boy could drive the truck and the children were all going to a beach near Nin the nest day. They wanted Chic to go with them? They were packed off by their mother with a large picnic, the kids in the back and Chic in the passenger seat. This really took him back to his army days and he was impressed by the lad's driving. The town was on a salt water lagoon accessed by an ancient stone bridge. They drove around to the far side where the lagoon was divided from the sea by a long beach of the finest silver sand. Josip parked up, it was already getting busy. The children showed Chic where it was safe to swim, they were like eels weaving in and out, diving and splashing, he sat on the beach watching, it was an unforgettable day. That evening he ate with the family, a delicious "pasticada"*(beef stew)* with dumplings washed down with plenty of red wine.

The whole family walked to church on Sunday. They invited Chic to go with them and he sat at the back, they were all taking communion and there was a lot of chanting. Nothing much happened on the sabbath apart from the daily routine of feeding the animals. Chic thought he should wend his way, but there did not appear to be any public transport on a Sunday. How was he going to get to Plitvice? He decided to change his plans and go to Rijeka instead. If Josip could give him a lift early on Monday morning, he could catch a bus from Starigrad and travel along the coast road. It was over one hundred miles but with a couple of stops he could make a day of it. It should be easy to find somewhere to stay in Rijeka, it was a fishing port, there would be plenty of hostelries. He settled up, said his goodbyes to the family and gave all the children a few dinars each. Josip was learning English and keen to practise on Chic, he chatted all the way on the twenty-five miles journey to Starigrad. They arrived in plenty of time for the bus, Chic thanked Josip for all his help and paid him handsomely for the taxi service. He gave him his business card, if ever Josip should come to England he was to get in touch, they parted with a handshake.

After buying his single ticket to Rijeka he boarded the bus, it was not due to leave for nearly an hour but already filling up, mainly with locals. Elderly ladies dressed in black carrying huge baskets of produce from the market, mothers with babies and young children, an old peasant with a dog and a few tourists. One middle aged woman had a cage with two hens in it and there were three teenage boys at the back of the bus larking about. Chic sat on the left by the window where he could look at the sea. The journey was interesting, the bus stopped in every town on route for five minutes or so and also dropped off and picked up passengers in the middle of nowhere, if someone wanted to get on, they just waved the bus down. On arrival at Karlobag, Chic got out to stretch his legs, he did not go far it was busy and he didn't want to lose his seat. When he boarded the bus, four soldiers followed him and sat behind. He thought they were speaking Russian and they were all smoking and drinking from a hip flask, their talking and laughter became more and more raucous. The journey to Senj had spectacular scenery with the mountains rising higher and higher as they approached the town, Chic concentrated on the view rather than his fellow passengers. It was noon when the driver parked up at the station, Chic decided to take his suitcase, look around the town and catch a later bus to Rijeka. He did not fancy being on the bus with the Russians for the rest of his journey.

Senj was extremely picturesque, nestled in a small bay at the foot of the mountains with its own castle. The harbour was busy with fishermen mending their nets and dozens of small boats were moored up in the harbour. It was the perfect place to grab something nice to eat. He found a cafe that served: "lepinja and batter junkie" *(bread rolls with fish soup,)* it was delicious. After an extremely strong cup of coffee he made his way back to the bus station. The next leg of the journey was much pleasanter, the bus was half empty with more tourists than locals. It seemed most local inhabitants took their afternoon siesta very seriously, but there was no chance of Chic sleeping, the coffee was keeping him very much awake. He arrived in Rijeka mid-afternoon just as the city was waking up. Another harbour packed with fishing boats with a few fishermen selling their catch, there was a gentle breeze and a calm blue sea that sparkled in the sunshine.

His first task was to find somewhere to stay, he did not have to look far, there was a sign saying "SOBA" *(room)* above a restaurant on the harbour wall. The door was open and a woman was preparing food in the kitchen. She called her husband who spoke good English, Chic said he wanted a bed for just one night and was going to Zagreb tomorrow. He was guided up three flights of stairs to a tiny attic room with a single bed and a cabinet, it was adequate, spotlessly clean with crisp cotton sheets and cheap. The washing arrangements were rather limited with a chamber pot under the bed but he had suffered worse. The owner said;

> *"You like? Me Ivan. You?"*
> *"Chic".*
> *"Ah yes! Chic. You want food?"*

Chic realised he did, he was suddenly very hungry. They did not start cooking until six, he was the first to sit down. He thought about ordering squid but it was served with black rice and he was not sure about that. He decided on sea bass instead, with potato fries, it was the best fish he had ever tasted. During the evening he wandered around the town, he wished he had more time to explore, the city was a hive of activity. The architecture was similar to Trieste, just a few miles away as the crow flies. It brought many memories flooding back, mostly good, some not so good. The harbour proved to be rather rowdy even into the early hours and he did not sleep well. He woke early and was anxious to get to Zagreb as soon as possible.

Chic was reluctant to go on another long bus journey, he had plenty of money left and decided to ask his hosts to book him a taxi to Zagreb, then he could relax. A big old green Fiat that had seen better days, turned up outside within minutes. A tall, skinny driver appeared wearing a flat cap and smoking a cigarette, he was talking nineteen to the dozen to Ivan, who turned to Chic and asked for the hotel address in Zagreb. It was on the edge of the city just north of the river, the driver nodded, he knew it well and introduced himself as David, Ivan's brother. They discussed a price, Chic quibbled a little as expected, he paid half the fare and off they went. Chic sat in the front, it was more comfortable despite the fumes from his chain-smoking chauffeur. The road was good and the scenery different again, they drove through immense forests, across mountain ridges and over vast rivers, the landscape was astonishing. David spoke pigeon English and asked Chic what he did as work. Chic thought it best to be vague and said he was an engineer. David laughed;

"That is good if we stop. No?"

Chic also laughed, despite not finding it funny. After about an hour and a half they passed a sign for Karlovac. David told Chic it was called the *"City of Parks"* and there was an old castle there, Chic made a note, he would look that up when he got home. He thought David had the makings of a good chauffeur, if he cleaned up his car, smartened himself up and stopped smoking. In less than an hour Chic was delivered to his hotel, he paid the rest of the fare with a healthy tip, he knew how good it felt to be appreciated. He checked in, booked a taxi to the airport for the following morning and then after a much longed for shower and change of clothes went off to explore Zagreb.

The city was a complex mix of ancient and modern, not unlike London. Chic was drawn to the medieval lanes of the Gradec district where shops and cafes lined the narrow streets. He needed to buy some souvenirs and found the perfect gift, local *"Licitar"* heart shaped biscuits decorated with peasant designs, he bought three; one each for Joyce, Jane and Edie. He spent the afternoon strolling around the Venetian gardens and then found his way to the old town again to get something to eat, he loved people watching. His holiday was at an end and he was ready to go home, he was feeling much refreshed and ready for new challenges ahead. There was not much to do at the airport, he bought a Daily Express to catch up on the news, along with his duty-free vodka and perfume for Joyce. his flight was only slightly delayed. On arrival in England he rang home from a payphone in the customs hall and by the time he walked through with his luggage, Joyce was waiting for him at the barrier. She threw her arms around him, she was very, very pleased to see him and told him she had been worried sick for the whole ten days. He just laughed and gave her a big kiss.

33. BACK TO WORK.

Chic still had some Dinar left and the next time he was at the airport he cashed them in for US dollars at the bureau de change. The exchange rate was at an all-time high, at two dollars to the pound. He didn't tell Joyce, he wanted a bit of independence, but he started investing his cash tips. Every time he was near a bureau de change, he checked the exchange rates and traded his strong currency to a weak one. The trick was to trade back to pounds at the optimum moment, he was regularly making a profit and building up a stash of cash that he hid in the garage. Chic studied the money pages, this hobby not only kept him amused whilst waiting for customers at airports and stations, but it was also making him money and best of all, it was tax free. Joyce knew that he dabbled, but he only told her the half of it, she would have put it all in the building society if she had known.

On returning from Yugoslavia, Chic was energised and decided to sort out the cars. He bought a three year old Zephyr to replace FPJ, it was becoming unreliable and sold two months later for £55. The following year MYU went for £60, he was left with FUU 286 C, and EYM 738 J; two black Ford saloons plus the Daimler. Then, Bob nearly wrote off FUU whilst driving up in London on a snowy winter's night. Chic was furious, he told him not to stray off the main roads in the snow, but Bob ignored him. He could not afford to have a car off the road for more than a few days and was forced to give away loads of work, the insurance company were slow to respond. The claim was not settled until April and Chic discussed with Joyce the possibility of winding down, they agreed to pull back to one saloon, with Chic doing the bulk of the driving. Joyce could always step in for short trips and their regular contract with the Blind Club and the chiropody trips. The insurance eventually paid up £115 and the car was sold a month later at a loss for £75.

Life slotted into a routine or at least as much of a routine as the Sherwood household ever had. There were early mornings, late nights, busy week-ends, car maintenance and endless jobs to do around the house. Bob was now married and they along with Joe and Maureen enjoyed hilarious nights out, outings and short holidays with Joyce and Chic; in between a heavy workload. Chic still suffered from depression and was burning the candle at both ends, but he didn't say much. His back ached and angina had reared its ugly head again. He did not want to take tablets for the rest of his life and turned to alternative medicine, in particular the naturopathic theory of biorhythms. He plotted his physical, emotional and intellectual cycles to identify the best times to carry out tasks and more importantly, when to rest. He tried hard to look after himself.

He wished he had kept a diary whilst in Yugoslavia, as he had back in the war but it was too late now. Sherwood Car Hire offered complimentary diaries to all their regular customers and Chic always carried one himself. His was mostly used for writing down quotes or trying out a bit of poetry, influenced by his daughter's writing as a teenager. She had received a much better education than he, thanks to the eleven plus and a place at Rosebery Grammar School. Chic had no aspirations for an academic life but he did like reading poetry. He discovered the poet, Patience Strong when he was in the army and now prescribed to the magazine; *"This England."* This sentimental poet was a regular contributor and Chic loved her style, the magazine was also useful for building up his knowledge about the English way of life. He used it to impress his customers with snippets of little known facts not unlike Michael Caine.

Now the Daimler was bringing in more wedding business, he designed a complimentary card for the bride and groom, with a witty quip:

With happiness through each matrimonial mile.
We drove you to it."

Sherwood Chauffeur Driven Car Hire had a strong core of loyal customers. In addition to the weddings, airport and station transfers there were regulars who liked to be taken to the shops, the chiropodist, or the doctor, as well as a head mistress who did not drive and enjoyed day trips to the seaside. There were several business clients from the financial and publishing sector and Chic always had a good story to tell with discretion of course. But his best came from the entertainment world. How the wax foetus in the film; *"2001. A Space Odyssey"* melted in the boot of his car on the way to Elstree Studios. The behaviour of the stage door Johnnies' when he drove Pearl Carr and Teddy Johnson to their theatre performances. His invitation to drinks at a popular comedienne's house party where he mingled with his favourite actors. And, how the famous medium Doris Stokes, told him he had; *"the gift."* He enjoyed his job, he had a good life and as Grandpa Charlie always drummed into him;

"He knew his place."

One account client from Kingston Hill, also owned a house in Cambridgeshire and property abroad. Mrs and Mrs Empedocles were good customers who although wealthy, enjoyed simple pleasures. She was an amateur entomologist and with her husband had been creating a butterfly sanctuary at their house in Caldecote. Sadly, he died in January 1973 leaving his wife and three sons. The following year in August, their eldest son Ian, committed suicide and Mrs E then lost her mother two months later. She used Sherwood Car Hire frequently during this time and subsequently, Chic's chauffeur services were required for dozens of airport transfers and trips back and forth to Caldecote. Her younger son Philip was a chemistry professor at an American university, where he lived with his wife and two children, he often travelled to London on business and visited his mother at the same time. Anthony, the youngest son by seven years, was twenty-seven, unmarried and still at home. On this particular occasion he was staying at Caldecote while his mother went on holiday to Malta. Chic drove her to the airport and was also booked to pick Philip up from Cambridgeshire and bring him back to Kingston Hill, before driving him to Heathrow for his return to the States. He had been working in London and planned to visit his brother before he returned home.

It was Thursday the 9th of December and Chic had been up early taking customers to Gatwick airport. He was snoozing on the window seat while Joyce prepared an early lunch, he needed to leave home by 1 pm, to arrive at Caldecote for mid-afternoon. Just as Joyce was thinking about waking her husband with a cup of tea she heard him cry out. She rushed into the lounge to see him with his head down, literally hanging on the edge of his seat. She thought he was having a heart attack. He looked visibly shaken and before she had a chance to speak, he stood up and said;

"Don't rush the lunch love. I won't be going to Cambridge."

He gave her a hug, she wanted to know what had happened, was he ill? He sat her down, he was fine but he had woken from a horrible dream. He still suffered nightmares where he was back in the army being shelled and surrounded by the unearthly screams of dying men. But this was different; he had seen a shadowy figure killed by a shot through the head. She told him it was only a dream and a cup of tea and something sweet would sort him out. He needed to get changed into his uniform and while he was upstairs freshening up, the phone rang; it was Mrs Empedocles calling from Malta. There had been a terrible accident and Philip was dead. She was flying back to London that evening and being met at the airport by the police. She would be in touch.

The next day the newspapers reported that Anthony had been remanded in custody for the murder of his brother. After he shot Philip with a crossbow, once through the heart and then twice more, he rang the doctor and the police to tell them what he had done. The case did not come to trial until the following April. It seemed that Anthony had purchased two cross-bows previous to the attack, because he thought Philip was planning to kidnap him over an argument about a fortune of coins left to Philip and Ian by their grandfather, before Anthony was born. The sad truth was that the family all agreed after Ian died, that Philip and Anthony should share the fortune, but they did not tell Anthony this because they thought him too unstable. On the 1ˢᵗ April 1976 he pleaded guilty to manslaughter and was detained at Broadmoor, thought to be suffering from paranoid schizophrenia. The whole sequence of events broke Mrs E's heart, she spent much of her remaining life in Malta and died three years later.

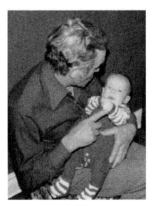

34. ANOTHER BABY.

Joyce and Chic were now grandparents and Chic could not believe the emotions it stirred within him. It took so long for them both to become parents, he never dreamed he would have a grandson, mother and baby were doing well and he was on cloud nine. Joyce could not wait to get to the hospital, they called Bob in to cover Chic's driving jobs. It was January and the roads were icy, it took nearly an hour to get to Farnborough Hospital, in Kent. Jane and Ken were in the middle of house renovations, they had no kitchen and were living upstairs with floorboards up in every room. The health visitor would not allow Jane to go home, the house was unfit for a baby and they would have to stay with Joyce and Chic until at least the kitchen was functional. Joyce was delighted, Chic was not so sure, they had a houseful with Edie now living there almost permanently. Then he thought back to when he was little, with him his brother and his parents all in one room and his cousin's family in the other, Grandpa Charlie slept downstairs in the front parlour. Joyce reminded him of when they rented a room in his parent's house before they moved to the Sunray Estate, it was only thirty years ago but a totally different world, they had all come a long way since then.

Jane and the baby only stayed for three weeks, once they were back home Chic began another bricklaying project, with the bricks he had reclaimed from inside the house. Their tiny garden was given brick edged flowerbeds, a potting shed with a reclaimed clay tile roof and a York stone patio. Both he and Joyce studied dozens of garden design books and went to the Royal Horticultural Society at Wisley to get ideas. He built another extension to the garage, also in brick with another porthole, he had kept the wooden template and it was a shame to waste it. He turned an old aluminium teapot upside down and fixed it to the wall, he was delighted when a robin set up home in it. Nothing went to waste, he found an old golf club and bent it in his vice to create a bracket for a hanging basket. He was a great fan of *"Gardener's World,"* Percy Thrower showed him how to grow tomatoes and train climbing roses along the yard wall, now Geoff Hamilton was inspiring his building projects. They had recently bought a new dishwasher, the old one still worked so he plumbed it in under the phone in the garage, it was great for washing his flowerpots.

35. MORE DAIMLER LIMOUSINES.

Chic had been thinking for a while about getting another Daimler and kept his nose to the ground. He walked up Beaconsfield Road once a week to go to the bank and always stuck his nose around the yard door at the undertakers, to have a chat with the lads. It turned out the company was upgrading its hearses and buying new limousines to match, they were getting rid of both the Daimler Majestics because they were too thirsty. Chic was very interested, one a 1963 C registration, the other 192 FLY, was nearly twenty years old. He could probably buy both if they were willing to give him a good price for cash. He got an excellent deal, less for the two than he paid for his first one back in 1973. The bottom had dropped out of the market due to a worsening oil crisis, no one wanted old fashioned gas guzzling vehicles, except Chic. His plan was to have one black and one white limousine for wedding work, keeping the other for spares. He drove them both back to the yard, by the time he had all three Daimlers parked up in the garage there was only room for one Zephyr.

The old limousine 192 FLY, was just about in working order but the bodywork was poor, Chic decided to cancel the insurance and take it off the road. The parts were worth their weight in gold as spares for his old girl and the new one. He wanted to get a white limousine on the road as quickly as possible and began preparing DYP for a respray. Every spare moment was spent in the garage, Joyce suggested he slept out there, he laughed and blew her a kiss. Chic was in heaven, he loved getting his hands dirty with the smell of oil and problem solving whilst listening to the radio. The evenings were drawing in and the weather had changed, it was getting too cold to spend his days and nights out in the unheated garage, but by the end of October DYP was ready to go off for her paint job. Chic had taken all the seats out and the door panels, there were a few repairs that he could carry out on the upholstery while the car was away. He selected the best from both cars, glued and stitched some of the leather, cleaned it all up and treated it with conditioner. In the middle of this process the original Daimler developed a fault with the electric windows, it was a dodgy connection behind the door panelling, he soon sorted it out.

The white Daimler was back before Christmas, the respray cost £450, the same amount that he paid to buy the first limousine. His new toy sat in the garage waiting for a full service, it had its first wedding

243

commitment in March. Chic had two months to prepare it for the MOT *(Ministry of Transport)* test in readiness for DYP's first job. January and February were always quiet, he dished out a few jobs to Bob and Jack and got on with what he really enjoyed, being a mechanic. He spent many hours at Surbiton Engineering, they had the equipment to rejig a few parts that Chic could not repair himself, they talked his language and all had a few laughs while they worked. The white Daimler Majestic limousine was looking magnificent for her debut with white ribbons adorning the huge bonnet. Chic in his grey suit with matching chauffeur's cap was proud as punch as he parked up outside the bride's house, to collect the bridesmaids. It was a local wedding at Saint Matthew's Church with a reception at Leatherhead Golf Club, everything went as planned and the bride and groom were thrilled.

Chic had developed a good relationship with a wedding photographer from Essex, who paid him £20 for every recommendation. The arrangement worked well for both of them and Sherwood Car Hire received a couple of interesting bookings in return, one for a TV advert. Chic thought it would be a bit of fun, there was a whole day of filming and the money was good. The day started at the crack of dawn in the Essex countryside, they finished filming late afternoon. Chic was required to drive in shot for just a few yards over and over again, the process was tedious but it was an experience and another story to tell his clients. He was given a video tape of the film, the BP advert appeared on Thames Television for a whole season. It was Chic's moment of fame.

He was now sixty years old and slowing down, both he and Joyce were much more selective with the bookings they accepted. They did not need to work themselves to the bone and it was time to sell the Zephyrs. Chic sold them privately and bought a dark blue Ford Zodiac with a V6 engine. It was a big old beast and not ideal for chauffeur work, Joyce hated it. The Zodiac proved to be a white elephant and was quickly sold on and replaced with a light metallic blue Granada. It cost him £2,450.00, he had never paid so much for a car. This purchase was more for private use, although Chic and Joyce both still drove a few regular customers. In 1981 both Daimlers were fully booked every week-end throughout the season, wedding fever had struck the whole country, it seemed that many young ladies wanted to be brides just like Lady Diana who was marrying her prince on Wednesday the 29 July 1981 at 11.20 am, it was another a public holiday. Beaconsfield Road was holding a street party in celebration and Joyce was on the organising committee with neighbours Vron, a district nurse and her husband Rob who was a policeman, along with others. Joyce wrote to the Mayor of Kingston-upon-Thames who accepted her invitation to attend the party at some point during the afternoon.

The party was due to start at 2 pm to enable everyone to watch the wedding on television first. The weather was perfect, dozens of trestle tables lined the footpaths, almost all the residents joined in and brought party food and drink. Bunting was stretched across the road, balloons hung on garden gates and a sound system set up outside The Tuck Shop. There were wacky races, dancing in the street and a fancy-dress competition reminiscent of the VJ celebrations back in June 1945. The Mayor and Mayoress turned up with a reporter from The Surrey Comet and Joyce was interviewed with Mrs Baigent who was the street's oldest resident and guest of honour. The party continued after dark but the music was turned off and everything cleared up before midnight. Total normality was resumed for the next working day. Chic thought about Joyce dressed up as Britannia nearly forty years ago. Now he was a husband, a father and a grandfather, he had his family around him and he was happy.

Joyce and Chic were going on more holidays and their grandson Sam, often came to stay with his dog Jethro. Chic enjoyed this family time, he had great fun with Sam teaching him carpentry and bit of tricycle maintenance. There were outings to: Chessington Zoo, the Trooping of the Colour, Wimbledon Theatre, the seaside and even a short trip away to Yorkshire. Edie was living with them permanently and Chic thought it time to sell the bungalow, but Joyce was reluctant. It was her last link with Foxton, they paid a gardener to mow the grass, but the other maintenance was a worry. It did not make good sense to leave the house empty, they were paying rates and heating to stop the pipes freezing and it was all money down the drain.

The following January, Edie died. Joyce organised her mother's funeral locally but her ashes were scattered at Cambridge Crematorium with her husband, Harry. This brought back unwelcome memories of her father's death and the winter months of December and January always remained difficult for Joyce. She suggested letting the bungalow but Chic did not want the aggravation, it was a good two hour drive away and not a practical proposition. They took several overnight trips to sort out the contents, although Edie could never be accused of being a hoarder she was a neat and tidy soul. The property was put on the market in March and sold very quickly. Joyce had been suffering from bronchitis and was told by the doctor she must give up smoking, this would be her third attempt, she was depressed and irritable. She dealt with her grief by throwing herself into fund raising for Esher Cancer Research. Chic was content to potter about, tinker with the cars and grow tomatoes. He decided to paint the exterior of the house. Some of the bungalow money was used to pay for a new roof and now he was keen to smarten up the outside. He was fed up with Joyce's moodiness, this would keep him occupied and out of the house for the whole summer. What an horrific summer it turned out to be.

36. ANOTHER WAR.

The news was also depressing. The IRA *(Irish Republican Army)* terrorists were making a nuisance of themselves, there was talk of links with the left wing Baader-Minehof Gang *(The Red Army)* who had been causing havoc in West Germany since the 1960s. Maggie Thatcher was Prime Minister and still arguing with the Trade Unions. Then on the 2ⁿᵈ of April, Argentina invaded the Falkland Isles and Britain was at war. Chic became more and more distressed as events unfolded, every day brought worse news throughout April and May. The surrender of the British Falkland Isles government, the two hundred miles exclusion zone, the sinking of the Argentinian ship General Belgrano and then in retaliation, HMS Sheffield. The pitched battles of Goose Green and Stanley changed the outlook again. Many countries were beginning to take sides and he feared along with millions of others the possibility of another world war. On the 3ʳᵈ of June, the Israeli ambassador was shot in Lebanon, now conflict had spread to the middle east and it was all reminiscent of those dark days when he was a young man. His nightmares returned, he dreamed of bloodshed and destruction. Then just when everyone was celebrating victory in The Falklands, the IRA bombed the London parks, killing soldiers, civilians and horses. He was fretting about his family. Was there a future for his grandson? Would he even reach adulthood? He kept all these worries to himself apart from a few vociferous political debates down at The Plough and Harrow on a Sunday lunchtime, with his best mate Joe and the other regulars.

The house looked very smart now the brick work was transformed from dark green to a subtle mushroom colour with white woodwork. It was a long job, Chic painted it all himself without any help or scaffolding, just one very tall ladder and a few wooden boards to protect the glass loggia roof. One morning, he was working on the upstairs facia board on the outside wall when he missed his footing and slid down the ladder from top to bottom. He landed with a hefty jolt, but managed to remain upright, it shook him up. Joyce heard the commotion from the kitchen and came rushing out the back gate to find Chic laughing with one of the neighbours who was on his way back from the allotments with a huge bundle of runner beans. She went back inside with a handful of beans for their tea. Chic decided to pack up for the day and ran himself a hot bath with Epsom Salts, he was already beginning to stiffen up. He was still getting nightmares, the tossing and turning was disturbing Joyce and she suggested he sleep in the back bedroom. He didn't mind, it was quieter there away from the traffic noise. When he woke the next morning he could hardly move, his back was giving him gyp. As soon as he was dressed he went down to the garage and hung from the rafters by his feet, to stretch out his spine. He did that every day until the pain and the bruising eased and never told Joyce the half of it, she would have stopped him driving.

There was a general election the following year and Maggie got in with a landslide victory, Chic was pleased about that. The doctor advised him to walk as much as possible, to help his back and his blood pressure. He was still taking aspirin and cod liver oil every morning and made a habit of walking to Worcester Park to visit his friends Joe and Maureen, who were always great fun. They were not very practical, Chic helped them out with decorating ideas and built a fireplace for them. He got on very well with their son Martin who was a staunch supporter of Arthur Scargill, the militant trade union leader, he and Chic liked to wind each other up. There always seemed to be someone on strike these days with the miners being the most militant, carrying out aggressive picketing with constant scuffles against blacklegs and the police. The CND *(Campaign for Nuclear Disarmament)* women were also demonstrating and clashing with the police over the US cruise missiles based in England.

In November a violent robbery was carried out at a warehouse near Heathrow airport. The following day Chic was meeting a client off a British Airways flight from San Francisco at Terminal One, there were police everywhere. When he arrived home, Joyce told him about the Brink's Mat robbery, a violent gang had got away with a huge haul of gold bullion and diamonds worth millions. More than Ronny Biggs stole in the Great Train robbery back in 1963. He wondered if the villains would ever be caught. Ronny Biggs was now swanning around South America after escaping from prison in 1965. It seemed to Chic that the least deserving often came out on top, there was no justice in the world.

Everyone was sick to death of the strikes, the protestors and the terrorists that were now part of normal life. Thatcher's Britain was in turmoil, but;
"The lady was not for turning."

Chic always tried to keep things light hearted, but some days it was a struggle. The television helped with comedy programmes like, *"It Aint*

Half Hot Mum" and repeats of *"The Morecambe and Wise Show"*. Eric never failed to make him laugh even when he knew what was coming. Joyce and Chic both loved the Sunday night variety shows; *"Live from Her Majesty's"* was showing on ITV. Chic had settled down with a glass of barley wine to watch the show hosted by Jimmy Tarbuck, while Joyce did her knitting. Tommy Cooper was the next act, all he had to do was walk on stage for the audience to dissolve into laughter. His glamorous assistant helped him dress in a golden coat, in readiness for a magic trick. He fell to the floor triggering spontaneous laughter, rocked a bit, sat up, groaned and then fell backwards making snoring noises, it looked like part of the act. When he did not get up the theatre curtain closed and the TV went to adverts. The show continued with Les Dennis. What had happened to Tommy Cooper? Perhaps he was drunk? The national news followed immediately afterwards, Tommy had collapsed and been taken to hospital. The next day the press reported that he had suffered a major heart attack and died whilst on stage in front of millions of viewers. He was six months younger than Chic.

Joyce wanted to celebrate their ruby wedding anniversary with a party. Chic was not that keen but he went along with it for a quiet life. Joyce and Jane planned the food, friends and relations were invited and a good time was had by all, apart from Chic. He smiled and joked his way through the proceedings for the sake of the family but he was not really in the mood. Arthur Scargill was still causing trouble and unemployment was rising again. This brave new world the Conservative party promised should not be suffering the same problems that his family experienced fifty years ago between the wars. Austin Rover were in trouble, it looked like the Japanese were taking over the car industry, that did not bode well particularly in Joyce's eyes. Her brother suffered dreadfully under the Japanese regime during WW2 and she was not about to forgive them, she refused to have anything Japanese in the house. Chic went to great lengths to conceal any Japanese connections to any gadgets that did enter their home, by 1985 it was almost impossible not to own something made in Japan.

The Granada had now been replaced with a Volvo and Joyce drove a little Triumph Acclaim. The fact that it was produced by the Japanese company Honda passed Joyce by, much to the relief of Chic who thought it a great little car. They were now on their fourth accountant, none of them a patch on Don Hamilton but it was still worth their while to keep the business going, for the tax relief if nothing else. Chic adopted a strategy of doing what needed to be done without asking Joyce, it worked most of the time. In fact half the time she didn't even notice, it saved many heated discussions and as a result they were back on good terms. Now they were worried about Jane and her family who were stuck out in Kent where the 1987 hurricane had done its worst.

The roads were blocked, power and telephone lines were down and they were incommunicado. Jane managed to make one phone call from a neighbour's mobile phone to tell her parents they were all OK and asked them to relay the news to Kens parents. Joyce and Chic were worried sick. A state of emergency had been declared, food parcels were being dropped and the army brought in to clear the roads and restore electricity. There was nothing they could do, they had to wait just like during the war. It was five days before the kids were able to get out to buy supplies but happily they were unharmed, despite an oak tree landing on the house and causing major damage. Chic drove over at the first opportunity to make sure they were really OK. There was no power for weeks with no telephone for months, but they were in a better position than most. They had a coal Rayburn providing heat, hot water and an oven with a petrol generator giving them lights and the television for keeping up with the news. They were used to frequent power cuts *(hence the generator)* and had been snowed in for over a week the previous winter. They were resourceful and it was no more than a nuisance to them, but it did not stop Chic worrying.

After a winter of worry with frequent visits to Kent, Chic decided it was time to think about selling the Daimlers, his pride and joy. He was enjoying life and wanted to free up his week-ends to enable him to spend time with friends and family. The wedding business had changed, now youngsters wanted pink Cadillacs and gold Rolls Royces or even wackier transport. He decided to put both limousines into auction. They went for a song, but no matter they were gone. All he had left of them was one number plate, 192 FLY, and he took down the enamel sign that hung by the front door.

SHERWOOD
CHAUFFEUR DRIVEN
CAR HIRE
Tel. 399-3303

No longer would he have to put up with drunks ringing the doorbell late at night after a session at the British Legion. No longer would he have to get up at 3 am to take clients to the airport to catch the first flight out. No longer would he have to park up outside hotels and restaurants for hours on the increasingly congested London streets, sweet talking traffic wardens to let him stay just a few more minutes. But he would miss the people watching and the banter. He had met many interesting people during his working life and seen some sights, he had plenty of memories to keep him going.

Both he and Joyce spent more time at Jane's house where there was always something needing doing, they were happy to help out with a bit of maintenance or gardening and always made time to play with their grandson who was growing up rapidly. Joyce thought it would be nice to have a week away to celebrate Chic's seventieth birthday on the 8ᵗʰ of August 1990, but it was high season and they decided to wait until September, when Joe and Maureen could join them. On Sunday the 5ᵗʰ August they were invited to Jane's house for lunch, it was a beautiful day with boiling hot sunshine. The journey took longer than usual because the roads were busy with day trippers. All was quiet when they arrived at the cottage, Sadie, the dog was wagging her tail at the gate.

Sam appeared from the backgarden grinning from ear to ear, he loved Granddad. Chic walked around the back and got the surprise of his life, all his best friends and family were there, his wife, daughter, son-in-law and grandson, his brother Charlie, with his wife, daughter and grandson, friends Joe and Maureen, Bob and Joan and Nora from the dance club. There were twenty guests and a good time was had by all. They played an hilarious game of charades, rode bicycles backwards and one guest who was a bit too fond of her drink fell in the pond. The whole day was a riot. Chic was fit and could not have had a better time, he would remember it forever.

The Chauffeur.

They will miss his gentle manner and his smiling face,
The driver in his uniform who went from place to place.
Doing more than just his share, always with a helping hand,
Many will remember him as a kind and cheerful friend.

Percy (Chic) Sherwood. 1971.

ENDWORD.

Two months later Chic was suffering from the most dreadful headache, worse than 1944, 1945 and 1963 combined. Reluctantly he went to the doctor who took some blood, the results were due within a few days but did not materialise and the pain got worse. One morning in April shortly after breakfast, Chic collapsed in the kitchen. Joyce rang 999 and an ambulance arrived within minutes. The paramedics thought he was having an epileptic fit and took him straight to casualty at Kingston Hospital. The next day he was moved to the Atkinson Morley in Wimbledon where they diagnosed an abscess on the brain. He was given major surgery and kept in intensive care for two weeks, where he suffered a heart attack.

Chic was moved again, this time to St Georges Hospital in Tooting, South London. He was still in intensive care when he suffered another heart attack. He was heavily dosed with morphine that triggered hallucinations, he was reliving the war. Everything he had tucked away deep in his brain for fifty years was now coming out; the horror, the fear, the death and destruction. After several months of hospitalisation, Chic was considered well enough to come home, he was now a frail old man who could do little for himself. Joyce took care of him but found it a strain, she was exhausted and often impatient with him. When she was telling him off, his eyes sparkled and with a chuckle he would say;

"Give me a kiss, Darling."

She couldn't stay cross with him for long.

He died on the 4ʰ June 1993 in Tolworth Hospital just a few yards from where he was born. Chic was seventy-two years old.

ACKNOWLEDGEMENTS.

When I embarked on this biographical novel I thought my research was complete. I discovered my father's diaries after my mother died in 2000 and transcribed them for my son in 2010 with the help of Percy's copy of *"Taurus Pursuant. A History of the 11ᵗ Armoured Division."* Two years ago I began posting snippets on my Face Book page and was surprised to be approached by Billy Leblond, the curator of Musee: La Percee du Bocage in Normandy. Billy's support has been invaluable, offering advice, source material and contacts. This gave me the confidence to set up a private FB group called "Percy's War Diary" and the idea of a daily blog following Percy's words. I was astonished to discover the interest this generated, with members contributing their own experiences and expert knowledge. Alain Brogniez, who manages the Brussels branch of the Royal British Legion, has helped me on many occasions to get my facts straight. Andrew Morgan, a military historian, has not only loaned me several books but also added significantly to my understanding of army life and events in Europe during WW2. He has kindly helped with the editing. I would like to thank Peter Whitaker's generosity in sharing his research and the war diaries for 12ᵗ and 612ᵗ Field Squadrons. Peter has put names to faces on photographs, our fathers trained and served together. Lastly, thanks to Kev Reynolds for giving the book a final edit before publication.

Chic had a long silent battle against PTSD as a result of his war experiences. But the army changed his life, he travelled and met his wife who was his rock, they worked together and faced every problem together with strong mutual friendships. Their best friends Maureen and Joe have helped me reminisce and reminded me of all the happy times Joyce was not in good health herself when Chic was finally admitted to Tolworth Hospital, but she never missed a day's visiting. Her health slowly declined after he died, she had lost her soulmate. Chic and Joyce's influence on my family life has been profound. When my husband Ken and I needed to earn a crust due to redundancy, we turned to operating a chauffeur service, the business thrived and kept us buoyant until retirement. Ken is my rock, he has advised, supported and encouraged me throughout, answered my questions, read transcripts, made endless cups of tea and given me pep talks when I considered giving up. He has also taken on my share of the housework and the gardening, to enable me to write for several hours a day, every day. Thank you, Ken.

Printed in Great Britain
by Amazon